LIGHT · COMPA

DE GAS LIGHT CO

LACLEDE GAS AND ST. LOUIS
150 YEARS OF WORKING TOGETHER, 1857–2007

by Bill Beck

FIRST EDITION
Published by Laclede Gas Company, St. Louis, Missouri
Copyright © 2007 by Laclede Gas Company
Design and Production by
Werremeyer, St. Louis, Missouri 63116

International Standard Book Number
978-0-9710910-1-6

Printed in the United States of America by
Advertisers Printing Company, St. Louis, Missouri 63110

Acknowledgements

It is customary in the writing business for the writer of a book to sit down and acknowledge those who have been helpful in the process. The only problem is that in a project like the history of Laclede Gas, the list of those who have contributed to making the book a reality is lengthy, and, I hope, inclusive.

Doug Yaeger, president, chairman and CEO of Laclede Gas, wanted the story of Laclede's 150 years in St. Louis told so that future generations don't forget the challenges that employees of every era faced and surmounted. Doug graciously submitted to several long, videotaped interviews and read every word of the manuscript in the draft copy stage.

George Csolak, Dave Arrow and DiAnne Voegtle on the Corporate Communications team at Laclede were the glue that tied the project together. George, who shares both a northern Minnesota and journalistic connection with the author, opened countless doors and spent hours explaining his vast lore of contemporary St. Louis history. Dave is the corporate memory, and his office houses thousands of pictures as well as back issues of Laclede Gas annual reports and employee magazines dating to the early 20th century. DiAnne, the department's administrative assistant, was a jack-of-all-trades, lining up dozens of oral history interviews and tracking down outrageous requests at the drop of a hat.

Mary Kullman, Laclede's chief governance officer and corporate secretary; Ellen Theroff, assistant vice president of administration and associate general counsel; and Rob Arrol from the Corporate Communications Department served on George Csolak's team charged with reviewing the draft copy of the manuscript. The team worked diligently and quickly and made suggestions that strengthened the final product immeasurably.

The beautiful design is the work of Ann Campbell and her team at Werremeyer of Webster Groves. Karin Roper and Cheryl Bonnett created the magic of combining text and photos. Bill Gorman of Advertisers Printing of St. Louis made an often painful part of the publishing process painless.

On the home front, research assistant Jim Richardson relived his days at The Rock Island Refinery when researching Laclede's gas exploration days in the 1970s. My wife Elizabeth and partner in Lakeside Writers' Group, kept the business going, edited all of the drafts and became a grandmother for the first time during Laclede's evolution from chapter outline to book.

So that's the team who is responsible for the book. They all deserve accolades for a job well done. But they need not take the blame for the errors, omissions and misinterpretations that inevitably creep into any 192-page book. I'm responsible for all those.

Bill Beck
Indianapolis, Indiana
August 17, 2007

Foreword

Laclede Gas and St. Louis have been partners for 150 years. It's a partnership that has evolved and grown with the region since we were chartered by the Missouri General Assembly in 1857, and named our company after one of the city's founders, Pierre Laclede.

Our community began humbly as a frontier village but has evolved into so much more. St. Louis' potential was apparent to Pierre Laclede, as he predicted in a 1763 journal entry, "I have found a situation where I am going to form a settlement which might become hereafter one of the finest cities in America." And it has, with Laclede Gas' active involvement and participation.

Almost from the beginning, Laclede Gas Light Company was a building block of the local business community and, in 1896, was chosen as one of only twelve stocks to be on the original Dow Jones list of New York Exchange-traded companies. Moreover, the company helped usher in the day of modern energy, as it pre-dated electricity and helped fuel the massive growth of industry and commerce during the mid to late 1800s.

Most St. Louisans would not recognize the company that served their great, great grandparents in the late 19th century. In those days, gas was "manufactured" by burning coal in the absence of oxygen in retorts, or furnaces, producing a fuel with a much lower heating content than today's natural gas. Most of the gas furnished in St. Louis before about 1890 was used to light municipal street lamps or to fuel industrial processes. When electric lighting became widespread in the 1880s and 1890s, Laclede adapted by developing a strong presence in residential heating and cooking.

In 1931, natural gas first came to St. Louis via deliveries from Mississippi River Fuel Company, and the company began mixing natural and manufactured gas to produce a higher quality gas for its customers.

Laclede Gas announced its decision to convert to straight clean-burning, efficient natural gas in St. Louis in the years following World War II, with the growth of the interstate natural gas pipeline industry. At about the same time, the company acquired the St. Louis County Gas Company from Union Electric. The development of substantial underground storage capacity in the late 1950s and early 1960s made natural gas the fuel of choice for St. Louis for the next half-century.

The company entered the St. Charles County market in 1963 when it purchased a controlling interest in St. Charles Gas Company, and it entered Jefferson County two years later when it purchased a controlling interest in Missouri Natural Gas Company. During the 1970s, the company engaged in natural gas exploration and development activities in Texas and Oklahoma that proved to be quite successful. As the 1980s dawned, the company started investigating ways to diversify its revenue base and made several profitable real estate investments, some of which the company continues to participate in today.

The deregulation of the natural gas industry during the 1990s and early 21st century has brought more change to Laclede Gas. In 2001, the company formed a holding company, The Laclede Group, to manage and operate Laclede's core natural gas delivery business, as well as develop diversified subsidiaries.

Through world wars and depressions, through good times and bad, Laclede Gas has changed and adapted to remain a vital and engaged partner to not only the city of St. Louis but to every municipality in our Eastern Missouri service area. We look forward to serving the residents of the region for the next 150 years.

Doug Yaeger
March 2, 2007

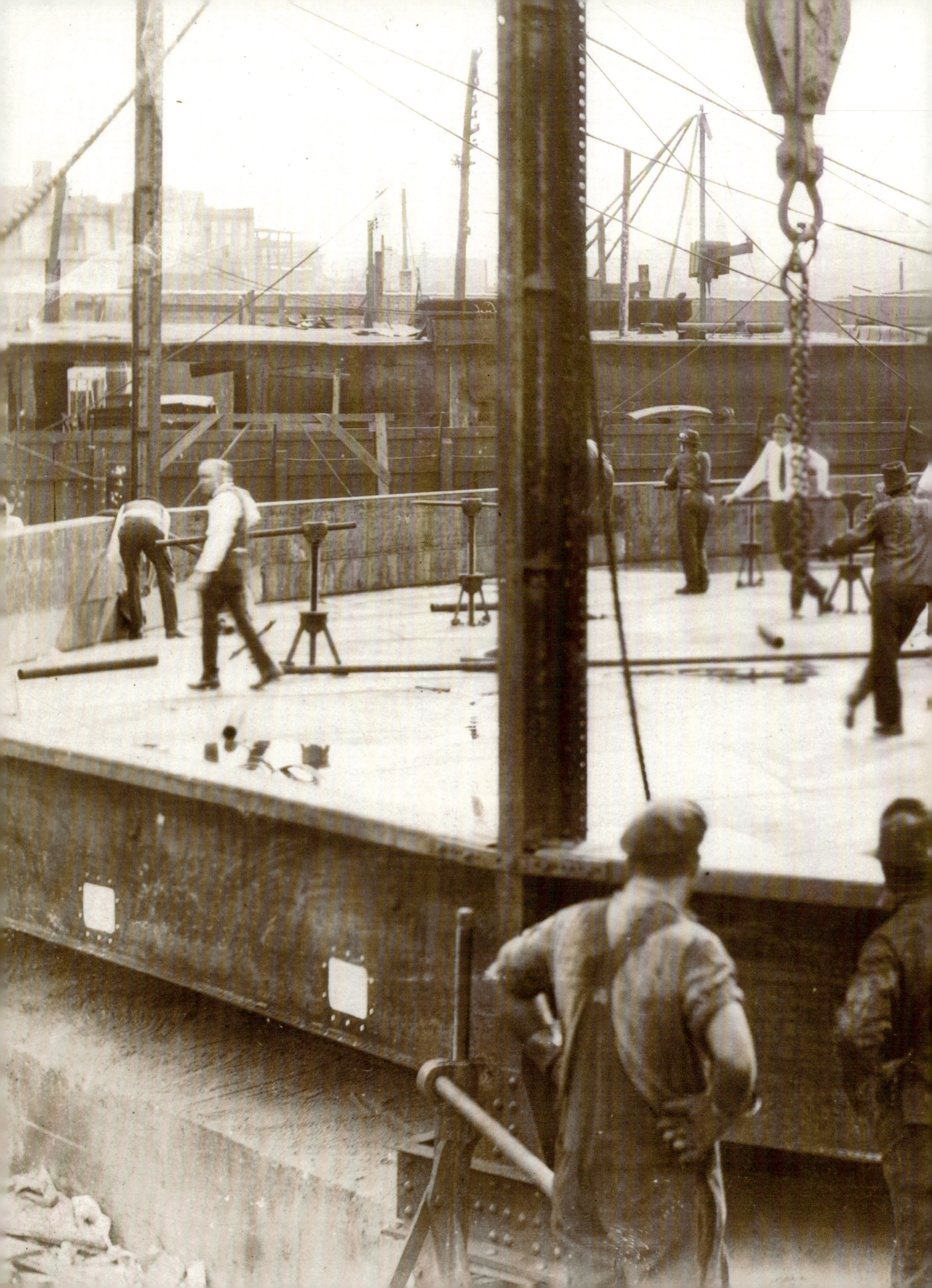

Table of Contents

1. In the Beginning..................8
2. Growing Pains..................20
   Interlude 1: The Town Gas Era..................32
3. Into a New Century..................36
4. 1017 Olive Street..................46
5. War and Peace..................58
6. The Roaring Twenties..................66
   Interlude 2: The Holding Company Era..................75
7. Natural Gas Comes to St. Louis..................78
8. The Conversion..................90
9. The Judge Otto Years..................100
   Interlude 3: The Natural Gas Era..................112
10. The H. Reid Derrick Years..................116
11. Energy Crisis..................130
12. Dealing with the Bubble..................142
13. Suburban Growth..................154
    Interlude 4: The Era of Deregulation..................167
14. The Laclede Group..................170
15. Building the Future on the Past..................182
    Index..................186

The French American merchant, Pierre Laclede Liguest stands guard over the city he helped found in 1764. Less than a century later, the gas company that has served St. Louis since 1857 honored Laclede by taking his name.

LACLEDE
FOUNDER OF ST. LOUIS
1764

CHAPTER 1

In the Beginning

Laclede Gas celebrates 150 years of continuous operations in the first decade of the 21st century. St. Louis, the home of Laclede Gas, was nearly a century old when a group of entrepreneurs and attorneys gathered in a downtown office in 1857 to incorporate a gas company named in honor of the city's founder, Pierre Laclede Liguest.

For more than a century, St. Louis was the jumping-off place for the American West. In 1857, when The Laclede Gas Light Co. was chartered, buffalo hunters were still setting out from the Gateway City for the Great Plains.

The city that Pierre Laclede founded as a fur trading outpost in 1764 owed its existence to a location astride the rivers that drained the interior of North America. Located 10 miles below the confluence of the Missouri and Mississippi Rivers, St. Louis from the earliest days was a launching point for travelers and explorers traversing a continent. Fur traders traveling south down the Mississippi River gained access to the Ohio River Valley less than a day south of St. Louis. Those paddling north up the Mississippi River in the 1760s could follow the Illinois River and a short portage east to Lake Michigan at the new fur trading post of Chicago.

Traders headed northwest along the Missouri River could paddle all the way to the Rocky Mountains. Portages in what is present-day Montana led traders west along the Columbia River to the Pacific Ocean or northwest to some of the richest beaver-trapping grounds on the continent. Canada in the 1600s and 1700s had a population of beaver estimated at more than 10 million.

St. Louis capitalized on its logistical advantages during the next 200 years. The fur trade gave way to steam transportation on the Mississippi and Missouri Rivers and then to railroads and later trucks. Business executives in the 19th and 20th centuries realized the truth of Pierre Laclede's 1764 discovery: St. Louis was superbly located for the gathering of raw materials and the marketing and transportation of finished products.

Gateway to the West

After the end of the French and Indian War in 1763, the French governor of Louisiana granted trading monopolies to merchants, hoping to stimulate trade in the Mississippi River Valley. Gilbert Antoine Maxent, a New Orleans businessman, applied for and won a six-year trading concession with the tribes on the Missouri River and the western basin of the Mississippi. Maxent entered into a partnership with Pierre Laclede Liguest, who agreed to found and manage a trading post in the Illinois country, often referred to as Upper Louisiana.

In August 1763, Laclede and his 13-year-old stepson, Auguste Chouteau, started upriver from New Orleans. It took four months to reach the confluence of the Missouri and Mississippi Rivers, and Laclede rejected the site because it proved too low and swampy for building a town.

Laclede and Chouteau retraced their route about 18 miles down the Mississippi until they encountered the limestone bluffs where St. Louis stands today. The area boasted a gently sloping plateau for river access, high bluffs to prevent flooding and outcroppings of stone for building, as well as plenty of timber. Laclede and Chouteau marked the site and immediately returned to Fort de Chartres (located in present-day Chester, Illinois) to recruit workers and gather supplies. One year later, the two came back to begin building the town they named St. Louis in honor of King Louis IX of France.

Laclede was so impressed with the location of the new settlement that he announced in 1764 he had "found a situation where I am going to form a settlement which might become, hereafter, one of the finest cities in America — so many advantages are embraced in its site, by its locality and central position, for forming settlements."

With the founding of the post, the French established a thriving fur trading community. The town quickly became a center for north-south commerce along the Mississippi River. The early settlement had no retail center. In the 1780s, there were two granaries, a bakery, a maple sugar works and a church.

Supplies were brought to St. Louis on keelboats, with cargoes of flour, sugar, whiskey, blankets, fabrics, tools and household goods dominating the river travel.

President Thomas Jefferson acquired French North America from the Emperor Napoleon in 1803. By the time of the Louisiana Purchase, St. Louis' population had grown to 1,100 people, and the city's merchants had established a bustling river landing. With city growth came new warehouses, supply stores and a pressing need for boat makers and repair shops.

After Meriwether Lewis and William Clark returned from exploring the Louisiana Purchase in 1806, their reports of beaver-trapping potential far to the northwest was of great interest to trappers in the infant United States. St. Louis became a hub for trappers in a new trade oriented to the far west. The city's merchants established a thriving trade outfitting travelers for their journeys far upriver.

In 1817, the steamboat *Zebulon M. Pike* docked at St. Louis for the first time, opening a new era in steam transportation along the Mississippi River. Steamboats became the mode of river transportation and gradually replaced the keelboat. By 1849, St. Louis was a major U.S. trading city, serving travelers passing through to the gold

Laclede named St. Louis in honor of King Louis IX, the crusader King of France

August 1763
Laclede and his 13-year-old stepson, Auguste Chouteau, started upriver from New Orleans.

PIERRE LACLEDE LIGUEST

Pierre Laclede Liguest, the namesake of Laclede Gas, came from France to found the city named for a medieval French king.

Laclede, who sometimes added the family name "Liguest" at the end of his signature to distinguish him from other relatives, was born in 1724 in Bedous, France. His contemporaries described Laclede as a striking man, about 5 feet 8 inches tall, erect, with a commanding presence, and a dark complexion.

Laclede's black eyes constituted one of his most impressive physical features. A man of restless energy, Laclede made frequent trips, arduous as the mode of transportation was in those days, between St. Louis and New Orleans.

After serving in the French army, he arrived in New Orleans as a "gentleman traveling for pleasure." Laclede was well-educated and known for his skill in fencing. He fell in love with Marie Therese Chouteau, a woman whose husband had deserted her in New Orleans. Since divorce was forbidden by both French and Spanish law, Marie Therese became Laclede's common-law wife. The couple had four children together. She already had one son, Auguste Chouteau, whom Laclede made his ward, as well as a clerk in his office.

Laclede became interested in the fur trade, and in 1763 partnered with Gilbert Antoine Maxent to win the exclusive right to trade with the Indians of the Mississippi and Missouri Rivers. Laclede headed upriver from New Orleans in his flatboat with his stepson and merchandise for his Indian trade on August 3, 1763. Laclede arrived at Fort de Chartres, some 20 miles above Ste. Genevieve, four months later.

During his stay at Fort de Chartres, he rode with a small party to the Native American village and settlement of Cahokia, crossed to the west side of the Mississippi River and explored the country to the mouth of the Missouri River. Laclede selected a site for the location of his trading post and marked it by blazing the trees. Laclede returned the following year and named the new site St. Louis, in honor of King Louis IX of France.

The end of the French and Indian War resulted in the cession of the lands east of the Mississippi to England in 1764. Many of the French fur trading families in the Illinois country crossed to the west side of the Mississippi River to live near Laclede's trading post. The migration encouraged the gradual growth of St. Louis over the next 40 years. The community grew slowly during the late 18th century. When the territory was transferred to the United States in 1804, the city of St. Louis numbered only 1,100 people.

Pierre Laclede lived for 14 years in St. Louis, looking after his trading and business affairs. The founder of the city fell deeply into debt and was in poor health by 1777, when he traveled to New Orleans to try to straighten out his tangled fortunes.

During his return trip to St. Louis in the spring of 1778, Laclede died on June 20 aboard his boat somewhere near the mouth of the Arkansas River. He was 54 years old. Laclede's friends buried the pioneer in the wilderness. If anything marked the place where his remains were laid, it was soon obliterated. A few years later, no trace of the burial site could be found.

It wasn't until 80 years later, in 1857, that the organizers of The Laclede Gas Light Company chose the intrepid Frenchman as the namesake for the industrial enterprise.

1830 to 1840
The population of St. Louis more than doubled from 6,694 to 16,649.

rush in California or leaving from nearby Independence to follow the Oregon Trail. St. Louis developed into a flourishing river town that boasted municipal improvements more often found in settled Eastern cities.

19th Century Growth

The development of the fur trade in Missouri in the 1830s and 1840s was made possible by the great improvements in river transportation, the most important of which was the introduction of the steamboat. River traffic increased so rapidly that by 1850, St. Louis was the nation's second largest port in point of tonnage, exceeded only by New York City. As river traffic increased, so did the population of St. Louis. During the 1840s, it was the largest city in the nation west of Pittsburgh.

The decade from 1830 to 1840 was one of prosperity and growth in the booming city. The population more than doubled. Many new Protestant churches were established, and the Catholic Diocese erected a beautiful new cathedral, which today is known as the Old Cathedral. Investors incorporated the city water works, and the public school system was

When Laclede Gas Light Co. was founded in 1857, drillers in the eastern United States had already discovered the nation's first supplies of natural gas.

started. The cornerstone of what would become St. Louis University was laid at Ninth and Green Streets. The college opened in 1829 and was the first institution of higher learning west of the Mississippi.

The St. Louis Gas Light Company

The city's municipal improvements would not be complete until residents could venture out on the downtown streets at night without fear of falling off board sidewalks or stepping into bottomless mud puddles. Calls for a gas lighting system began in the 1830s. Baltimore had lighted its streets as early as 1816, and by the 1830s, dozens of U.S. cities were illuminated by gas lights. Philadelphia lighted its streets with gas in 1836. The news of gas-lit streets was telegraphed across the nation to St. Louis.

The Missouri Legislature advanced the gas lighting cause on February 4, 1837, when it enacted special legislation calling for the incorporation of the St. Louis Gas Light Company. St. Louis Gas Light was given "the sole and exclusive privilege of vending gas lights and gas fixtures in the city of St. Louis and its suburbs."

St. Louis was the seventh city in the United States with a gas company, and the first city west of the Mississippi River. The city was singularly unfortunate in that the gas company attempted to accomplish the expensive process of building a gas plant and laying gas mains in city streets at a time when St. Louis was facing unsettled economic conditions. The Bank Panic of 1837 depressed the price of cotton by more than 50 percent and laid up much of the Mississippi River fleet for the next several years.

As a result, St. Louis Gas Light did not complete its first plant for the manufacture of gas at Second and Rutger

February 4, 1837
The Missouri Legislature advanced the gas lighting cause when it enacted special legislation calling for the incorporation of the St. Louis Gas Light Company.

The cornerstone of what would become St. Louis University was laid at Ninth and Green Streets. The college opened in 1829 and was the first institution of higher learning west of the Mississippi.

The Bank Panic of 1837 depressed the price of cotton by more than 50 percent and laid up much of the Mississippi River fleet for the next several years.

Streets until 1841. It was not until 1847 that the plant sent out its first gas to illuminate the streets of St. Louis.

Residents eagerly followed the progress of the St. Louis Gas Light Company crews. "We understand that the expectations of the Engineer, Mr. Lee, are, that he will be able to let on the gas to the public lamps, this evening, and supply private burners at the same time, throughout the district in which the main pipes have been laid down," the St. Louis Republican reported on November 6, 1847.

"It will require some time to exhaust the atmosphere from the gasometers, pipes, etc., and until this is accomplished, the light will not be as brilliant as it will prove to be when the atmospheric air is entirely removed. We shall, however, regard this evening as the real epoch of the introduction of gas light into our streets."

The news of the successful lighting of gas lamps downtown was received with much the same jubilation as the news that arrived on a steamboat just weeks before that General Winfield Scott's U.S. troops had stormed the Hill of Chapultepec, defeated General Santa Ana and taken Mexico City.

"The gloom of our street was dispelled for a portion of last evening by the first burst of gas light," the city's Weekly Reveille reported on November 8, 1847. "It is no longer a dream from which we are to wake in disappointment."

Disaster and Rebirth

Between 1840 and 1850, St. Louis continued rapid growth in both size and population. An important factor in the growth of the city's population was the large influx of immigrants, particularly from Germany and Ireland. The Germans, many of whom had fled the 1848 revolution in their homeland, arrived in such numbers that by the early 1850s, city ordinances were published in German for their benefit.

City officials established the park system in 1844 with the purchase of Lafayette Park from the old St. Louis commons. The transit era opened with the introduction of an omnibus line by Erastus Wells. In the year before city streets were first illuminated by gas, the city organized the police department and incorporated the Mercantile Library. In 1847, St. Louis was connected to the East by telegraph.

St. Louis suffered two disasters in 1849. A great fire devastated 15 city blocks along the riverfront and destroyed 23 steamboats. At the same time, the city suffered a serious outbreak of cholera that sickened and killed thousands of residents. The epidemic resulted in the draining of Chouteau's Pond in the early 1850s. The pond had become polluted by industrial waste and was far from the idyllic picnic site it had been in the 1820s and 1830s.

The city adopted new building codes after the fire requiring buildings erected after 1850 to be constructed in stone rather than wood to alleviate the threat of future fires. The structures that emerged following the fire were built with an emphasis on fireproofing. They were typically four or five stories in height, supported by heavy brick walls

1849
A great fire devastated 15 city blocks along the riverfront and destroyed 23 steamboats.

faced on the street front with stone or cast iron facades.

A new method of land transport, which would later sound the death knell of the steamboat, began to influence St. Louis in the 1850s. The rapid development of the railroads had an immense impact on the nation's economy in the 1850s. Railroads spread from the East to reach the Mississippi River opposite St. Louis about 1850. Construction of the first railroad west of the Mississippi began in 1852. The first line across Missouri was called the Pacific Railroad, and it became the nucleus of the Missouri-Pacific system. It was built westward to Jefferson City by 1855, but because of the Civil War, did not reach Kansas City until 1865.

Soon after construction began on the Pacific line, the Iron Mountain Railroad was built south from St. Louis to tap the rich mining sections of southern Missouri. The North Missouri Railroad (later the Wabash) was built to the north and west. St. Louis and Missouri in general came late to the building of railroads because of the innate conservative nature of the state and the fact that Missouri had magnificent waterways on which to move goods.

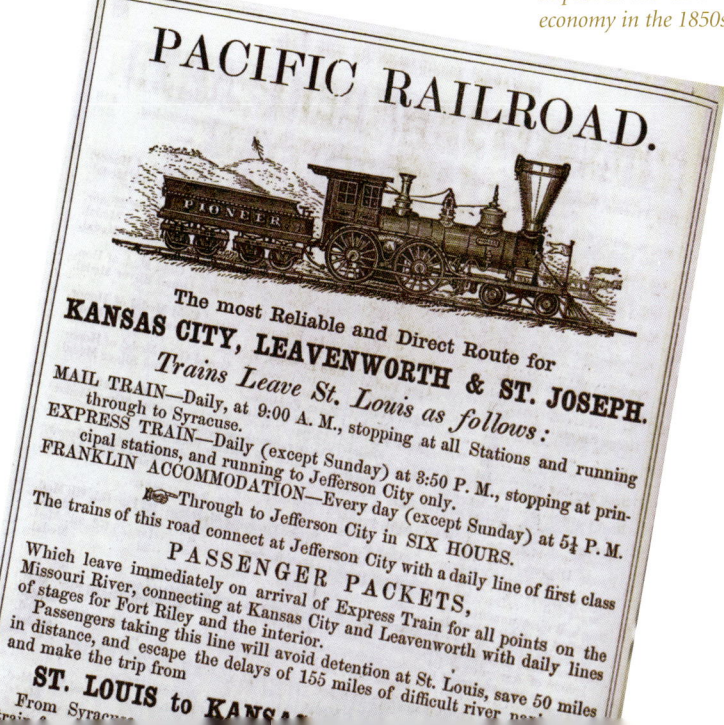

One factor in the growth of St. Louis was the Agricultural and Mechanical Fair, established in 1855 in what is now Fairground Park. The event began as a small country fair, but it gradually grew into a large exposition of more than

The rapid development of the railroads had an immense impact on the nation's economy in the 1850s.

1855
One factor in the growth of St. Louis was the Agricultural and Mechanical Fair, established in what is now Fairground Park.

100 acres with pavilions devoted to the arts and sciences, a zoological garden and a race course. The fair was held in the fall of each year and attracted hundreds of thousands of visitors to the city, many of whom remained as residents.

The Laclede Gas Light Company

St. Louis was in the national spotlight in 1857. In March, the U.S. Supreme Court decided the Dred Scott case, ruling that a person descended from slaves is not a citizen. Scott, a Missouri resident, had accompanied his owner to Illinois and Missouri, both free states. When he returned to St. Louis, he went to the state courthouse to argue that he should be permanently free. Missouri's Supreme Court and a federal appeals court both ruled against Scott, but he took his case to the U.S. Supreme Court. Justice Roger Taney's ruling paved the way for the nation's divisive Civil War four years later.

The Dred Scott case had become a national issue, but local issues continued to dominate the St. Louis political scene. By 1857, most residents were decidedly unhappy with the service provided by the St. Louis Gas Light Company. The service was plagued by interruptions and was the frequent target of high rate complaints.

On March 2, 1857, just a few days before the Supreme Court handed down the Dred Scott decision, the Missouri Legislature passed an act creating two additional gas companies. One of the new companies was named The Laclede Gas Light Company. It was given a franchise to serve customers in the city of St. Louis. The second new firm, the Carondelet Gas Light Company, was formed to serve customers south of St. Louis along the Mississippi River.

The original shareholders of Laclede Gas Light Company were St. Louis merchants and attorneys. The new corporation issued 600 shares of common stock at $100 par value per share. The single largest shareholder, with 160 shares, was attorney Charles Gibson. Brothers Archibald and Hamilton R. Gamble owned 50 shares apiece, as did Edward Bredell, Samuel Gardner, James Hughes and Henry A. Clover. Merchant John Riggin owned 80 shares, and Chester Harding owned 20 shares. Francis H. Manter, named interim president while the corporation was organized, owned 40 shares of stock.

The first shareholders' meeting was held in the office of attorney Henry A. Clover at Seventh and Locust Streets in

The Dred Scott case, decided by the Supreme Court one week after the founding of Laclede Gas Light Co., contributed to the Civil War four years later.

the summer of 1857. Clover reported that approximately 15 people attended. "Most of the parties were lawyers," Clover noted, "and anticipated a legal contest with the St. Louis Gas Light Company." The $600,000 the shareholders raised through the initial public offering was immediately applied to the purchase of land for the construction of a new gas plant at Mound and Mullanphy Streets to serve prospective street lighting customers.

The fact that three gas companies served customers in the St. Louis metropolitan area was a source of immense civic pride. The 1857 *St. Louis City Directory* noted that "the city is lit with gas. Most of the private houses, all hotels, halls, churches, stores and most offices are thus supplied with gas."

But before the shareholders could marshal the resources needed to manufacture and distribute gas to end-use customers, St. Louis was involved in a great Civil War that determined the fate of the American Republic.

Civil War Years

By 1860, on the eve of the tragic Civil War that would divide a nation, St. Louis had become a mature city. It made the transition from a town entirely dependent upon river traffic to a commercial metropolis with both river and rail connections. The city's population in 1860 was 160,733, more than double the population in 1850.

When the Civil War broke out, St. Louis was the most important city in the West, and Missouri was a keystone

St. Louis in the 1850s was a mixture of 19th century urban modernity and frontier American town.

1860
The city's population reached 160,733, more than double the population in 1850.

150 Year Anniversary 17

1861
Some 200,000 men served in the war from Missouri. Approximately 110,000 enlisted on the side of the Union, and 90,000 served on the side of the Confederacy.

of the Union cause. The country's major western lines of communication and travel were anchored in the state by the California, Oregon and Santa Fe Trails. Missouri ranked eighth in population in the United States, making it an excellent manpower resource for the federal armies. The state was rich in deposits of raw materials that included lead for bullets and iron for cannonballs. Its agricultural production alone could feed an army.

Missouri was a microcosm of the United States in 1861. Some 200,000 men served in the war from Missouri. Approximately 110,000 enlisted on the side of the Union, and 90,000 served on the side of the Confederacy. Missouri sent more men to war in proportion to its population than any other state. Approximately 27,000 Missourians, both military and civilian, were killed during the Civil War. The state of Missouri supplied 94 volunteer infantry regiments, 46 independent companies and six artillery batteries during the war.

At the start of the war, Confederate victories at Wilson's Creek and Lexington encouraged Governor Claiborne Jackson to call a special legislative session in Neosho. The pro-Confederate politicians passed an Ordinance of Secession, and the Confederate government recognized Missouri as the 12th Confederate state. At the same time, pro-Union Missouri legislators met in Jefferson City and declared the state's loyalty to the Union.

Missouri was recognized as the 12th Confederate state after Confederate victories at Wilson's Creek and Lexington.

Missouri now had two governments and representation in both the U.S. Congress and Confederate Congress.

Missouri was the site of 28 battles during the Civil War, ranging from major engagements such as New Madrid and Westport to minor skirmishes like Boonville and Mt. Zion Church. The period of conflict in Missouri exceeded three full years, from June 17, 1861 to October 28, 1864.

The Battle of Wilson's Creek, the first major engagement of the Civil War west of the Mississippi River, marked the beginning of the Civil War in Missouri. For the next 3½ years, the state was the scene of savage and fierce fighting, mostly guerrilla warfare, with small bands of mounted raiders destroying anything military or civilian that could aid the enemy. By the time the conflict ended in the spring of 1865, Missouri had witnessed so many battles and skirmishes that it ranked as the third most fought over state in the nation.

The Battle of Westport, nicknamed the "Gettysburg of the West," was the largest battle fought west of the Mississippi River. Like Gettysburg, the Battle of Westport was a failed Confederate attempt to sever Union territory at the point of attack. The engagement was the last big battle in the state and essentially ended the Civil War in Missouri. Perhaps in no other slave state that did not secede was support for the Confederacy so determined and so costly in lives and property as in Missouri. The political fight for control of nearby Kansas, characterized by violence and bitterness, had made Missourians excessively partisan.

Thomas C. Fletcher, Missouri's governor in 1865, signed the proclamation stating that slavery would be abolished in Missouri "now and forever." Missouri independently abolished slavery before the 13th amendment to the Constitution abolished it everywhere in the United States.

The attorneys and merchants who organized Laclede Gas Light Company in the spring of 1857 put their business venture on hold during the Civil War. Hamilton R. Gamble was elected governor of Missouri during the war on a pro-Union platform. His brother, Archibald Gamble, served as St. Louis' ninth postmaster.

Francis H. Manter, the company's first interim president, commanded a brigade in the first division of the 15th Army Corps under General William Tecumseh Sherman at the Battle of Jackson and the Siege of Vicksburg in 1863. Manter was killed in action the next spring in Arkansas. Charles Gibson, the company's largest shareholder, left St. Louis for Washington, D.C., where he established a successful contracting business. Samuel Gardner was named the U.S. customs collector for Missouri.

The end of the war in the spring of 1865 ushered in a postwar era of peace and prosperity that lasted for nearly 30 years. Laclede Gas Light Company would become one of the St. Louis' most successful firms during the 1870s and 1880s.

1865
Thomas C. Fletcher, Missouri's governor, signed the proclamation stating that slavery would be abolished in Missouri "now and forever."

Residences on Kennett Place in the early 1890s. Relatively undeveloped until the 1850s, the Lafayette Square neighborhood became a suburban sanctuary for the city's wealthiest families.

Growing Pains

Thousands of soldiers and sailors returned to St. Louis in the summer of 1865, eager to resume their lives after four long years of war. For Laclede Gas Light Company, however, the years following the Civil War were consumed by one battle after another with the competing St. Louis Gas Light Company and the city of St. Louis.

The fights over service territory would only be settled in 1873 when the three parties to the struggle signed a Tripartite Agreement that designated franchise territories for each gas company. And the war between Laclede Gas Light Company and St. Louis Gas Light Company would not officially end until 1889 when Laclede acquired the assets and franchises of its longtime competitor.

The roots of the battle between the two gas companies stemmed from the March 1857 special act of the Missouri Legislature chartering Laclede Gas Light Company and Carondelet Gas Light Company. The language of the act authorized Laclede Gas Light "to do the business of making and vending gas, etc., within all that part of the city of St. Louis lying west of Seventh Street and east of Grand Avenue…"

The Legislature had given Laclede Gas Light wide-ranging powers to light the streets, make and vend gas, erect gas lights and gas fixtures, and bury pipes, fixtures and equipment in order to carry on its business. But the Legislature included several restrictions in the act that were to plague Laclede Gas Light for much of its early history. In a March 3, 1857 amendment to the act passed the previous day, the Missouri Legislature struck the utility's right to a "sole and exclusive" franchise. The Legislature also noted that the St. Louis Gas Light Company, by virtue of its 1837 franchise, had the right to exclude Laclede Gas Light Company, as well as any person or firm that wanted to make and sell gas in the city, from doing so.

In other words, Laclede Gas Light Company had to get permission from St. Louis Gas Light Company to extend its lines west of Seventh Street and east of Grand Avenue. In the years following the Civil War, Laclede Gas Light built a gas plant on land it owned at Mound and Mullanphy Streets. But St. Louis Gas Light would not allow its newer competitor to lay distribution lines in the city.

Isaac Lionberger, a St. Louis attorney who would later serve Laclede Gas Light as a corporate officer, noted that "the Laclede charter appeared valueless except that perhaps it gave a right to the company to negotiate with the St. Louis company for a surrender of part of its exclusive rights." In any case, Lionberger pointed out, St. Louis Gas Light could afford to wait its rival out. The exclusive charter of the St. Louis Gas Light Company did not expire until 1890, while Laclede Gas Light's charter expired in 1887.

Realizing it was unlikely that St. Louis Gas Light would ever agree to allow Laclede Gas Light to make and sell gas in the city, Laclede Gas Light went back to the Missouri Legislature for relief. In 1868, the Legislature passed an act that amended Laclede Gas Light's original 1857 charter. The amendment, while declaring that nothing in the 1868 act would be construed to affect the vested rights of St. Louis Gas Light, did remedy Laclede Gas Light's chief complaint. It authorized the company

St. Louis attorney Isaac Lionberger figured prominently in Laclede Gas Light's franchise fights with competitors during the 1870s and 1880s.

JOHN PINKNEY KEISER

John Pinkney Keiser, Laclede Gas Light Company's first president, still holds the record for longest term served as company president. The Mississippi River steamboat captain was president of Laclede for 32 years, from 1868 to 1900.

Keiser was born September 23, 1833 in Boone County, Missouri. Keiser's father built the first gristmill in the county as well as the first steam mill west of St. Charles, Missouri. He also built the first paper mill in the state.

John P. Keiser first attended school at Pittsburgh, Pennsylvania, while his father was superintending the building of a steamboat. He attended Catholic School in St. Louis in the old Walnut Street Cathedral. In 1848, Keiser boarded at a private school in Hermann, Missouri, to study the German language, and later attended Jones' Commercial College in St. Louis, as well as the Howard School of Fayette, Missouri, where he completed his studies.

At the time he left school, the river transportation business was experiencing an era of great prosperity. In 1852, before he was 20 years of age, Keiser shipped out on the steamer Clendenin, with Captain Henry W. Smith, to learn river navigation. In 1853, he received his first government license as a pilot on the Missouri River.

Keiser gradually worked himself up in the fleet. In 1856, at age 23, he became commander of a steamer of the Lightning Line. In 1858, Keiser bought his first steamer, the Isabella, which yielded him rich returns in the years before the Civil War. During the Civil War he was owner and commander of several steamers. For a time following the war, Keiser was in the commission business in St. Louis with his brother, Charles W. Keiser. But the discovery of gold in Montana and the increase in passenger and freight traffic took him back to the river transportation business once again.

During the years Keiser was actively engaged in steamboating, he built, owned and controlled 58 river steamers. He was identified with the construction of the Eads Bridge for a time as general supply agent and also was successful as general manager of the Carondelet shipyards.

Keiser was made general superintendent of the Memphis & St. Louis Packet Company, which subsequently was renamed the St. Louis & New Orleans Anchor Line. He was president of the Anchor Line from 1882 until 1884, when he disposed of his entire interest in the steamship firm and severed his connection with the river interests. During the years he spent managing his transportation interests, Keiser served as president of the Laclede Gas Light Company, a position he ably filled until the company transferred its property to a reorganized corporation in 1889.

Following his retirement from the presidency of Laclede, Keiser turned his attention to private business interests, rounding out a career in which he enjoyed an enviable reputation for honor and integrity of character. He was for many years a valued member of the Merchants' Exchange and was also a member of the St. Louis University and Noonday Clubs.

He married Miss Laura R. Hough of Jefferson City, Missouri, on September 27, 1864. Keiser died on July 27, 1901, at Penatangueshene, Ontario, while spending the summer with his family

---

to do business throughout the city, as it existed in 1868 and as its city limits might be established in the future. The 1868 act repealed the section of the 1857 charter giving the city the right to purchase Laclede Gas Light's property, and it authorized the company to increase its stock beyond the $2 million originally authorized. Finally, it extended the rights and franchises originally conferred for 60 years to a period of perpetuity. In effect, the Legislature had granted Laclede Gas Light a St. Louis franchise that would last forever.

The Tripartite Agreement

The fact that the 1868 act amending Laclede Gas Light's charter seemed to contravene several provisions of Missouri's 1865 constitution, especially concerning the perpetual franchise, provided grist for lawsuits for the next 30 years. But the 1868 act did unequivocally grant Laclede Gas Light the authority to make and sell gas in St. Louis. In 1873, the company began extending lines from its plant at Mound and Mullanphy Streets west of Seventh Street. St. Louis Gas Light promptly brought suit to restrain what it called "the invasion of its exclusive privilege."

1873
The company began extending lines from its plant at Mound and Mullanphy Streets west of Seventh Street.

1870
Bolstered by new immigrants, St. Louis grew from a town of 16,000 people in 1840 to an industrial metropolis of more than 300,000.

Laclede Gas Light's defense was handled by some of the city's leading attorneys. W.B. Napton, a Princeton University graduate, served as attorney general of Missouri in the 1830s and as a justice of the Missouri Supreme Court from 1838 to 1851. He would be re-appointed to the state Supreme Court in late 1873 and serve until 1881. James O. Broadhead, a Virginian who moved to St. Louis in 1859, was another member of the defense team. Broadhead served as Provost Marshal for Missouri and surrounding states during the Civil War and would help write the charter of the city of St. Louis in 1875. From 1878 to 1879, he was the first president of the American Bar Association.

Charles Gibson, one of the company's largest shareholders, provided legal advice to the defense team. Gibson, who had studied law under Edward Bates, the former Attorney General of the United States, returned to St. Louis after representing Missouri's interests in Washington, D.C. during the Civil War.

Before the case could go to trial, the two gas utilities reached an out-of-court compromise, which the city approved. The competition had become so disruptive during the early 1870s that both gas companies had installed mains on the same streets and offered deals to entice new customers.

The stakes had become too big for city officials to idly sit by while the community's two gas utilities tried to destroy each other. Bolstered by new immigrants, St. Louis grew from a town of 16,000 people in 1840 to an industrial metropolis of more than 300,000 by 1870, and the city's brewing industry was one of St. Louis' economic development success stories. The breweries supplied local taverns via horse-drawn wagons. They also served customers, directly in lavish beer gardens abuzz with oompah bands and singing clubs.

The Bavarian Brewery of Eberhard Anheuser was one of 50 breweries in St. Louis in 1870. Anheuser, a soap manufacturer, had taken over an insolvent business in 1860 and made it profitable. But it was his son-in-law, Adolphus Busch, who would spearhead the company's global expansion and become St. Louis's merchant king of beer.

During the late 1800s, Anheuser-Busch was one of the city's thriving businesses. Adolphus Busch and other brewers hosted a Bavarian exhibit called the "Tyrolean Alps" with a restaurant seating 3,000 people. Anheuser-Busch was by the 1890s the world's largest brewery. It covered an area equal to 60 city blocks, employed 5,000 people, and each day brewed 6,000 barrels and shipped nearly 800,000 bottles of beer.

During the late 19th century, beer gardens opened in St. Louis every spring.

24 Laclede Gas Company

By the 1890's, Anheuser-Busch was the largest brewery in the world.

The fight between Laclede Gas Light and St. Louis Gas Light imperiled the city's industrial development efforts. As a result, the Tripartite Agreement signed in 1873 set specific boundaries for the two utilities. Laclede Gas Light was assigned an exclusive franchise to serve the area of the city north of Washington Avenue and agreed to pay St. Louis Gas Light $700,000 for all of its pipes, fixtures and customers in the city's north end.

For its part, the city dropped its lawsuit against St. Louis Gas Light Company, alleging that it had the right to purchase the assets of the city's original gas company.

The Eads Bridge

Laclede Gas Light had a hand in illuminating one of the wonders of the age. In 1874, James Buchanan Eads, an Indiana native who had grown up in St. Louis, designed and built the first road and rail bridge to cross the Mississippi River. The rise of railroads in the decade following the Civil War had allowed Chicago to eclipse St. Louis as the transportation hub for the Midwest. The Eads Bridge, which the city approved in 1867 and Eads completed in 1874, was an attempt by St. Louis to regain its position as the logistics center for the region.

Eads sunk his piers 100 feet below the river bottom and used three steel arches averaging 500 feet in length to hold up his bridge. A dozen men died in the airless caissons beneath the water, placing the piers in the riverbed. The work was the deepest ever done at the time, and when the bridge was completed in 1874, it was hailed as a marvel of modern engineering, much like the Gateway Arch nearly a century in the future.

Laclede Gas Light installed gas lights across the entire length of the $7 million bridge which Eads opened in 1874 by having 15 fully loaded 50-ton locomotives driven across the span. At night, the gas lights blazing on the bridge became a new landmark for St. Louis.

1870
Laclede Gas Light was assigned an exclusive franchise to serve the area of the city north of Washington Avenue and agreed to pay St. Louis Gas Light $700,000 for all of its pipes, fixtures and customers in the city's north end.

By the 1890s, St. Louis manufacturers such as the Excelsior Stove Works were providing a market for gas produced by Laclede Gas Light.

1874
When the bridge was completed in 1874, it was hailed as a marvel of modern engineering.

Laclede Gas Light also was very active in installing light fixtures along the St. Louis Riverfront at the foot of the Eads Bridge. The utility's gas light's illuminated the bustling factory and warehouse district along First Street and Second Street, lighting up such St. Louis businesses as the Cutlery Factory in the 600 block of Second Street, the Old Judge Coffee Building in the 700 block of Second Street, the Excelsior Stove Factory in the 600 block of First Street and the Raeder Place Building in the 700 block of First Street.

Back in Court

In 1879, both Laclede Gas Light and St. Louis Gas Light were back in court, this time as defendants in a suit filed by the city of St. Louis. Years later, Isaac Lionberger recalled that "the city, becoming dissatisfied with the price charged for gas, brought suit to annul the Tripartite Agreement on the grounds that the Laclede Company had not by the act of 1857 the right to do business east of Seventh Street or west of Grand Avenue." Furthermore, the city claimed that the 1868 act was unconstitutional, and that Laclede Gas Light therefore had no power to enter into the 1873 contract with the city and St. Louis Gas Light Company.

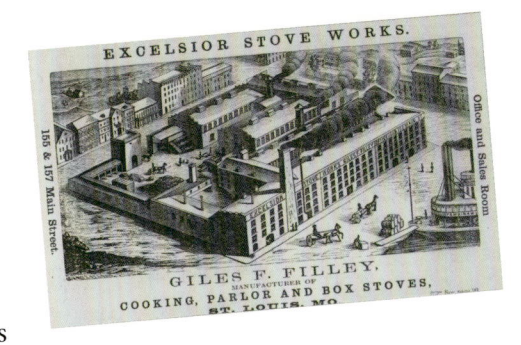

The Circuit Court of St. Louis ruled in favor of the city, voiding the Tripartite

The 1874 Eads Bridge was a St. Louis landmark that boasted gas lights provided by Laclede Gas Light across the entire length of the half-mile span.

26 Laclede Gas Company

Agreement. Laclede Gas Light took the matter to the Court of Appeals, which affirmed the lower court's decision. It wasn't until the Missouri Supreme Court overturned the appeals court decision that Laclede Gas Light and its officers could finally breathe a sigh of relief. With the 1879 Supreme Court decision, Laclede Gas Light and the city settled into a relationship based on the inviolability of the 1868 amendments to the 1857 charter.

"After this case was disposed of," Lionberger explained, "Mr. Marshall, who represented the city in the litigation, advised the Laclede company that in view of all the cases decided, our charter was not only valid but perpetual."

Lionberger further noted in 1917 that "the Supreme Court of the State in every case brought before it had predicated its position on the validity of the act of 1868." Had the Supreme Court ruled otherwise at any point during the 1870s, the utility would likely never had survived to the turn of the 20th century, let alone the 21st century.

Let There Be Light

For Laclede Gas Light Company, the 1880s brought the opportunity to showcase the strides that gas light illumination had made during the years following the Civil War. New Weslbach Mantles and an improved underground distribution system allowed Laclede Gas Light to increase the candlepower rating of the fixtures, as well as to provide for ingenious displays of gas lighting.

Lee Liberman, later Laclede's president and CEO, explained in 1987 that the 1880s were "the golden age of gas illumination, highlighted by such massive undertakings as the 1882 'Carnival City of America,' featuring gas-lighted arches with 21,000 globes of various colors."

The forerunner of today's electric and neon lights and signs, gas illumination in the 1880s and 1890s provided St. Louis with a source of civic pride. The city's business community collected $20,000 for the 1882 Carnival and supervised the placement of gas pipes and arches along and over the sidewalks and along 44 blocks of the city's business district. A historian noted that the display was "better than anything England or Continental Europe could provide."

The parade capping the 1882 Carnival festivities was lit by gas, and the route through the city was decorated by gas-lit fixtures resembling trees. Ten years later, Laclede Gas Light again displayed its skills at gas illumination when it lit the Columbia Exhibition of 1893. The Exhibition included a gas-lit arch highlighting each president of the United States.

During the 1890s, one of the highlights of each year in St. Louis was the Veiled Prophet Parade, sponsored by one of the city's many civic clubs. Laclede Gas participated actively in the annual event, lighting the streets with gas-lit arches and providing gas torches for most of the floats.

William S. Dodd, who served as treasurer of the company in the early 1900s, recalled how some of the spectacular lighting effects were achieved. "About the time of the Spanish-American War when the American eagle was a part of all

1882

The city's business community collected $20,000 for the 1882 Carnival and supervised the placement of gas pipes and arches along and over the sidewalks and along 44 blocks of the city's business district.

A trolley car passes under the gas-lit presidential arch at the 1892 Columbia Exhibition in downtown St. Louis. Arches, or 'flambeaux,' were commonly used to illuminate American cities during the 1890s.

1882
Sunbury was the site of the first three-wire installation for a direct current central station generator.

displays," he said, "the men at the service stations created the outlines of an eagle by bending pipes along a chalk drawing on the floor of one of the shops. Holes were then drilled in the pipes and burners attached, which we later lighted to outline the design."

For Laclede Gas Light President John Keiser and the company's executive staff, the 1882 and 1892 celebrations were an affirmation of the power of gas to illuminate the city's streets and places of business. But by the mid-1880s, Laclede Gas Light and St. Louis Gas Light Company were beginning to feel the impact of a powerful new competitor.

The Second Industrial Revolution

The village of Sunbury in central Pennsylvania on the Susquehanna River was perhaps an unlikely place to usher in a new era in world technology. Sunbury was the site of the first three-wire installation for a direct current central station generator. As such, it is the common ancestor for every electric utility in America as well as the world.

Thomas Edison himself spent a fair amount of time in Sunbury and the nearby communities of Tamaqua and Shamokin in the spring and summer of 1882, helping his local agents to wire up the system and get it running — which they did on July 4, 1882.

The local newspapers were full of awe for the miracle that Thomas Edison had wrought for their small community. Many described it as the dawn of the second industrial revolution. But it would be very expensive to bring the new technology to fruition.

Edison basically franchised his operation to the local investors. In a precursor of the capital-intensive nature of the electric utility industry, the investors in the Sunbury franchise came up short on the money they owed Mr. Edison. In lieu of cash, they prevailed upon the Wizard of

Menlo Park to take stock in their venture, which he did in September 1882.

It didn't take long for the newfangled invention of electric power generation to work its way westward. The site of the first hydroelectric central power station in the Western Hemisphere was located along the banks of the Mississippi River in downtown Minneapolis. It was built at the St. Anthony Falls by the Minnesota Brush Electric Company and began operation on September 6, 1882 to furnish arc lighting service for commercial businesses in part of the city. The next year, the station began supplying arc street lighting for the entire city of Minneapolis.

The prime motive power for the hydroelectric station was a Francis-type hydraulic turbine. Water for the turbine came from the pool created by a timber crib dam, which was later replaced by a concrete dam. The water was conveyed through a 200-foot-long steel pipe and discharged to the tail-race. The head was about 30 feet, and the turbine drove a line shaft to which were belted four 40-light and one 20-light Brush arc dynamos. The total output of the station was about 100 kilowatts. The power was transmitted by pole line one-quarter of a mile to Washington Avenue.

It didn't take long for electric power to work its way down river from St. Anthony's Falls to St. Louis. It came in the form of transportation. The Gateway City had enjoyed horse-drawn streetcars since about the time of the Tripartite Agreement in 1873. In 1886, the St. Louis Cable and Western Company was incorporated to operate a cable car line from Sixth and Locust Streets to Vandeventer Avenue via Franklin Avenue. The cable cars were operated by a steam engine that ran a large wire cable just below grade. The cars were equipped with grips on their undercarriage that fastened on to the cable, which allowed the cars to move through the streets at about 5 mph.

In 1887, the city authorized several street railways doing business in St. Louis to use electricity as motive power for the cars. The Lindell Railway Company, the Union Depot Railway Company and the Mound City Line all electrified in the early 1890s. They operated electric streetcars that attached to overhead distribution lines by means of an eight-foot-long wooden troller, which gave the cars the nickname "trolley." The three St. Louis streetcar lines consolidated in 1899 as the St. Louis Transit Company.

The competition with electric companies threatened to take away much of Laclede Gas Light's business. But Laclede Gas Light, along with the rest of the gas distribution business in North America, was quick to react to the threat posed by electric power competition for lighting load in the 1880s and 1890s. Within a generation, the gas industry in general, and Laclede Gas Light in particular experienced a change from 90 percent lighting load to a 90 percent cooking and heating load.

The company noted early in the 20th century that the threat from electric utilities threatened Laclede Gas Light's very existence. "The gas companies in St. Louis were no different than others throughout the nation," the utility told shareholders, "except that the local companies were blessed with a citizenry

1886
The St. Louis Cable and Western Company was incorporated to operate a cable car line from Sixth and Locust Streets to Vandeventer Avenue via Franklin Avenue.

1889
The three St. Louis streetcar lines consolidated as the St. Louis Transit Company.

Although Laclede Gas Light lost much of its lighting business to electric power competitors at the turn of the 20th century, the St. Louis utility grew its business on the strength of gas cooking.

that was conservative to a degree and not too quick to accept change. This, fortunately, gave the companies time to make readjustments."

One readjustment that Laclede Gas Light made was to promote the sale of gas stoves in the 1880s and 1890s, one of the first gas utilities in America to do so. John Ringen, a German immigrant fleeing the 1848 upheavals in his native land, established his own tin shop in the 1850s in St. Louis. In the 1870s, Ringen and his partner, George A. Kahle, began making and selling cooking stoves, washing machines and other household appliances. The cooking stoves were dubbed "quick meals," and the two men incorporated the Quick Meal Stove Company and the Ringen Stove Company to make and market the popular appliances.

In the early 1880s, Ringen began manufacturing a gas range under the Quick Meal brand name. Ringen went on to form the American Stove Company with other manufacturers from Cleveland and Chicago in 1901, and in later years, it introduced the brand name "Magic Chef." But in the 1880s and 1890s, Quick Meal gas ranges gave Laclede Gas Light Company a lucrative new market.

Consolidation

By the time the streetcar companies were brought together in a single company in 1899, the gas companies had been consolidated for a decade. The cutthroat competition of the 1880s had proved to be too much for St. Louis Gas Light Company.

The Laclede Gas Light Company was so nimble in its strategic marketing initiatives, it was able to utilize economies of scale to drive the price of gas in St. Louis down throughout the 1880s. In 1873, when the Tripartite Agreement was signed, the price charged for gas delivered to city street lights was $4.50 per 1,000 cubic feet. By the mid-1870s, competition had dropped the price to $3.50 per 1,000 cubic feet, and the price continued dropping through the late 1870s and into the 1880s. The price dropped to $3.00, and then to $2.50, "and finally," an 1893 St. Louis directory pointed out, "the Laclede company forced the price down to its lowest notch by reducing the price of its product to $1.18-¼ per 1,000 cubic feet, at which price it has remained."

30 Laclede Gas Company

Unable to compete with Laclede Gas Light Company, the Carondelet Gas Light Company and the St. Louis Heat and Power Company approached Laclede Gas Light about the possibility of being acquired by the city's dominant gas franchise. In early 1889, Laclede Gas Light purchased the two smaller gas utilities for $500,000 in cash and stock. The acquisition gave Laclede Gas Light the Carondelet gas plant at the far southern edge of the city, which positioned Laclede Gas Light for industrial growth in the 1890s and 1900s.

Meanwhile, St. Louis Gas Light Company was flirting with bankruptcy and concerned that the city would refuse to renew the company's franchise when it expired in 1890. In 1886, St. Louis Gas Light negotiated a 30-year franchise extension with the city, for the payment of $1.5 million.

The payment to the city depleted St. Louis Gas Light's cash reserves. In 1889, St. Louis Gas Light Company quietly let it be known that it was for sale. Isaac Lionberger, the distinguished St. Louis attorney who served Laclede Gas Light Company as vice president, went to New York City to arrange financing for the purchase. Lionberger put Laclede's board in touch with Henry Bowly Hollins.

Harry B. Hollins was from old New York money. His wife was New York socialite Evelina Merseole Knapp, and the couple's doings dominated the society pages of The New York Times. In 1878, Hollins organized the banking and brokerage firm of H.B. Hollins & Co., specializing in making a market in railroad and industrial stocks.

In 1888, Hollins added investment banking to his resumé. Hollins boasted of his relationships with some of America's wealthiest venture capitalists, including William K. Vanderbilt and J.P. Morgan. Hollins and Morgan, whose offices were across the street from each other at the corner of Wall and Broad Streets, were business partners in the acquisition of a number of properties in the Midwest during the 1890s and 1900s.

Hollins arranged a $4 million financing for the purchase of the St. Louis Gas Light Company. Laclede Gas Light Company reorganized and sold stock to H.B. Hollins & Co. to pay for the acquisition. Laclede Gas Light agreed to abide by the 1886 agreement that St. Louis Gas Light forged with the city of St. Louis for the extension of the franchise, even though Laclede Gas Light's perpetual franchise superseded that of St. Louis Gas Light Company. Laclede Gas Light also moved its administrative offices from Station B at Main and Mullanphy Street and from its retail offices on Pine Street downtown to St. Louis Gas Light Company's more modern facilities at 411 N. 11th Street.

Laclede Gas Light Company faced the 1890s with an optimistic spirit. St. Louis had recaptured fourth place among American cities in the 1890 Census with a population of more than 450,000 people, and even the Panic of 1893 could not long dampen the economic strength that St. Louis exhibited in the 1890s. Laclede Gas Light intended to fuel that economic growth into the new century.

1889
Laclede Gas Light purchased the two smaller gas utilities for $500,000 in cash and stock.

INTERLUDE 1

The Town Gas Era

For the first 90 years of its existence, Laclede Gas, like most gas distribution companies in North America and Europe, manufactured and sold what was commonly called town gas. Derived from burning coal in the absence of oxygen, low-British Thermal Unit (BTU) manufactured (or town) gas lit the streets of North America for much of the 19th century. In the early 20th century, manufactured gas played an increasingly important role in gas utilities' penetration of residential and commercial cooking and heating markets.

Gas technology was a phenomenon of the Industrial Revolution. Europeans developed the concept of burning coal in airless retorts to produce a low-BTU manufactured gas as early as the 1750s. The technology crossed the Atlantic to North America shortly after the War of 1812, and Americans quickly learned to use what they called town gas for cooking, heating and lighting.

In the beginning, what little light was shed over the cities and streets of America was cast by gas street lamps and whale-oil or kerosene lamps in homes and shops.

The First Gas Utilities

Soon after Rembrandt Peale founded the first gas lighting company in America in Baltimore in the summer of 1816, entrepreneurs elsewhere on the East Coast began to envision the soft glow of gas lamps lighting up the night sky.

On February 7, 1817, Peale and his investors erected the first gas light in the United States at the corner of Market and Lemon Streets, now the intersection of Baltimore and Holliday. Just two years before Peale's establishment of the Gas Light Company of Baltimore, British troops had burned the District of Columbia during the War of 1812.

Residents of the District of Columbia tried to emulate Peale's success by establishing a gas lighting company as early as 1817, but the cost of erecting gasworks and laying mains in the streets meant that the city had to make do with its whale-oil street lamps for another 30 years. Gas lights offered the luxury of forgoing wicks, tallow and excessive smoke, but the gas was difficult to manufacture. Essentially, it involved burning coal in large boilers and then mixing the resulting gas with water or fuel oil to increase the BTU content and candlepower rating of the coal gas.

Gas and water utility services were 19th century technologies that paved the way for the introduction of natural gas utility service in the 20th century. During the 1820s and 1830s, gas service spread throughout the East Coast. The Boston Gas Light Company organized in 1822, followed a year later by the New York Gas Light Company. Philadelphia got gas service in 1836, and most communities of any size east of the Appalachian Mountains had at least rudimentary gas service by the mid-1840s. The formation of the St. Louis Gas Light Company in 1837 marked the introduction of gas distribution service west of the Mississippi River.

The development of a canal barge and rail infrastructure in the United States east of the Mississippi River after 1840 meant that coal quickly became the fuel of choice for producing manufactured gas. By the 1850s, vast coal reserves had been developed in Pennsylvania and Virginia. As settlers moved west, they discovered and developed new reserves of coal in Indiana, Ohio, Illinois and Iowa.

By the beginning of the Civil War in 1861, there were few communities in the Midwest and Mid-Atlantic states that did not have easy access to a supply of coal for making manufactured gas. The resulting gas was a methane/hydrogen combination that had a BTU content of between 400 to 550 BTUs per cubic foot.

Prior to the Civil War and the development in the early 1870s of enrichment techniques of injecting coal gas with fuel oil, town gas typically produced 17 to 19 candlepower, or the light produced by one candle.

Simple and Primitive

Delivery of town gas to consumers in the 1840s was simple and primitive. In the early days of the industry, most gas pipes in service were made of wood. Gas crews took a hollowed-out log that had an inside diameter of three inches and was tapered at one end and fit the sections into each other. Joints frequently were reinforced with iron bands that were sealed with lead or coal tar residue from the gas plant.

Following the Civil War, town gas companies like Laclede Gas, the Washington Gas Light Company, the Philadelphia Gas Works and Brooklyn Union Gas Company were frequent purchasers of surplus military equipment. Old musket barrels often were pressed into use by the gas utilities as service pipes for homes and businesses.

Early coal gas plants in St. Louis first used water to quench the burning coal, and then purified the resulting gas to remove sulfide, cyanide and ammonia. Much of the residue consisted of coke, which is an almost pure form of carbon that the utility then sold to foundries for the production of iron and steel and to local gas companies for home heating. By the turn of the 20th century, Midwest utilities such as Laclede Gas and the Citizens Gas Trust in nearby Indianapolis operated thriving coke businesses as a sideline to the gas manufacturing process.

The organizers of Midwest and East Coast gas companies were quick to convert to a new water gas process when it was introduced in the mid-1870s. All of the Pennsylvania gas utilities made use of the coal carbonization process that had been brought to the United States from Europe prior to 1820. Coal carbonization involved the distillation of coal in the

Gaslights illuminate downtown St. Louis circa 1895.

absence of air, which in essence drove off approximately 30 percent of the coal by weight as gas and residual chemicals.

The coal gas process was simple, and it produced manufactured gas inexpensively. But the gas produced was low-BTU, and even lower in candlepower. That problem was resolved by Thaddeus S.C. Lowe.

Born and raised on a New Hampshire farm, Thaddeus Sobieski Coulincourt Lowe spent most of his life tinkering with chemistry and gases. During the Civil War, President Abraham Lincoln named Lowe chief of the Union Army's Corps of Aeronautics. His observation balloons flew over the war's battlefields. Lowe and his cohorts reported back to the federal Army of the Potomac on the disposition of the Confederate troops spread out below them.

In 1872, Lowe experimented with the manufactured gas processes of the day. According to the history of the Philadelphia-based United Gas Improvement Corporation (UGI), which later patented the talented inventor's process, "Lowe exposed water gas vapors to a thin stream of petroleum naptha, enriching the gas with hydrocarbons from the oil. The enriched, or carburetted, water gas burned with a far brighter flame than coal gas."

Not only was the flame brighter, the process was actually cheaper than coal carbonization. In 1874,

The gaslights on this store were a typical outdoor installation of the "gay nineties."

Lowe helped build the first carburetted gas plant at Phoenixville, Pennsylvania, northwest of Valley Forge. Lowe's process boosted the concentration of hydrogen and carbon monoxide in the gas, thereby enriching it and making it more suitable for illumination. By the turn of the century, water gas was well on its way to becoming the predominant gas manufacturing process in America.

A Watershed Decade

The 1880s were a watershed decade for the gas industry in America. UGI created the nation's first utility holding company in the years after 1882, when it began expanding its reach well beyond Philadelphia. UGI sold the Lowe patents when it acquired town gas companies in communities across the eastern half of the nation, including Nashville, Tennessee; Des Moines, Iowa; Concord and Manchester, New Hampshire; Allentown, Pennsylvania; Savannah and Atlanta, Georgia; Vicksburg, Mississippi; and Hammond, Indiana. The North American Companies, which had been incorporated in the late 1880s to invest in railroad securities, branched out into control of gas and electric companies during the 1890s.

The gas industry scored a technological coup late in the 1880s when UGI secured the patents for the Welsbach Mantle from its Austrian inventor. The Welsbach Mantle was a cloth and metallic wick for gas lights and was a decided improvement in both candlepower and durability over its predecessors. The improvement allowed town gas companies to retain at least part of their lighting business well into the 20th century.

The 1880s also brought the first major competition to the nation's gas industry. Thomas Edison's discovery of a workable incandescent lighting system between 1879 and 1883 effectively began the process of shutting town gas producers out of the residential and commercial lighting markets.

The great expense of building incandescent lighting systems and wiring homes for electricity, however, coupled with the efficiency of the Welsbach Mantle, made the process of replacement long and drawn out. In reality, it was 20 years before incandescent electric lighting irrevocably captured the home lighting market in America from manufactured gas suppliers.

Edison himself had been so sure that incandescent lighting systems would quickly run town gas companies out of business that he put together a syndicate in the early 1880s to take short positions in gas company stocks. Edison was an inventive genius, but his business decisions frequently left something to be desired. In the case of the short gas stocks, Edison and his syndicate were thwarted by a brilliant marketing stroke on the part of the town gas companies.

Realizing by the mid-1890s that, even with the introduction of the Welsbach Mantle, gas lighting was likely to be supplanted by incandescent electric lighting, the nation's gas companies smoothly shifted marketing gears. Beginning in the years immediately prior to the turn of the century, gas companies began heavily promoting what they called "fuel gas" for residential and commercial heating and gas for cooking. By the early 1900s, board of director minutes for companies like the predecessor of Brooklyn Union Gas Company routinely reported on the number of gas ranges sold.

The gas industry's decision in the 1890s to not compete with incandescent electric lighting and to focus instead on heating and cooking created the marketing foundation of the modern industry. When town gas was replaced by natural gas, the industry had a customer base which readily took to the more efficient fuel source. And by the 1890s, the first town gas companies in the Midwest were beginning to convert to natural gas.

The 264 foot Ferris Wheel dominated the grounds of the St. Louis World's Fair in the summer of 1904. Held to celebrate the centennial of the Lewis and Clark expedition, the fair attracted attendees from around the world. Laclede Gas Light erected thousands of gas lights on the grounds, casting a soft glow across the Missouri night sky.

CHAPTER 3

Into a New Century

Laclede Gas Light Company was in the nation's spotlight as the United States celebrated a new century in the summer of 1904. The St. Louis World's Fair brought thousands of visitors to the Gateway City. "Meet me in St. Louis, Louis" was on everybody's lips, and the fair introduced the country to a great new way to eat ice cream.

In the 1890s, the intersection of Broadway and Chestnut was the heart of the St. Louis commercial district.

The ice cream cone resulted when a concessionaire at the fair experimented with folding a warm waffle and filling it with ice cream.

Laclede Gas Light was the gas supplier to the fair. The company's thousands of gas bulbs and arches lit the fair grounds well into the Missouri summer night. St. Louis was a vibrant community at the turn of the 20th century, with a population of more than 575,000 people and an economy driven by transportation, brewing and metalworking.

The city's downtown district had expanded north and south along Broadway during the late 1880s and 1890s. With the widespread introduction of Elisha Otis' elevator and Werner Siemens' invention of an electric elevator in 1880, skyscrapers became a fixture on the St. Louis downtown scene in the 1890s. The United States Custom House and Post Office, known today as the Old Post Office, a model of Second Empire architecture, anchored the business district when it was built in 1884.

The Wainwright Building, one of the first steel frame structures built in the United States, was designed by architect Louis Sullivan in 1891. Two years

38   Laclede Gas Company

later, a 15-story building rose in the 700 block of Olive Street, kitty-corner from the Old Post Office. In 1896, the 16-story Chemical Building went up downtown.

The city's streets in the late 1890s increasingly were choked with the newfangled horseless carriage. Automobiles, however, would not replace the electric street railways that crisscrossed St. Louis in the 1890s until well into the 1910s. In 1899, all of the trolley companies serving St. Louis had consolidated into one company, the St. Louis Transit Company. Under Mayor Rolla Wells, the City Water Department had upgraded its facilities in the years before the St. Louis World's Fair, making the city's water supply one of the safest in the country in 1900.

A Golden Era

Laclede Gas Light Company was very much a part of the growth of St. Louis during the 1890s and early 1900s. Reorganized in 1889 by H.B. Hollins Company of New York, Laclede Gas Light experienced a golden era during the 1890s. The company began producing water gas at its Station A during the decade by passing steam over hot coke to produce carbon monoxide and hydrogen. The resulting stream combined to form a gas of about 500 BTU per cubic foot, nearly double the BTU value of the coal gas produced previously.

The company provided gas to the Columbia Exposition of 1893, including a centerpiece gas-lit arch featuring each president of the United States. It also negotiated a profitable contract with the 1904 Louisiana Purchase Exposition for a supply of gas to the World's Fair Ground.

Laclede Gas Light faced increasing competition from predecessors of Union Light, Heat & Power Company for the important street lighting business in St. Louis. Laclede Gas Light's 1891 purchase of Municipal Electric Lighting & Power Company for just over $3 million allowed the company to use much of Municipal Electric's assets and franchises to purchase the stock of Phoenix Light, Heat & Power Company in 1896 to serve customers in the underground district downtown.

Even with increasing competition from electric power suppliers, 90 percent of the company's revenues in 1900 came from gas lighting. The company at the time had 64,000 meters. But Laclede Gas Light embarked upon an ambitious diversification project in the 1890s and 1900s in an attempt to carve a niche in the residential and commercial heating and cooking segments of the city's utility business.

1900
Even with increasing competition from electric power suppliers, 90 percent of the company's revenues in 1900 came from gas lighting.

Laclede Gas Light workers monitor the fire in a gas retort at one of the company's plants early in the 20th century.

Emerson McMillin, one of the nation's most successful utility executives, built Laclede Gas Light into one of America's better-run gas companies during the 1890s.

LT. EMERSON McMILLIN

MARION McMILLIN

MURRAY McMILLIN

J. H. McMILLIN

ANDREW McMILLIN

LT. MILTON McMILLIN

The McMillin Brothers

By the turn of the 20th century, Laclede Gas Light Company was valued at more than $15 million, an immense amount of money for the era. Much of the growth in the company's business and revenue was due to the enlightened management of the company's president and his management team between 1889 and 1903.

The Remarkable Mr. McMillin

Osirus Emerson McMillin was born on April 16, 1844 in a river community similar in history and culture to St. Louis. Ironton, Ohio, and its sister community across the Ohio River, Ashland, Kentucky, were among the earliest iron producing communities west of the Appalachian Mountains.

McMillin went to work in a local iron foundry at the age of 10, banking and stoking charcoal furnaces 12 hours a day. Two years later, he was placed in charge of the boilers and steam engines at the foundry, and at the age of 14, McMillin was promoted to oversee the production of the foundry's charcoal.

In 1861, the 17-year-old McMillin joined five of his brothers and enlisted in the 18th Ohio Infantry Regiment to fight in the Civil War. Three months later, the unit was reorganized as the 2nd West Virginia Cavalry Regiment. McMillin, who participated in 38 battles and was wounded several times, ended the Civil War a lieutenant in the 2nd West Virginia Cavalry. Three of his brothers died in combat or succumbed later to wounds or disease.

McMillin returned to southeastern Ohio in 1865 and worked as a traveling salesman, schoolteacher and construction foreman. In 1867, McMillin "labored in laying the first gas mains in Ironton and assisted in the installation of the gas works, becoming the company's first secretary," a longtime Ironton journalist later recalled. McMillin was named superintendent of the Ironton Gas Works in 1869. He spent the next decade expanding the new gas plant and investing in iron and coal properties around Ironton.

McMillin was an early investor in the Findlay, Ohio gas fields, which John D. Rockefeller and other Cleveland investors made into the nation's first natural gas field during the 1880s. In 1879, McMillin was asked to join the Columbus Gas Works in the state's capital city. Columbus Gas had been one of Ohio's least profitable gas companies, and McMillin was able to turn the company's fortunes around and post a profit. In 1888, McMillin put together an investment syndicate to purchase control of Columbus Gas. Grateful stockholders named the Ironton resident president of the company.

McMillin branched out across the Midwest and began acquiring distressed gas properties, making them operationally efficient and selling them for a profit. One of his first forays outside Ohio occurred in 1881 when he leased the facilities of the Sioux City Gas Light Company for $2,500 a year. McMillin eventually ousted the original shareholders, purchased the Iowa gas company in 1885, hired a competent plant manager, and arranged bond financing in 1888 to expand the Sioux City plant's capacity.

In 1888, McMillin incorporated the Sioux City Light, Heat & Power Company to serve the growing meatpacking

1869
McMillin was named superintendent of the Ironton Gas Works, and spent the next decade expanding the new gas plant and investing in iron and coal properties around Ironton.

Late 1880s
McMillin was a prolific writer and a frequent contributor to the technical and trade journals of the time.

metropolis on the Missouri River north of Omaha. Rather than fight the introduction of electric power into the community, McMillin incorporated the electric utility to give the gas company a presence in the then emerging electric light and power business.

During the late 1880s, McMillin's business career was just beginning to attract national attention. McMillin was a prolific writer and a frequent contributor to the technical and trade journals of the time. He was particularly insistent that gas companies could compete effectively with the electric utilities that were then springing up in America's cities. McMillin preached consolidation of gas companies that had traditionally competed among themselves for customers. Eliminate redundant systems and administrative processes, McMillin argued, that gas could be delivered to customers at a lower price while increasing profits for gas company shareholders.

The Master Stroke

In 1889, McMillin laid the foundation for his emergence as one of the nation's first great captains of industry in the utility business. McMillin and George Shepherd Page, a New York investment banker, learned that St. Louis Gas Light Company was for sale and that its major competitor, Laclede Gas Light Company, was in search of financing to underwrite the purchase. At the time, McMillin had cash to invest in suitable utility properties having sold his ownership stake in Sioux City Gas Light Company to United Gas Improvement Company, the Philadelphia-based holding company that was in the process of amassing gas utility properties nationwide. McMillin negotiated the sale of his stake in the Iowa utility to Samuel Bodine, who would serve as the holding company's president and chief executive officer between 1900 and 1920, and Randal Morgan, the Philadelphia holding company's longtime outside counsel.

McMillin and Page approached Sir Julian Goldsmith, the London-based owner of more than 100 gas companies in Great Britain and on the European continent. Sir Julian raised funding from his old friend, the Duke of Sutherland, and several other wealthy investors. McMillin and Page were named the American agents of the American Industrial Syndicate, Ltd. of London and immediately began negotiations with the trustees of St. Louis Gas Light Company and the board of directors of The Laclede Gas Light Company.

Through the English syndicate, McMillin was introduced to H.B. Hollins & Co., a New York investment banking house that specialized in financing gas and railroad properties. When the English investors backed away from the reorganization of the St. Louis gas companies, Harry Hollins agreed to finance the project — if McMillin was willing to serve as president of the reorganized utility.

McMillin's agreement to become president of Laclede Gas Light was predicated on Hollins' promise to appoint a president by the beginning of 1890. Despite this, McMillin was president of Laclede Gas Light Company for the next 14 years, from 1889 to 1903.

Emerson McMillin & Company, Bankers

McMillin's familiarity with gas utility operation and skill at putting together the reorganized Laclede Gas Light Company convinced Hollins to back the Ohioan in his own investment banking firm. In 1891, McMillin opened Emerson McMillin & Company, Bankers at 40 Wall Street, in a suite of offices upstairs from H.B. Hollins & Co. offices.

During the next decade, McMillin & Company financed more than $50 million in gas company capitalization. The McMillin banking house cleared more than $300,000 in profit when it introduced the Welsbach Commercial Company and its revolutionary gas mantle to the U.S. market in the mid-1890s.

In 1894, McMillin formed the East River Gas Company to provide gas to customers in the five boroughs of New York City. He built a gas plant on Long Island, sunk a tunnel under the East River and piped the gas to customers in New York. McMillin's financial backers included New York multi-millionaire August Belmont and Ernest Lehman, whose Lehman Brothers investment banking firm was beginning to make its mark on Wall Street.

During McMillin's tenure as president of Laclede Gas Light Company, he built one of the first and most successful utility holding companies in North America. By the early 1900s, Emerson McMillin & Company held a controlling interest in nine U.S. gas and electric companies, including the Binghamton, New York Gas Works; the Consolidated Gas Company of New Jersey; the Detroit City Gas Company; the Grand Rapids, Michigan Gas Light Company; the Milwaukee Gas Light Company; the Southern Light & Traction Company; the Western Gas Light Company in Milwaukee; the American Light & Traction Company; and the San Antonio Traction Company.

McMillin also served as a director of several other gas and electric utilities, including the St. Paul Gas Light Company, the San Antonio Gas & Electric Company, and the Denver Gas & Electric Company. At the turn of the 20th century, McMillin began a philanthropic career that lasted until his death. The Emerson McMillin Observatory on the campus of the Ohio State University in Columbus was his most memorable gift, although he also funded the university's law library and a natural science museum. In many ways, McMillin's business practices were as visionary as his philanthropic activity.

Economic Incentives

Emerson McMillin was one of the more farsighted business executives of his era. In the mid-1880s, even before he consolidated Laclede Gas Light Company, McMillin instituted a sweeping set of employee relations reforms at Columbus Gas that he would introduce at Laclede Gas Light five years later. McMillin banned alcohol from the company's plants, began offering retention bonuses to his long-term employees, created a profit-sharing plan and established an employee stock ownership plan.

Alcoholism in 19th century America was an occupational hazard in many manufacturing work sites. Workers at gas houses sometimes came to work drunk

1894
McMillin formed the East River Gas Company to provide gas to customers in the five boroughs of New York City.

1895
McMillin launched a profit-sharing plan for Laclede Gas Light employees.

and stored bottles of alcohol on the premises. Accidents frequently occurred, and temperance activists made the local gas house a common target of their protests.

McMillin, who told associates he never tasted liquor until he was in his 30s, quickly established a zero tolerance policy for liquor on the job at all of his properties. Shortly after being named president of Laclede Gas Light, McMillin posted a placard to the front gates of the company's gas plants stating that any employee caught drinking on the job would be fired without cause.

"Old employees were disposed to treat the edict as a huge joke," a contemporary account noted. "But they were not slow to discover that beneath the genial, sympathetic persona of the new manager was a will of iron."

With the liquor problem addressed, McMillin quickly moved to deal with the high rate of labor turnover at Laclede Gas Light. The intense heat of stoking gas batteries in the stifling humidity of a St. Louis summer made work at Laclede Gas Light an ordeal. Crews would disappear for hours or days at a time, causing service to suffer. Workers frequently quit in the middle of a shift.

To remedy the situation, McMillin established an attendance bonus for his workers. Employees who had not missed a day's work in the previous quarter were entitled to a bonus of $10. Perfect attendance for a year's time entitled the employee to an extra $25, making the potential bonus for the year $65.

In 1895, McMillin launched a profit-sharing plan for Laclede Gas Light employees. The company paid a percent dividend to shareholders after recovering from the economic downturn of the Panic of 1893. Employees were awarded a 5 percent bonus of their total wages each year that the company paid a dividend to shareholders. Laclede Gas Light also urged employees to become shareholders themselves.

A New Century

The waning days of the 1890s were a golden era for Laclede Gas Light Company. The St. Louis utility and the community recovered remarkably quickly from the economic dislocation caused by the Panic of 1893. More disruptive was the massive tornado that devastated St. Louis on May 27, 1896. The cyclone, which carved a path across St. Louis and East St. Louis from southwest to northeast, struck the city just after most downtown offices and businesses closed for the day. The F4 tornado, one of the strongest ever recorded in Missouri, dipped down repeatedly across the metropolitan area for the next half-hour.

Before the storm's fury was spent, 400 residents had been killed, and more than 1,200 St. Louisans were injured. The storm tore out more than 300 feet of the eastern approaches to the Eads Bridge. Laclede Gas Light's Station A and Station C, at the foot of the landmark bridge, were both heavily damaged, although the two plants were back in partial operation by the weekend. The winds blew freight trains off the tracks near the bridge.

The Union Depot Railway powerhouse, which supplied the city's streetcar system and commercial arc lighting for St. Louis, wasn't so fortunate. The

Laclede Gas Light sustained severe damage at its Station A and Station C manufactured gas plants during the tornado outbreak in late May 1896.

smokestack towering over the electric plant toppled, and the roof of the massive building was blown away. A contemporary account noted that the facility appeared to have been bombarded by artillery shells. It was well into June before the electric company restored streetcar and lighting service to the city.

With its recovery from the tornado complete by late summer, Laclede Gas Light Company moved to more fully compete with Union Depot Electric Company when it incorporated Phoenix Light, Heat & Power Co. to serve the underground district in the downtown area. Sanctioned by the Keyes Ordinance, the establishment of Phoenix Light, Heat & Power capitalized on Laclede Gas Light's 1891 purchase of Municipal Electric Lighting & Power Co. Laclede Gas Light used the assets of the existing electric utility to fund the expansion of the new electric company.

As a new century dawned, Laclede Gas Light Company was a profitable, growing gas utility. In 1900, the company served 64,106 meters and distributed 235.5 million cubic feet of gas to customers through 419 miles of mains. The company was one of 40 gas, electric and streetcar utilities that made up American Light & Traction Co., a holding company McMillin incorporated in 1900.

The new century, however, would bring about sweeping changes for Laclede Gas Light Company.

1900
The company served 64,106 meters and distributed 235.5 million cubic feet of gas to customers through 419 miles of mains.

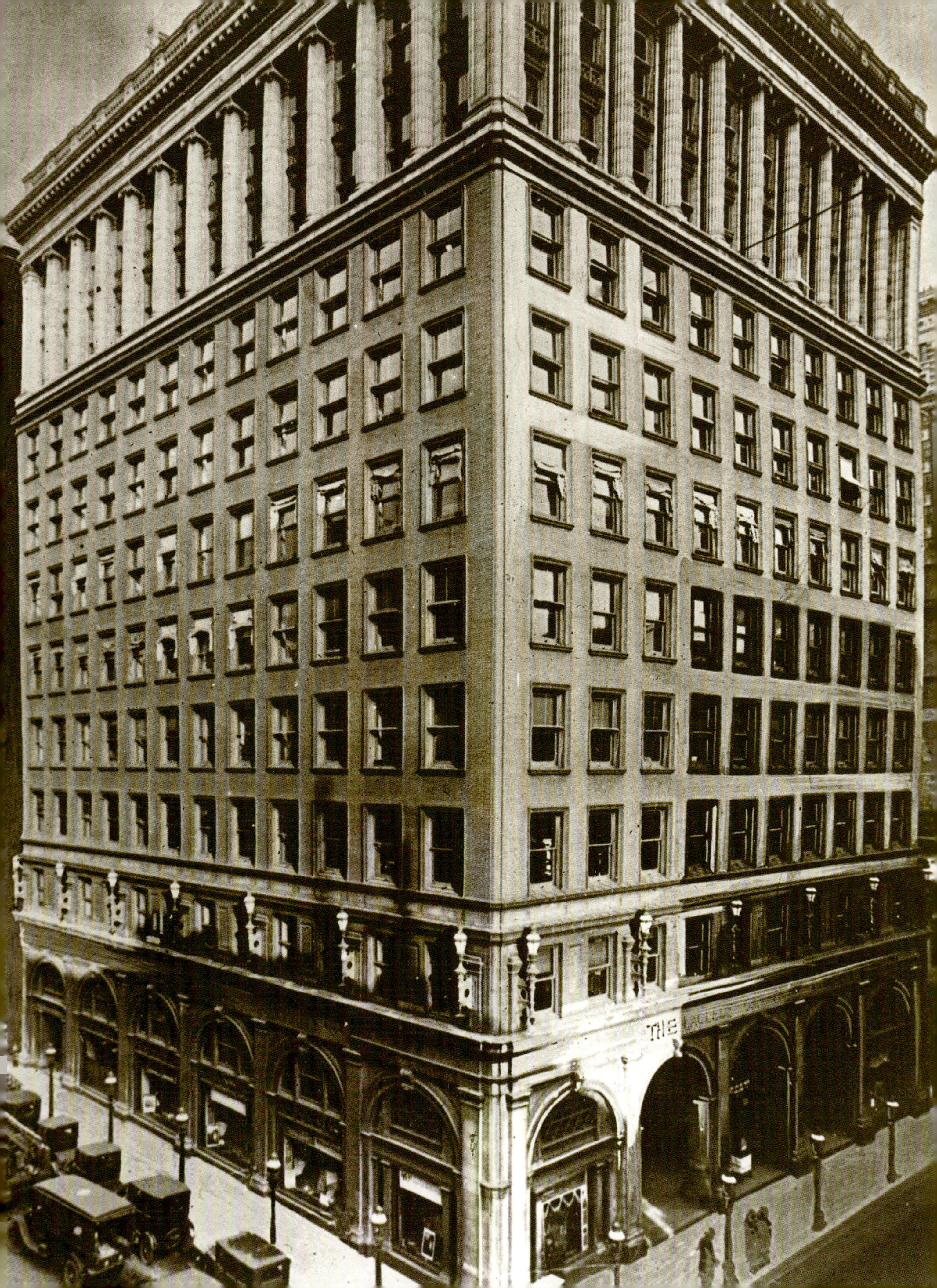
THE

CHAPTER 4

1017 Olive Street

The new century was only three years old when Laclede Gas Light Company was sold. In 1903, American Light & Traction Co., the holding company Emerson McMillin had incorporated three years before, sold its St. Louis gas properties to the North American Company.

The Laclede Gas Light headquarters at 1017 Olive Street was a fixture on the downtown St. Louis skyline from 1913 to 1970.

Then one of the most successful utility holding companies in the nation, the North American Company served electric, gas and street railway customers in some of America's largest metropolitan communities.

McMillin's decision to sell Laclede Gas Light Company perhaps stemmed from the makeup of his holding company, American Light & Traction. Most of the utilities in the holding company were, as the name implied, involved in the electric light and street railway business. In 1901, McMillin consolidated his wide holdings into American Light & Traction and spent the next three years acquiring electric and street railway properties from Muskegon, Michigan to San Antonio, Texas.

By 1903, McMillin was nearing his 60th birthday and had served as president of Laclede Gas Light Company for 14 years. McMillin also ran a successful investment banking firm in New York City. In 1902 and 1903, he began to liquidate some of the holdings he had been compiling since the mid-1880s.

McMillin sold more than half of the 40 properties controlled by American Light & Traction in 1903. The holding company was valued at more than $40 million at the time, and McMillin used the proceeds of the asset sales to fund his philanthropic activities, including scholarships for needy Ohioans.

Laclede Gas Light Company was the first property McMillin disposed of. The firm was well-managed and had made substantial capital investments in improving the productivity of the company's gas plants and distribution system. In 1903, Laclede spent nearly $1 million to augment the capacity of the gas distribution system by putting a high-pressure belt line encircling St. Louis into operation. At the same time, Laclede Gas Light entered into a contract with the Pintsch Compressing Company to install a Pintsch gas manufacturing plant at Station A at Second and Rutger Streets.

A compressed gas made from naptha, Pintsch gas primarily was used for the illumination of railroad cars. Invented by Julius Pintsch of Berlin, the gas was widely available in the late 19th and early 20th centuries. When compressed, the oil gas possessed an illuminating power six times greater than the gas Laclede Gas Light made at Station A. Laclede Gas Light installed a pipeline from the Pintsch gas plant at Station A to a holder station at 14th and Gratiot Streets. From there, the compressed gas was distributed to the adjacent railroad yards.

Laclede Gas Light servicemen wore a badge that identified them as a representatives of the St. Louis utility.

Laclede Gas Light prided itself on reducing the price of gas to residential customers between 1899 and 1903 "to a greater extent in St. Louis than in any other city in the United States." Gas at the time cost $1 per mcf for St. Louis residents, lower than the $1.25 per mcf paid by residents New York City, Washington, D.C., Baltimore, Boston, Chicago and Louisville. Residents of Philadelphia paid $1.50 per mcf in 1903.

"Money is made not by high prices," the company pointed out in a 1903 marketing campaign, "but by large sales. Large sales can only be had by giving satisfaction to consumers, and thereby inducing the largest possible percentage of the population to use gas to the exclusion of other modes of lighting."

McMillin and Laclede Gas Light Company had created an environment that stressed customer service at a time when many gas companies were the deserving targets of civic reformers. Laclede Gas Light in 1903 joined with the American Express Co. to operate a network of St. Louis drugstores, many open nights and weekends, that handled Laclede Gas Light bill payments.

The North American Company

McMillin sold Laclede Gas Light in 1903 to one of the nation's best-managed utility holding companies. Henry Villard, an early associate of Thomas Edison, had founded the North American Company in 1890 to finance the consolidation of streetcar service in Milwaukee, Wisconsin. Villard had reorganized the Northern Pacific Railway in 1889; the debt restructuring had left the railroad independent and Villard a millionaire. Villard incorporated North American Company on June 14, 1890 to control some of the smaller city street railway properties he had been amassing since the mid-1880s.

From its inception, North American's philosophy was to acquire utilities in heavily populated metropolitan areas and then make them profitable by applying economies of scale to its holdings. Villard was proud of his German heritage and was interested in purchasing utilities in communities with a large German-American population. Villard's second purchase for North American Company after the Milwaukee street railway property was the predecessor to Cincinnati Gas & Electric Company.

By the early 1900s, North American Company owned utilities in Milwaukee and Cincinnati, as well as the Cleveland Electric Illuminating Company, Pacific Gas & Electric, Detroit Edison and the Butte Electric & Power Company. North American entered the St. Louis market shortly before the turn of the 20th century when it began acquiring shares of the city's Union Electric Company. In 1905, North American Company took control of the United Railways Company, the parent firm for the city's electric street railways.

As part of its customer information outreach activities during the early 1900s, Laclede Gas Light printed thousands of postcards explaining how to read residential gas meters.

1899 to 1903
Laclede Gas Light prided itself on reducing the price of gas to residential customers "to a greater extent in St. Louis than in any other city in the United States."

For most of the 1890s, the major holding of the North American Company was The Milwaukee Electric Railway and Light Company (TMERL), which served electric and traction customers across a broad swath of southeastern Wisconsin. Known to Wisconsin residents at TMERL, the Milwaukee firm dominated the interurban street railway lines north of Chicago.

New Management

McMillin's sale of Laclede Gas Light Company to North American Company in 1903 brought a new management team to the St. Louis gas utility. The president of the North American Company at the time was Charles Wetmore, a Marquette, Michigan native who had attended Harvard College and parlayed a Harvard Law School degree into a career in finance in New York City. Wetmore had been nearly ruined in 1893 when Lake Superior iron ore mines and shipping interests he had invested in defaulted during the Panic of that summer. But influential friends, including confidantes of John D. Rockefeller, had rescued Wetmore's career. By 1903, Wetmore was serving as the full-time president of Detroit Edison and the part-time president of North American Company.

George R. Sheldon served as the board chairman of the North American Company in 1903. A Harvard College graduate like Wetmore, Sheldon was a prominent banker in New York City and a colleague of Henry Bayne, a TMERL executive and Republican National Committeeman. Another TMERL executive, William Nelson Cromwell, served as the secretary of North American Company. The white-maned Cromwell was one of the most accomplished Wall Street attorneys in early 20th century America.

The new management named John I. Beggs president of Laclede Gas Light Company to succeed Emerson McMillin. Beggs was the recently named president of North American's flagship Milwaukee electric street railway subsidiary. Like McMillin, he was an absentee president for Laclede Gas Light, traveling to St. Louis for board meetings once a month and as needed.

Fortunately for Beggs and Laclede Gas Light, the president's presence wasn't often needed. The day-to-day operations of the utility were in the hands of Edward G. Cowdery, who served as the firm's vice president and general manager. Cowdery's executive team included Charles Holman, the secretary of the gas company, and Charles A. Tucker, the utility's treasurer.

Cowdery, a Massachusetts native and a graduate of the Institute of Technology in Boston, came to St. Louis from Milwaukee, where he had been the general manager of the Milwaukee Gas Company and had come to the attention of Cromwell, Beggs and the executives of the North American Company.

Cowdery arrived in St. Louis as the city was beginning its preparations for the 1904 World's Fair. Laclede Gas Light's new general manager quickly involved the gas company in planning for the fair. "Almost from the outset," a contemporary profile reported, "he inaugurated a policy which had for its foundation the broad principle that the measure of a great public utility's success is the extent to which it is able to hold the favor of the general public."

Cowdery's tenure as general manager of Laclede Gas Light only lasted four years. In 1907, he resigned and was succeeded by Holman. By that time, North American Company was quietly shopping Laclede Gas Light Company to interested buyers.

The Walker-Busch Syndicate

Rumors spread through St. Louis for much of the spring of 1909 that North American Company was seeking a buyer for its share of Laclede Gas Light Company. It wasn't that Laclede Gas Light was unprofitable. The St. Louis subsidiary of the holding company made money. But Wetmore, the management and board of North American were far more comfortable operating electric utilities and electric street railway companies than they were running gas utilities. Of the major metropolitan properties that the company operated in 1909, the vast majority were electric or street railway utilities.

Most of the gas utilities that North American did operate were combination utilities such as Cincinnati Gas & Electric Company and Pacific Gas & Electric Company. While offering Laclede Gas Light for sale, North American continued to buy shares of Union Electric, the St. Louis electric utility.

What was somewhat surprising was the identity of the proposed buyer. Emerson McMillin, the president and chairman of American Light & Traction, was negotiating to re-purchase the St. Louis gas utility the holding company had sold to North American just six years before. McMillin and American Light & Traction offered to buy Laclede Gas Light Company from North American Company for $93.50 a share in a combined cash and stock buyout.

Spring 1909
Rumors spread through St. Louis that North American Company was seeking a buyer for its share of Laclede Gas Light Company.

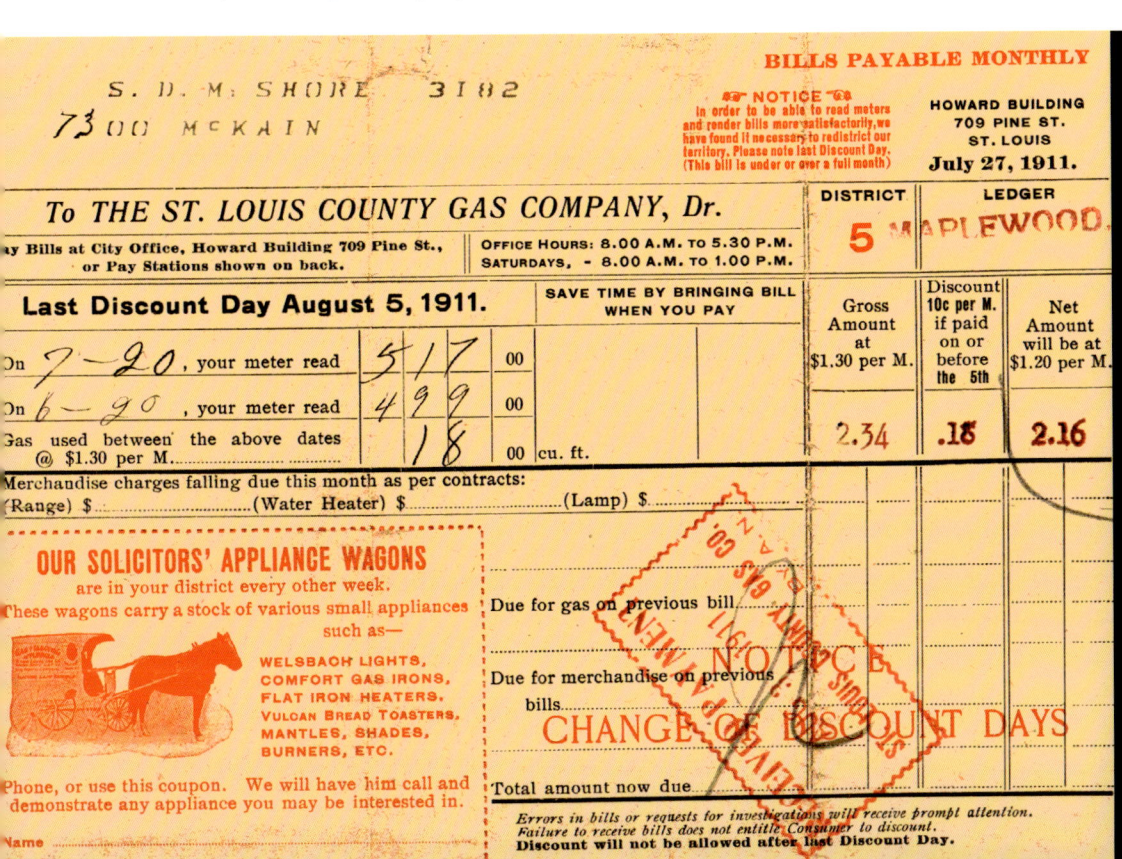

The St. Louis County Gas Company, which would become a part of Laclede in the late 1940s, was headquartered just down the street from Laclede's general office during the 1910s.

1910
$7 million purchase of Laclede Gas Light Company ushered in a new era for the St. Louis utility.

American Light & Traction's offer was nearly accepted. But at the North American Company's board meeting in New York City on June 10, 1909, the deal quickly unraveled. St. Louis newspapers reported that the proposed sale to McMillin had fallen apart when "G.H. Walker, Adolphus Busch, Charles H. Huttig and John I. Beggs had appeared at the meeting unexpectedly and filed a protest on behalf of all of the directors, with two exceptions, against the sale of Laclede to the American Light & Traction Company."

The opposition offered to buy the St. Louis property for $97.50 a share in cash, a far superior price to what McMillin and American Light & Traction were prepared to pay.

The Walker-Busch Syndicate, as it became known in the local newspapers, was comprised of some of St. Louis' most influential residents. George Herbert Walker operated perhaps the most successful brokerage houses in the Midwest. His grandson, George Herbert Walker Bush, and his great-grandson George Walker Bush became the 41st and 43rd presidents of the United States, respectively. Busch owned the city's largest and best known breweries, and Huttig was a prominent St. Louis investor. Beggs, the only non-St. Louis resident in the syndicate, was Laclede Gas Light's president.

North American Company quickly accepted the Walker-Busch Syndicate's offer, and the New York City investment banking house of Salomon & Co. acted for G.H. Walker in lining up investment capital for the acquisition. With its cash offer, the syndicate quickly controlled 74,000 of Laclede Gas Light's 85,000 shares. The news that Walker, Busch and Huttig were involved in the purchase of the city's hometown gas utility was greeted with approval in the St. Louis business community.

"St. Louis capitalists felt, too, that the city's interests probably would be served well if the company were controlled by local capital," a contemporary newspaper account noted, "and directors of the Laclede Gas Light Company gave their support to the Walker-Busch Syndicate to this end."

The new owners hinted that St. Louis might well expect big changes in the delivery of gas to the community. Walker, Busch and Huttig controlled some 240,000 acres of land in Caddo Parish, Louisiana, which already held promise of becoming the nation's biggest deposit of natural gas. Busch told the Post-Dispatch that the syndicate intended to begin laying pipe at once from the Caddo fields to St. Louis.

Busch's optimism wasn't warranted. It wouldn't be until the 1920s that investment bankers devised a foolproof method of estimating natural gas reserves in the ground, a necessity for financing long-distance transport of natural gas. And not until the late 1920s did the steel industry introduce corrosion-resistant alloy pipe capable of carrying natural gas across the country.

Still, the $7 million purchase of Laclede Gas Light Company ushered in a new era for the St. Louis utility. And the knowledge that Busch had subscribed for $1 million of the local company's

52 Laclede Gas Company

Laclede Gas Light's Station A was the utility's backbone manufactured gas plant in 1910.

stock was a vote of confidence in Laclede Gas Light.

Expanding the System

The Walker-Busch Syndicate purchased a well-run metropolitan gas utility in 1909. During the next five years, the new owners made substantial capital investments to expand the system.

Laclede Gas Light's main manufacturing facility at the time was Station A, located at Second and Rutger Streets. The longtime St. Louis gas plant made water gas for city use from seven standard Lowe water gas sets, installed between 1891 and 1904. In 1910, the new owners of Laclede Gas Light installed two new 11-foot Lowe water gas sets with separate air blowers in adjacent buildings at the Rutger Street site. The total daily generating capacity of the company's water gas plant at the time was 15 million cubic feet.

Laclede Gas Light in 1909 also made coal gas at the Rutger Street site. In 1910, shortly after the Walker-Busch Syndicate acquired control of the utility, Laclede Gas Light embarked upon a major upgrade of its coal gas facilities at Station A, installing a retort house around the corner at Convent Street. The new facility included 20 benches, each with eight retorts 20 feet long.

Three years later, in 1913, Laclede Gas Light installed a similar-sized retort house at Rutger Street that included 16 benches, each with eight retorts 16 feet long. Together, the two new retort houses gave the utility a daily capacity of 6 million cubic feet of coal gas.

Rutger Street also housed four rotary gas pumping units, eight water-tube boilers and the Pintsch gas plant for making railroad gas. In 1910, crews installed a low-pressure turbine to capture the exhaust steam at Station A. The turbine generated 500-volt DC current for use in the gas plant and for delivery to the company's growing network of electric distribution lines.

The older and smaller Station B at Main and Mullanphy Streets consisted of five standard Lowe water gas sets producing about 4 million cubic feet of water gas a day. The station also housed one retort facility that included 16 benches, each with eight retorts 16 feet long. The coal gas retort house at Station B had a daily capacity of .5 million cubic feet of coal gas. Chemical laboratories for the

1910
Shortly after the Walker-Busch Syndicate acquired control of the utility, Laclede Gas Light embarked upon a major upgrade of its coal gas facilities at Station A, installing a retort house around the corner at Convent Street.

daily testing of gas were maintained at both Station A and Station B in 1910.

Station E

In 1911, Laclede Gas Light made a major commitment to diversify utility services and to compete with North American Company, its recent owner. The St. Louis utility completed and put into operation an electric generating station at Mound Street and the Levee that year.

Crews installed a 1,000-KVA turbine-generator and two 3,500-KVA turbine-generators at the site, which Laclede Gas Light engineers named Station E. The new turbine-generators were fed cooling water from the nearby Mississippi River by Worthington surface condensers with steam-driven dry vacuum pumps, motor-driven hot well pumps and turbine-driven circulating pumps.

The electric plant boasted two 75-kilowatt exciters to regulate the turbine-generators and two 500-kilowatt synchronous motor generator sets. A main switchboard was equipped with electrically-operated oil switches, bus bar and high-tension equipment for the transmission of power to downtown St. Louis. The boiler plant consisted of eight 500-horsepower water tube boilers.

"A very complete coal and ash handling facility has been provided, which handles the coal from the cars into an overhead bin, from which it is fed by gravity to the boilers," a 1914 report noted. "The ashes are in turn handled by the same equipment from hoppers under the boilers into an overhead bin from which they are loaded directly into cars."

In 1911, the company operated electric substations at Sarah Street and Evans Avenue, the site of one of Laclede

The Station H telescoping gas holder was one of several in metropolitan St. Louis that stored gas during for peak use during the 1910s and 1920s.

As early as 1906, Laclede Gas Light began a customer outreach program to instruct St. Louis residents in the most efficient ways to use gas for cooking. Laclede also helped customers finance the purchase of gas appliances.

LACLEDE · GAS · LIGHT · COMPAN

OF THE LACLEDE GAS LIGHT CO
USE GAS   US

FUTURE HOME OF
THE

Between 1907 and 1917, Laclede Gas Light made hundreds of thousands of dollars in improvements to its system. At top, workers lay the foundation for a new telescoping gas holder. At bottom, masons finish the stone facade of the company's new general office building at 1017 Olive Street.

Gas Light's largest gas holders, and in the basement of an office building at 410 N. Seventh Street downtown.

A Gas Fairyland

For Laclede Gas Light Company, the biggest expansion of 1911 was the utility's announcement that it had purchased a large lot at the northeast corner of Eleventh and Olive Streets downtown. Laclede Gas Light had long since outgrown the corporate headquarters at 716 Locust Street, and the new St. Louis owners of the utility wanted to demonstrate to the community that Laclede Gas Light was becoming one of St. Louis' most influential corporate citizens.

Laclede Gas Light hired the St. Louis architectural firm of Mauran, Russell, Crowell to design a 12-story classic revival skyscraper. William DeForest Crowell, a Massachusetts native who arrived in St. Louis the year before, designed the 125,000-square-foot building in a mixture of classic and renaissance styles. The new skyscraper would be the first of a number of downtown buildings Crowell designed during the next nearly 40 years, including the Bell Telephone Co. building, the Railway Exchange building, the Missouri-Pacific Railroad building and the Federal Reserve Bank of St. Louis.

Groundbreaking took place early in the spring of 1912, and the building was completed by the early summer of 1913. When costs approached $1 million, Laclede Gas Light scaled back on plans for the building. Contractors built 10 floors and a mezzanine instead of the originally planned 12 stories.

But when the building finally opened in late July 1913, it was hailed as a "gas fairyland" by local reporters. The new building was framed by 13 ornamental street lights along Eleventh and Olive Streets, as well as 13 bronze brackets on the exterior wall holding gas lights. Inside, on the first floor and mezzanine, large grates held gas logs for heating the floor space.

The basement of the building contained the company's appliance salesroom, as well as a model house to demonstrate the appliances in action. A marble staircase led to the first floor, where St. Louis residents could apply for gas service or pay their gas bills. A mezzanine overlooking the first floor housed meeting and public rooms. The remaining floors were occupied by the utility's large and growing office staff.

Employees made the move from 716 Locust Street from noon to midnight on Saturday, July 26, 1913. A trio of three-ton electric trucks were pressed into service to move employee property to the new building, making 50 trips apiece. The last truck, carrying 65 cases of stationery, pulled up at 1017 Olive Street just 10 seconds before midnight.

With the move to the new headquarters complete, Laclede Gas Light Company looked forward to new challenges and opportunities. The onset of war in Europe less than a year later, the change to a new method of manufacturing gas in 1916 and increasing competition with the city's dominant electric utility would offer Laclede Gas Light ample challenge in the years ahead.

July 26, 1913
Employees made a 12-hour move from 716 Locust Street to 1017 Olive Street.

During the 1910s, St. Louis residents became familiar with Laclede Gas Light Co. electric signs, located on rooftops around the metropolitan area.

CHAPTER 5

War and Peace

Life in St. Louis was good in 1915. America remained at peace that summer, although much of Europe was embroiled in a second year of war. Imperial Germany and France were stalemated in trench warfare that bisected the French countryside from the Belgian border to the Jura Mountains. German armies were more successful in Russia and Poland, routing Tsarist divisions at the battles of the Masurian Lakes and Tannenburg.

1915
St. Louis was one of about a dozen U.S. cities in eight states to ban the showing of D.W. Griffith's racist "Birth of a Nation" when it debuted in the summer of 1915.

More than a few of St. Louis' citizens hoisted a tankard to the success of German arms in 1915, when it still wasn't apparent whether the United States would intervene on the side of either Germany or Great Britain and France in what was still referred to as "the European War."

A more pressing question for most residents of the city was when each of the city's two major league baseball teams would start showing some success. The Cardinals continued their record of futility, which had seen the National League club finish no higher than third in any season since 1909. Fans at Robinson Field had reason for optimism in 1914 when the Redbirds finished the season 81-72, but the team returned to its dismal ways in 1915, finishing in six place at 72-81.

As bad as the Cards were, the American League Browns were far worse. Led by field manager Branch Rickey, who would go on to integrate Major League baseball with Jackie Robinson and the Brooklyn Dodgers 30 years later, the Browns finished the 1915 season in sixth place, nearly 40 games out of first place. The Browns' 1915 record of 63-91 was actually an improvement over the 1910 to 1912 clubs that lost more than 100 games each season three years running.

Residents who didn't follow the fortunes of the city's baseball teams could avail themselves of St. Louis' libraries, parks and recreational facilities. The city's population supported a network of neighborhood beer gardens, and round-the-clock streetcar service made the city's downtown the hub of commercial and entertainment activities. Motion pictures were the latest technological advancement, and a host of movie theaters sprung up downtown to cater to cinema patrons. But St. Louis was one of about a dozen U.S. cities in eight states to ban the showing of D.W. Griffith's racist "Birth of a Nation" when it debuted in the summer of 1915.

The Coke Plant

Another technological advance that made its debut in 1915 was Laclede Gas Light's coke plant. Prior to 1915, most of the gas supplied to St. Louis residents was coal gas and carbureted water gas. The coal gas was produced in D-type bench ovens with a byproduct of domestic coke. The water gas was produced by enriching hydrogen gas from Lowe water gas sets with oil, which, in turn, was mixed with the coal gas to produce a gas with a higher BTU rating.

The basic gas manufacturing process involved baking coal in airtight ovens, or retorts. Gases and other byproducts were driven off as the coal cooked in the ovens. When the process was complete, the solid remainder of the coal was coke. Primarily composed of pure carbon with small quantities of ash and volatiles, coke burned far hotter and more efficiently than coal.

"Coke is an old commodity of commerce," Henry Stith, the manager of Laclede Gas Light's coke plant wrote in 1921, "for the Chinese appear to have used it some 2,000 years ago. We also find traces of its manufacture in the

Laclede's Gas Light's coke station on Catalan Street included a fully-equipped chemistry laboratory.

middle ages for use in the arts and for domestic purposes."

Stith went on to note that coke first had been manufactured in the United States in 1841, and by 1842, manufacturers were shipping coke down the Ohio River from West Virginia to Cincinnati. The successful use of coke as a blast furnace fuel was first demonstrated in 1859 in Pittsburgh. Gas was initially manufactured as a byproduct of cooking coke in Syracuse, New York in 1893.

'An Advanced Step in Gas Production'

Always alert to improved methods of operation, Laclede Gas Light began studying the advantages of the newer, more up-to-date byproduct coke plants after the Walker-Busch Syndicate acquired the utility from the North American Company in 1909. In 1913, Laclede Gas Light began the construction of a byproducts coke plant at 527 Catalan Street in Carondelet. The plant, which was completed in 1915, was located near the far southern boundary of St. Louis at the confluence of the River Des Peres and the Mississippi River.

Between 1913 and 1915, work crews erected 56 Koppers byproduct coke ovens at the Carondelet site. Rectangular in shape, the Koppers ovens were 40 feet long, 16 to 24 inches wide, and 6 to 12 feet high. Coke plant crews could cook coke in 18 to 20 hours. Later, in 1920, Laclede Gas Light added eight experimental Belgian byproduct coke ovens at the plant that were capable of producing coke in 12 to 15 hours.

Laclede Gas Light was one of the first customers of American Koppers, which had been acquired from German control by U.S. investors early in 1915. The new owners moved the headquarters of the U.S. firm to Pittsburgh. Between 1915 and 1921, Koppers installed nearly 4,000 byproduct coke ovens in the United States.

The 180-acre site at Carondelet had ample room for the Koppers ovens, the coal and coke storage facilities, rail spurs, the spray pond, the gas holder, the byproducts building, the power house, machine shop and various storage tanks. Construction was delayed by the Panic of 1913, but the facility was built in a

1915
Laclede Gas Light finished construction on a byproducts coke plant at 527 Catalan Street in Carondelet.

150 Year Anniversary **61**

little more than one year after ground was broken in the spring of 1914. When completed, the capital investment for the new coke plant totaled just over $2 million.

From the start of commercial production, the byproduct coke plant at Catalan Street was a profitable venture. Laclede Gas Light produced a high-BTU gas for industrial purposes, as well as coke for the home heating market. "The sale of by-products was lucrative and helped to keep down the cost of gas," the company reported to shareholders in 1920.

In the 1890s and early 1900s, St. Louis had emerged as a major Midwestern center for iron foundries. Sand casting of iron had been first demonstrated in East St. Louis in 1891, and American Steel Foundries used its sand casting patents to dominate the industry in the early 20th century. Castings were used to make railroad wheels and other heavy equipment, and foundries such as American Steel were eager customers for the 600 BTU gas produced by the Carondelet byproducts coke plant.

The byproduct coke produced at the Catalan Street plant also was in high demand by Granite City Steel, which had been founded by the city's Niedringhaus brothers in 1895. Located across the Mississippi River in Granite City, Illinois, the steel works boasted two 22-ton open hearth furnaces and four rolling mills capable of producing 20,000 tons of finished steel a year. By 1908, the plant was making four tons of bar steel and tinplate a day and employed more than 2,000 men on the 15-acre site in the planned community.

An adjacent stamping plant, NESCO, had 1.25 million square feet under roof, occupied 75 acres of land, and employed more than 4,000 workers, many of them Slovak, Greek, Serb, Croat and Bulgarian immigrants. Both NESCO and Granite City Steel purchased coke and enriched coke byproduct gas from Laclede Gas Light Company.

The company's coke plant produced coke for St. Louis-area steel mills and foundries, as well as for sale to St. Louis residents for use as heating fuel.

As soon as the Catalan Street plant went into commercial operation, Laclede Gas Light began marketing coke to St. Louis homeowners through the city's fuel dealers. Most St. Louis residents heated their homes with soft coal mined in nearby southern Illinois and southwestern Indiana. Soft coal burned with a prodigious amount of white smoke, and on winter mornings, a pall of dirty, gray smoke often shrouded St. Louis. As early as 1892, the city passed its first smoke ordinance, but smoke pollution continued to be a problem until well into the 1940s.

Laclede Gas Light purchased its coking coal from mines in the Youghiogheny River Valley of Pennsylvania and West Virginia and had it shipped by river barge to St. Louis. Youghiogheny coal burned with far less smoke than the soft coal of the Illinois Basin.

"The beneficial effect of this new enterprise on the city of St. Louis will be felt in all civic circles in a degree equal to that which prevailed at the solution of problems involving schools, parks, traffic regulation, streets and sewage systems," noted The Gas Record, the gas industry's national trade publication. "St. Louis in past years successfully coped with these problems, and this year she likewise has solved the difficulties arising from an unsatisfactory city water supply. Now her principal remaining trouble, the smoke nuisance, promises an early abatement in the enormous new supply of modern and economical fuel gas and gas coke, which the Laclede Gas Light Co.'s new plant will make available."

Laclede Gas Light crews used a steam "bottle" locomotive to move carloads of coal around the coke plant yards.

The Byproducts Business

Laclede Gas Light reaped the biggest profits from the coke plant at Catalan Street through the sale of byproducts chemicals. Byproducts included various hydrocarbons, ammonia, cyanide, sulphur and phenolics. As America's pharmaceutical, chemical, plastics and cosmetics industries became more sophisticated in the early 1900s, byproduct compounds from the coke gas stream were in increasing demand.

Coal tar, one of the major byproducts, was used to make creosote. Companies such as Koppers in Pittsburgh and Republic Creosoting Co. in Indianapolis purchased coal tar from byproduct coke manufacturers to make creosote, which was used to coat wood for building purposes. Benzene, toluene and xylene, all stripped off during the gas-making process in the byproduct coke ovens, had innumerable applications in America's growing chemical industry.

Benzene production skyrocketed between 1915 and 1918, thanks to the installation of so many byproduct coke ovens during the period. Benzene production increased twenty-fold, from 2.5 million gallons in 1915 to 44 million gallons three years later. But it was World War I that gave the production of byproduct coke oven compounds new importance.

Wartime

The Democratic Party met in St. Louis in the summer of 1916 to re-nominate former New Jersey Governor Woodrow Wilson for the presidency. Wilson had captured the White House in 1912 when former President Teddy Roosevelt had entered the race on the Bull Moose ticket against incumbent Republican President William Howard Taft. Roosevelt and Taft had split the Republican vote, allowing Wilson to eke out a narrow victory in his quest for the White House.

In 1916, President Wilson campaigned on a platform of peace, vowing that he would do all he could to avoid sending American boys to fight and die in a European war. But when Germany resumed unrestricted submarine warfare in the late winter of 1917, Wilson and Congress responded in kind. In April, the United States declared war against Germany and its allies. Russia exited the war following the Bolshevik Revolution in the fall of 1917, leaving Great Britain, France and an untested America to face the Germans on the Western Front.

In the spring and summer of 1917, the United States had to develop a munitions industry to outfit and equip the millions of American soldiers called to the colors. For much of the 1890s and the early 1900s, the bulk of America's chemical supplies had come from Europe. A large percentage of that supply was imported from Germany. Americanization of the Koppers Co. in 1915 had brought an important chemical asset to the United States. For two of the compounds derived from the gas stream of byproduct coke ovens were absolutely essential to fighting a modern war.

Phenol and toluol, two of the common byproducts that Laclede Gas Light separated from the gas stream in its coke ovens, were the building blocks for the modern explosives industry. "The new war was fought with the products of coal," one historian noted.

Phenol was a critical ingredient in the manufacture of picric acid, which was employed in the manufacture of detonators. Phenol also was used to make ammonium picrate, which served both as a propellant powder and a charge in high explosive artillery shells.

Even more important to America's war effort was toluol, which was refined into toluene. Toluene is the second 't' in TriNitroToluene, which most recognize as TNT. Invented in Europe in 1907 as a replacement for nitroglycerine in commercial explosives, TNT quickly became the preferred explosive of all of the combatants during the First World War.

The tremendous increase in the number of Koppers byproduct coke ovens after 1915 helped the United States to solve its phenol and toluol shortage. But the federal government urged America's gas utilities to increase production of manufactured gas in order to increase the production of phenol and toluol.

On October 24, 1917, members of the executive committee of Laclede Gas Light Company met in closed session in the boardroom at 1017 Olive Street to hear from representatives of the U.S. War Department. The government officials asked the Laclede Gas Light executives to build stripping plants at Station A and Station B for the production of toluol, "the source of all the government's explosives. The only source from which it could be obtained was from coal and water gas."

Laclede Gas Light and the nation's gas utilities stepped up to the task of increasing gas production. Toluene production jumped from 623,000 gallons in 1915 to 8.8 million gallons in 1918. The artillery barrages that paved the way for American Expeditionary Force offensives at Belleau Wood, Chateau Thierry and the Meuse Argonne in 1918 were a product of the byproduct coke ovens at Carondelet and hundreds of other sites across the United States.

Return to Normalcy

Gas service personnel who had served with the military forces during World War I began to return to Laclede Gas Light Company in the winter and spring of 1919. The company's revenues fell that year as foundries and steel stamping plants that had absorbed much of the coke and coke gas the company had produced during World War I made the transition to civilian manufacture. Laclede Gas Light, which had expanded manufactured gas operations at the urging of the federal government during the war, immediately began marketing excess coke capacity for home heating applications.

"We advertise coke in the daily press and have demonstrators who are provided with automobiles and call on every new coke customer to show him how to regulate the drafts to get satisfactory results," Henry Stith, the company's coke operations plant manager, wrote shortly after the war. "Coke makes no smoke, no soot and very few ashes. As it does not make any smoke, it is not necessary to have a large smoke pipe such as is needed to carry off the smoke when soft coal is burned."

Laclede Gas Light demonstrators noted that "coke burns freely and therefore should be burned with a very light draft. As it is lighter in weight than anthracite or soft coal, it is necessary to carry a larger amount of fuel in the furnace. The ideal way of burning coke is to open the dampers slightly and get the fire started, then shut off the pipe damper and all drafts, and hold this heat in the furnace."

In the early 1920s, Laclede Gas Light increased marketing efforts, focusing on the benefits of firing coke in the furnaces of smaller stores and downtown buildings. The company argued that the soft coal burned in many of the inadequately vented furnaces in the downtown business district poured out "large volumes of smoke which is blown and carried into stores and offices, causing great damage to fine fabrics, draperies, stationery and the temper of the afflicted."

Laclede Gas Light Company entered the 1920s full of optimism, focused on marketing clean-burning fuels to a growing industrial, commercial and residential population. The growth of St. Louis during the decade would spark corresponding growth at Laclede Gas Light Company. But the St. Louis utility would struggle with events outside its control, including two more changes in the utility's management structure.

1918
Toluene production jumped from 623,000 gallons in 1915 to 8.8 million gallons.

A Charleston contest in front of the old City Hall in 1925. The Charleston was a dance craze that swept the nation during the Roaring Twenties.

CHAPTER 6

The Roaring Twenties

Laclede Gas Light Company marked a major milestone in 1924 when it added the company's 200,000th customer. In just 67 years, the St. Louis gas utility had become a powerful force for economic, industrial and social development in its hometown.

1925

Crews installed a manufactured gas plant at the coke station on Catalan Street to increase the daily output capacity by 5 million cubic feet.

In 1925, total revenue for the year was $11.85 million, making Laclede Gas Light one of the city's largest corporations. The utility also was one of the city's most profitable ventures, returning $1.77 million to shareholders after paying millions of dollars in franchise fees and taxes to the city. The company's total assets were more than $50 million, and stockholders' equity was nearly $18 million.

Laclede Gas Light took its mission to provide gas to St. Louis City residents seriously. The mid-1920s were one of the more prosperous eras in the nation's history up to that time. In the wake of World War I, America had become a manufacturing powerhouse, supplying the world with automobiles, farm machinery, machine tools and consumer appliances capable of running on gas or electricity.

The economy in St. Louis boomed during the decade, with thousands of residents working at Granite City Steel and in the city's numerous gray iron foundries. Thousands more worked for the Missouri Pacific and the two dozen other long-haul and short line railroads that used St. Louis as a terminal hub. By the mid 1920s, the St. Louis Terminal Association, the joint venture switching organization that handled traffic through St. Louis, interchanged more than 10,000 freight cars a day; some 300 passenger trains arrived or departed Union Station every 24 hours. Still more St. Louis residents bottled beer, forged stoves, pumped oil in refineries or handled insurance policies at downtown office buildings.

'Ample Distribution Capacity'

To keep up with the growth in industrial demand, Laclede Gas Light embarked on a program to upgrade the city's gas manufacturing and distribution system. In 1925, crews installed a manufactured gas plant at the coke station on Catalan Street to increase the daily output capacity by 5 million cubic feet. Crews also built a new, 2-million-cubic-foot gas holder at Station A and reinforced the belt line distribution system by extending a 30-inch main from the coke station to Bancroft Avenue, a distance of about five miles. In 1926, Laclede Gas Light completed a high-pressure main to the northwest part of St. Louis. The company told shareholders that the new main gave the city "not only ample production capacity, but ample distribution capacity for its present needs."

Laclede Gas Light also moved to strengthen its gas supply situation during the mid-1920s. In the years immediately following World War I, St. Louis became the terminus of long-distance pipelines bringing crude oil from the newly developed oil fields of Texas and Oklahoma. The spectacular rise of the automobile and the corresponding growth of paved roads fueled an unquenchable thirst for petroleum products. Several huge petroleum refineries were built on the east bank of the Mississippi River between 1921 and 1925.

In 1926, Laclede Gas Light negotiated a contract with Standard Oil Company of Indiana and Roxana Petroleum Corporation to purchase approximately 6 million cubic feet of still gas a day

Two workers from a Laclede Gas Light crew pause in their work of coating an underground main for installation, circa 1925.

produced in the refinery process. The Illinois and Missouri Pipeline Company built a pipeline under the Mississippi River to the Carondelet Coke Station. From there, the gas was piped through mains to Stations A and B.

"In addition to the value of this large supply of gas," the company told shareholders, "there is an added value in that this Company is protected from an increase in operating cost due to a rise in the price of oil."

The Home Service Department

From the turn of the 20th century on, Laclede Gas Light promoted gas heating and cooking to customers. The company's sale of appliances that could be financed through payment on the gas bill increased the consumption of gas. As early as 1906, Laclede Gas Light published brochures explaining how to cook with gas. At the time, the company established a Woman's Department on the fourth floor of its headquarters at

Laclede Gas Light's traveling cooking school brought gas cooking tips to thousands of St. Louis families during the 1910s and 1920s.

1926
The department began sponsoring a daily cooking tips broadcast on KSD, the radio station of the St. Louis Post-Dispatch.

716 Locust Street. By 1915, the company was sponsoring a "chuckwagon" that visited St. Louis neighborhoods for demonstrations on the ease and efficiency of cooking with gas.

In 1924, Laclede Gas Light formalized the promotional efforts when it established the Home Service Department and named St. Louis native Helen Wetherall the company's first Home Service Director. Wetherall and her staff of Home Service advisors focused on the development of the modern kitchen, offering scientific and practical tips to thousands of St. Louis residents during the next half-century. Laclede Gas Light was one of the first gas companies in America to start a Home Service Department.

Wetherall and her staff quickly established a rapport with St. Louis homeowners. By 1926, more than 25,000 women had attended free cooking classes in the Home Service Department kitchens in the basement of 1017 Olive Street. Every Saturday morning, 110 St. Louis Girl Scouts crowded into the department's kitchen for cooking lessons that helped them qualify for cooking and baking merit badges.

Laclede Gas Light Company and its Home Service Department operated a telephone hotline for St. Louis cooks seeking recipes, tips or advice when roasting a Thanksgiving turkey in a gas oven. Several generations of St. Louis women learned to dial Central 3800 "for any sort of recipe or general data on the home."

In 1926, the department began sponsoring a daily cooking tips broadcast on KSD, the radio station of the St. Louis Post-Dispatch. The Home Service Department also encouraged the purchase of furnaces for home heating. By the mid 1920s, Laclede Gas Light boasted more gas home heating per capita than any other city in the United States.

The Home Service Department efforts were rewarded with new business. Laclede Gas Light added 4,290 new customers during 1925, bringing the total customer count to 209,040.

Laclede Gas Light also looked after the well-being of its growing family of

70   Laclede Gas Company

employees during the 1920s. In 1925, the company gave life insurance policies varying from $500 to $1,500 to all employees at Christmas. The life insurance policies varied depending on the employee's term of service with the company.

New Owners

After operating under the same ownership for 15 years, Laclede Gas Light was acquired by a Chicago-based organization in 1924. The 1920s were a time of great ferment in the utility industry, with electric and gas utilities frequently changing hands. It was an era of low interest rates and easy credit terms in the Wall Street investment community. Holding companies were extremely active during the period, and utilities put up for sale quickly attracted a willing buyer at a higher price. The Walker-Busch Syndicate that had owned Laclede Gas Light since 1909 found by 1924 that its investment in the company was worth more in a sale than it was in the operating return the owners could reasonably expect.

The 1924 purchaser of Laclede Gas Light was a conglomerate made up of investors who were well-known in North America's gas and power business. The lead investor was Pittsburgh-based Koppers Co., which had supplied the coke oven batteries for Laclede's Carondelet Coke Plant just 10 years before. Other members of the syndicate included the Montreal Light, Heat & Power Co. and the Royal Bank of Canada.

Named chairman of the board was Charles A. Munroe, a Chicago gas company executive who had organized the cartel to purchase Laclede Gas Light. An associate of Samuel Insull, who controlled the utility infrastructure in

1924
The purchaser of Laclede Gas Light was a conglomerate made up of investors who were well-known in North America's gas and power business.

LACLEDE POWER & LIGHT COMPANY

On January 18, 1926, shortly before he sold Laclede Gas Light Company to Utilities Power & Light Corporation, Charles A. Munroe organized a new company in St. Louis. The incorporation of Laclede Power & Light Company was a recognition on Munroe's part that Laclede Gas Light could compete against Union Electric Light & Power Company in the rough and tumble world of electric power generation, transmission and distribution.

Laclede Power & Light was organized for the purpose of acquiring the electric properties of Laclede Gas Light that were located outside the downtown underground district. The new company also acquired the properties of the Phoenix Light, Heat & Power Company. Laclede Power & Light agreed to lease physical properties and franchises from the parent gas company for a period of 26 years.

The Missouri Public Service Commission fixed the lease price to be paid to Laclede Gas Light at $394,000 a year. Laclede Power & Light also had the option to purchase the electric light business from Laclede Gas Light Company for a price of $5.25 million on or before February 1, 1953.

Stockholders of the Laclede Gas Light Company were given the first right to purchase stock in the new power and light utility at a ratio of one to ten. Laclede Power & Light issued 13,200 shares of stock in the January 1926 initial public offering. Laclede Gas Light's stock aggregated 132,000 shares of stock.

Union Electric Light & Power Company, an operating subsidiary of North American Company, was Laclede Power & Light's main competitor in the 1920s and 1930s. Union Electric derived much of its power supply from the Keokuk Hydroelectric Project north of St. Louis on the Mississippi River and from the Bagnell Hydroelectric Plant on the Osage River west of St. Louis. Union Electric also operated the Cahokia Steam Plant in East St. Louis, Illinois. First opened for commercial power production in 1923, Cahokia had a generating capacity of 235,000 kilowatts by 1930, making it one of the largest and most efficient coal-fired plants in the Midwest.

1910s
Munroe helped Insull build the Public Service Company of Northern Illinois into one of the nation's fastest-growing electric utilities.

Chicago and much of the Midwest, Munroe was a Vermonter who had arrived in Chicago with a law degree at the turn of the 20th century. The then 26-year-old Munroe promptly came to Insull's attention in 1901 when he engineered a raid on Chicago's biggest potential electric customer, the city's elevated street railway system.

Insull at the time was in the process of building his Commonwealth Edison Co. into one of the nation's strongest electric utilities. In the 1910s, Munroe helped Insull build the Public Service Company of Northern Illinois into one of the nation's fastest-growing electric utilities.

During World War I, Munroe was at Insull's side when the Chicago utility magnate helped organize the Illinois economy for wartime production. When the war ended in late 1918, Insull launched a takeover of People's Gas, the ailing Chicago manufactured gas utility. Munroe converted People's Gas to coke gas production. At the time, he became acquainted with H.B. Rust, the president of Koppers Co. By 1924, People's Gas was one of the more profitable gas utilities in America; the Chicago gas company's stock more than quadrupled between 1919 and 1924.

In 1924, Munroe learned through his contacts at the American Gas Association that Laclede Gas Light was for sale. He contacted Koppers' H.B. Rust, and the two men put together financing for a buyout offer of $1.5 million to the Walker-Busch syndicate. Munroe, who rarely visited his St. Louis investment, named G.B. Evans president of Laclede Gas Light Company to succeed C.L. Holman, the firm's president from 1912 to 1925.

A graduate of the University of Wisconsin, Evans had devoted his entire life to Laclede Gas Light. He had joined the company as a structural engineer in 1903, and with the exception of two years as a private consultant, Evans had worked for the St. Louis utility since. In the early 1920s, Evans had been named the firm's vice president of operations and was responsible for the tremendous expansion of the Laclede Gas Light system in the years following World War I.

The Harley Clarke Years

The Munroe syndicate's ownership of Laclede Gas Light lasted only three years, although Munroe was rumored to have split a profit of $26 million with his partners during his short tenure at the St. Louis utility. The years of the Munroe cartel ownership were not particularly good for Laclede Gas Light or its reputation in the community.

On the morning of September 9, 1925, an explosion in the basement of 1017 Olive Street rocked the downtown area. Fire Department officials suspected a gas explosion, although they were never able to conclusively prove the source of the blast. The explosion killed four members of the utility's maintenance staff and injured 42 employees and visitors on the first two floors of the utility's headquarters building.

Laclede Gas Light came under added public scrutiny in the spring of 1927 when it filed a rate increase with the Missouri Public Service Commission. The new rates, scheduled to go into effect

St. Louis fireman put out the remnants of the blaze in the lobby of the Laclede Gas Light Building following a September 1925 explosion in the basement of the Olive Street building.

in the summer of that year, represented a rate increase of 29 percent for residential customers and a drop in rates for the firm's industrial customers. Laclede Gas Light argued that the new rates would allow it to more effectively compete against coal for new and existing manufacturing customers. Residential customers were upset, however, when the company proposed to cut back the BTUs in residential gas from 600 to 570, a 5 percent drop in energy efficiency.

The new rate had barely taken effect when Munroe announced early in 1928 that he and the organization had sold control of Laclede Gas Light Company to Harley L. Clarke's Utilities Power & Light Corporation of Chicago.

Clarke was another Insull friend and confidante, although the flamboyant Chicagoan was much closer to Samuel Insull's brother, Martin. In 1924, Martin Insull ran Middle West Utilities, the Insull family holding company that operated electric and gas utilities in a broad swath of North America, from Vermont to Texas. Clarke, along with utility financiers Albert and Victor Emanuel of New York and Burt Howe of Grand Rapids, bought, sold and traded operating utilities on the fringes of the Insull empire.

Between 1925 and 1932, Clarke built Utilities Power & Light Corporation into one of the most diverse utility holding companies in the United States. Unlike the North American Company, which had owned Laclede Gas Light early in the 20th century, Utilities Power & Light did not concentrate on utility properties in metropolitan areas. Nor did the Chicago-based company follow the lead of Martin Insull's Middle West Companies, which primarily operated electric light and power companies in rural areas.

Instead, Utilities Power & Light bought and operated gas, electric and street railway utilities in metropolitan areas such as St. Louis and rural areas of Missouri, Iowa, Nebraska, the Dakotas and Minnesota. By 1930, Clarke's Utilities Power & Light Corporation provided electric and gas service to customers in 16 states.

Clarke was a pillar of Chicago society, chairman of the Chicago Civic Shakespeare Society and frequent guest of the Insulls. In 1930, Clarke headed a syndicate of New York and Chicago banks that engineered a hostile takeover of Fox Films Corp., the predecessor to Twentieth Century Fox.

Clarke exercised control of Utilities Power & Light Corporation through a 10-year voting trust that held all of the shares in the company that Clarke owned. His control of less than $5 million of the holding company's $143 million in shares outstanding allowed Clarke to effectively control the company. Utilities Power & Light Corporation was a profitable venture during the late 1920s and early 1930s. For the year ended December 29, 1930, the Chicago-based holding company that controlled Laclede Gas Light reported a profit of just under $5 million.

By that time, however, America was sinking into the throes of the worst depression of the 20th century. The first casualties of that economic upheaval would be the nation's electric and gas utility holding companies.

1928
Munroe announced early in 1928 that he and the organization had sold control of Laclede Gas Light Company to Harley L. Clarke's Utilities Power & Light Corporation of Chicago.

INTERLUDE 2

The Holding Company Era

For nearly 50 years, from 1889 until the late 1930s, Laclede Gas Light Company was an operating subsidiary of one or another utility holding company. At various times in its history from the late 19th century and early 20th centuries, Laclede Gas Light was affiliated with American Light & Traction Co., North American Company, Middle West Utilities, Utilities Power & Light Corporation and Ogden Corp.

Laclede Gas Light wasn't alone in its ownership by holding companies during the period. At one time in the 1920s and early 1930s, operating subsidiaries of holding companies produced more than two-thirds of the manufactured gas consumed in the United States. According to the Federal Trade Commission, gas operating companies controlled by 44 utility holding companies produced almost 210 billion feet of manufactured gas in 1930 and 452 billion feet of natural gas during 1930.

Holding companies were even more dominant in the nation's electric power sector. By 1932, the 18 largest holding companies in North America generated almost 40 billion kilowatt-hours of electricity, 52.3 percent of all of the electric power generated by privately owned companies in the United States. The same 18 utility holding companies reported net income in 1932 before federal income taxes of $125 million.

The Origin of the Holding Companies

The United States in the late 19th century was undergoing an industrial transformation the likes of which the young republic had never before experienced. Inventors such as Thomas Edison, Elihu Thomson, Nikola Tesla and Theodore S.B.C. Lowe brought about a revolution in the American economy with their introduction of workable utility systems that substituted machinery for labor in the scheme of the nation's productivity.

Transforming the economy, however, necessitated huge amounts of capital. New York, Chicago, Philadelphia, Boston and San Francisco emerged as centers of U.S. investment capital during America's Gilded Age from 1880 to 1910. One of the most sought-after investments during the era was electric and gas utility companies.

Much like the Internet and dot com boom on Wall Street exactly a century later, the utility investment mania created as many losers as winners. Building water gas sets and piping gas to residential and commercial customers were extremely expensive undertakings, as were constructing electric generating stations and wiring cities, towns, homes and businesses. Many of the early electric and gas utility entrepreneurs discovered that the cost of providing service exceeded the revenue that could be generated from selling electricity or gas.

Competition, even in the nation's largest cities, was fierce before the advent of utility regulation in the early 1900s. Laclede Gas Light Company was unable to expand until after its 1889 absorption of the St. Louis Gas Company. Panics on Wall Street that dried up capital in 1893, 1907 and 1913 exacerbated the problem, causing many utilities to seek protection in bankruptcy court between 1880 and 1920.

Entrepreneurs in the gas industry were quick to realize the benefits of consolidating ownership of utility properties in holding companies. One of the first holding companies in America was the United Gas Improvement Company. Started by Philadelphia investment banker Randal Morgan to operate the Philadelphia Gas Works in 1897, UGI, as it was known to a generation of utility investors, became one of the most successful gas holding companies in the nation by the 1920s. At that point, UGI operated gas and electric companies in Pennsylvania, New Hampshire, Massachusetts, Connecticut, Delaware, Maryland, Pennsylvania, Tennessee and Arizona.

Emerson McMillin's American Light & Traction Co., which owned Laclede Gas Light from 1889 to 1903, also owned gas companies in Milwaukee and Detroit.

Another early and very successful holding company was North American Company. Founded by John I. Beggs, Laclede Gas Light's president from 1903 to 1909, the North American Company originally was established in the 1890s as a holding company for the Milwaukee Electric Railway & Light Company. During the next quarter century, the North American Company acquired control of the street railway systems in St. Louis, Portland and Cleveland. By 1925, the North American Company also controlled Potomac Electric Power Co., Detroit Edison Co. and Pacific Gas & Electric Co. At the time of the Great Depression, the North American Company's assets exceeded $2 billion.

'Dogs and Cats'

The success of UGI and North American Company spawned other holding companies during the years immediately following the turn of the 20th century. One of the most successful was an offshoot of General Electric Company (GE). In 1905, Sidney Zollicoffer Mitchell, a courtly Alabamian who was a vice president of the electrical manufacturer, went to his boss, Charles Coffin, with an intriguing proposition. Mitchell pointed out that GE owned the securities of numerous small-town electric utilities that had pledged their stocks as collateral for the purchase of GE generating equipment.

When the utilities became overextended and filed for bankruptcy protection, GE, as a secured creditor, ended up owning them. Mitchell suggested that these "dogs and cats" be combined into a holding company, which would operate the utilities in question. The holding company could then acquire other utilities; provide the operating utilities with management, financial and engineering expertise; and achieve economies of scale by creating regional utilities.

Mitchell's insight led to the creation of the Electric Bond and Share Co. in 1905. Bond and Share, as it became known to Wall Street, quickly emerged as one of the nation's pre-eminent utility holding companies. Bond and Share subsidiaries included such regional utilities as Florida Power & Light, Pennsylvania Power & Light, Utah Power & Light, Nebraska Power Co., Pacific Power & Light, and Minnesota Power & Light.

Mitchell pioneered the concept of diversity in utility economic development. He often explained to investors that utilities could not move their plants, wires and pipes in the case of an economic downturn. Mitchell modeled Bond and Share on the insurance industry philosophy of spreading the risk, "so that effects of a poor wheat crop in Kansas or a bad orange crop in Florida might be offset by a good cattle year or an oil boom in Texas or good apple prices and first-class farming conditions in Oregon and Washington."

Bond and Share's diversity was copied by J.P. Morgan's United Corporation, Henry M. Byllesby's H.M. Byllesby & Company and Harry Daugherty's Cities Service Company. But by far, the utility executive who came to personify the holding company in the popular mind was Samuel B. Insull. Once the private secretary to Thomas Edison, the British born Insull moved to Chicago in the 1890s to take over management of a struggling electric utility.

During the next 15 years, Insull turned Commonwealth Edison into the nation's most profitable utility. After 1910, Insull began acquiring other nearby utilities in Illinois, Indiana and Wisconsin. Within a decade, Insull's Middle West Utilities holding company had become synonymous with the progress of a society that was driven by electric and gas utility infrastructures.

The Fall of the Holding Companies

For most Americans, the date of the onset of the Great Depression was October 29, 1929. Black Tuesday ushered in the collapse of Wall Street and the demise of the holding companies. Just over three-and-one-half years later, on June 6, 1932, Middle West Utilities missed a $20 million bond payment, opening the way to a receivership that shocked both Wall Street and the nation.

The collapse of the Insull empire was emblematic of the abuses that were plaguing the holding companies by the end of the 1920s. Utility holding companies had acquired the reputation of being "widows and orphans" stocks, paying dividends come what may. But unscrupulous operators had pyramided debt on to operating companies, watering stock of sub-holding companies and inflating the value of operating companies by flipping them from one owner to the next.

In 1928, the Federal Trade Commission began a series of hearings on holding company abuses that captured headlines until the mid-1930s and resulted in a compilation of more than 70 volumes of testimony. Wilbur Foshay, the owner of an obscure Minneapolis holding company, preceded Wall Street into collapse in the summer of 1929. The holding companies, many of them leveraged with mountains of debt, began struggling. When Insull's Middle West Utilities went under in the spring of 1932, the resulting panic wiped out thousands of investors and served warning to those who had parked their life savings in utility stocks.

Franklin Delano Roosevelt, then the governor of New York, made the Insull collapse a key part of his campaign platform in the 1932 presidential race. When Roosevelt trounced incumbent President Herbert Hoover in November of that year, he immediately charged Congress with passing legislation to break up the holding companies.

Congress responded by passing the Public Utility Holding Company Act of 1935, which FDR immediately signed. The major provision of the legislation essentially required utility holding companies to divest non-contiguous operating utilities.

When the U.S. Supreme Court ruled the act constitutional in 1938, the die was cast for the breakup of the holding companies. Although World War II intervened, the Securities and Exchange Commission oversaw an orderly process to carry out the provisions of the 1935 legislation. Most operating subsidiaries of holding companies were spun out as independent companies in initial public offerings that took place between 1939 and 1949.

The lobby of the Laclede Gas Light Building at 1017 Olive struck a patriotic theme during World War II. Coke and manufactured gas from Laclede was critical to the smooth functioning of the steel mills, foundries and other defense industries that called St. Louis home during the war.

CHAPTER 7

Natural Gas Comes to St. Louis

The 1930s and 1940s were perhaps two of the most difficult decades in the history of Laclede Gas Light Company. After enjoying strong growth during the 1920s, the company's revenues and earnings stagnated through most of the 1930s as St. Louis coped with near economic collapse during the Great Depression. The 1940s brought new challenges, as Laclede Gas Light focused on providing gas for America's defense efforts during World War II.

By 1933
The national unemployment rate hovered around 25 percent by the spring.

Underlying the economic peaks and valleys of the 15 years between 1930 and 1945 were two events that would mark the transition between the Laclede Gas Light of the past and the modern corporation. In 1931, natural gas first came to St. Louis via a pipeline from Louisiana. Although Laclede Gas Light was unable to fully convert all of its residential and commercial cooking and heating customers to the new fuel until after World War II, the company almost immediately began mixing natural and manufactured gas to produce a higher quality gas of 800 BTU for its customers.

The second event that occurred during the Great Depression and in the early 1940s was the demise of the holding company structure that essentially had owned Laclede Gas Light since 1889. Harley L. Clarke, the Chicago holding company executive who had purchased control of Laclede Gas Light from Samuel Insull associate Charles Munroe, watched helplessly as the value of his stock plummeted from $230 a share in 1927 to $73 a share in April 1932.

That same week, creditors filed bankruptcy petitions against three of Insull's holding companies. The receivership of America's best-known utility holding company empire was a warning signal for the entire industry.

By 1936, Clarke's Utilities Power & Light Corporation, the holding company that owned Laclede Gas Light, was itself bankrupt. Laclede Gas Light passed through the hands of two more holding companies, the Atlas Corp. and the Ogden Corp., before it was finally reorganized in 1941 as Laclede Gas Corp.

The Great Depression

In many ways, Laclede Gas Light survived the Great Depression better than the city of St. Louis did. The descent into the Depression was inexorable following the collapse of Wall Street in October and November of 1929. Between the Black Tuesday drop on October 28, 1929 and the federal bank holiday in March 1933, more than 9,000 U.S. banks failed. The national unemployment rate hovered around 25 percent by the spring of 1933.

The unemployment rate in St. Louis bottomed out at nearly a quarter of the work force in early 1933. Dozens of industries and foundries in the city and nearby East St. Louis, Illinois fled the region for new locations in the South, while several hundred thousand African-Americans arrived in the city from the rural areas of the Mississippi Delta. The flood of new immigrants swelled the ranks of the unemployed. By 1930, there were soup lines on the streets of St. Louis and East St. Louis.

The city experienced a rash of Depression-induced holdups in 1931. In 1932, thousands of Bonus Marchers from the south and west converged on St. Louis. Unemployed veterans from World War I who hoped Congress would pass a veteran's bonus law, the Bonus Marchers marshalled forces to march on Washington, D.C. Many stayed at the nation's largest "Hooverville," a collection of tarpaper shacks on the banks of the Mississippi River named for the beleaguered president of the United States.

The city did what it could to alleviate suffering, putting thousands of residents to work building public works projects, including Memorial Plaza, which was

St. Louis was the beneficiary of a number of city, state and federal public works projects during the Great Depression. Here, work continues on clearing the site for Memorial Plaza in 1933, while cranes hover over the yet-to-be-completed Municipal (Kiel) Auditorium.

funded by a 1934 municipal bond issue. The next year, St. Louisans voted for a large bond issue to finance construction of the Jefferson National Expansion Memorial on the city's riverfront; part of the project was financed by the federal government through the National Park Service.

For Laclede Gas Light, one of the overriding realities of the Great Depression was the plateau in the city's population growth. In 1930, St. Louis was the 7th largest city in the United States. Ten years later St. Louis had dropped by 5,000 people to a population of just over 816,000. Because it was constrained from expanding outside the city limits, Laclede Gas Light was facing a potential shrinkage of its customer base at a time when much of that base was unemployed.

'Business Inactivity Due to the Depression'

Laclede Gas Light's total revenue for the year ended December 31, 1930 was $11.06 million, which resulted in a net profit of $1.03 million. Revenues wouldn't again approach $11 million in any single year until after the end of World War II. Total company assets in 1930 were $64.56 million and total shareholders' equity was $24.2 million.

In the early 1930s, the city of St. Louis began an extensive street widening and paving program as an emergency employment measure. As a result, Laclede Gas Light had to strengthen a large number of pipe connections to St. Louis homes and businesses. The utility also overhauled many miles of gas mains so that the company's underground facilities would be protected under the new, heavier pavements, the company told shareholders in the 1930 annual report.

Revenues declined in 1931, 1932 and 1933. Total revenue for 1931 was $10.2 million, which resulted in a net profit of less than $1 million. Revenue for the year ended December 31, 1932 was $9.25 million, and revenue for the

1930
St. Louis was the 7th largest city in the United States. Ten years later St. Louis had dropped by 5,000 people to a population of just over 816,000.

THE GASHOUSE GANG

For nearly a century, St. Louis has had a love affair with its Cardinals. From Rickey to La Russa, Hornsby to Musial, McGwire to Eckstein, the Cardinals have forged a legacy of winning unmatched in the National League — 17 pennants (most in the senior circuit), 11 world championships, eight division titles and 37 Hall of Famers.

Perhaps the most famous of the Cardinals' many talented teams was the Gashouse Gang, a nickname applied to the 1934 Cardinals, a rag-tag group of major league baseball players if ever there was one. The collection of hard-nosed, slightly offbeat characters were known as much for their crazy antics as for their baseball talent. The group included Pepper Martin, Frankie Frisch, Leo Durocher, Joe Medwick, and the Dean brothers, Dizzy and Daffy.

The Cardinals, by most accounts, earned the nickname from the team's shabby appearance and rough-and-tumble tactics, though there are two commonly circulated origins of the name:

- One story says that the team couldn't afford more than one uniform per player. After a particularly grimy game against the Boston Braves, the team boarded a train to Brooklyn for an early doubleheader, and had no time to launder their uniforms. The next morning, as the team arrived in the hotel lobby, one news writer claimed that they resembled the gangs of the Gashouse District in Lower Manhattan. The name stuck to describe the scrappy, reckless play of the team.
- The other story says that Frank Graham, a reporter for the New York Sun, was talking with Leo Durocher about the team. Graham commented half-jokingly that the team might be good enough to play in the American League. Durocher responded, "They wouldn't let us play in the American League. They'd say we were just a bunch of gashouse players." Graham, and eventually the rest of baseball, used the name from then on.

Workers at Laclede Gas knew that Durocher's reference was to the fine, but not quite major league caliber, amateur baseball played by teams from Laclede Gas and other companies in the industrial leagues around St. Louis each summer.

Despite the Cardinals' general lack of decorum, they managed to scrape together a fantastic season. Led by player/manager Frankie Frisch and the hard-nosed Durocher, the 1934 Cardinals won 95 games. They captured the National League pennant and beat the Detroit Tigers in seven games to win the World Series.

The team featured five regulars who hit at least .300, a 30-game winner in Dizzy Dean, and four all-stars, including Frisch. Not among the all-stars was RIP Collins, the first baseman who led the team in 16 offensive categories, including a .333 batting average, a .615 slugging percentage, 35 home runs, and 128 runs batted in.

The Gashouse Gang nickname is still used occasionally to describe the St. Louis organization.

---

year ended December 31, 1933 was $8.8 million. "The business inactivity due to the depression has resulted in a decline of approximately one percent in the number of meters connected to the mains," the company reported in its 1931 annual report. "There has been no major construction activity during this fiscal year due to the business downturn."

In 1932, the message was much the same. "Revenue declined slightly from the previous year due to the curtailed use of natural gas by all classes of customers and a reduction in rates that became effective August 1," Laclede Gas Light reported in its 1932 annual report.

By 1933, the company was treating the erosion of business as normal. "The net increase in main mileage was only 2.43 miles," Laclede Gas Light noted in its annual report, "and there was a two-and-one-half percent decrease in the number of meters connected to the mains. This is a nominal decrease in view of the current business conditions."

A more serious problem in the mid-1930s was a drop in total assets and shareholder equity, which affected the company's ability to raise money in the bond markets. Revenues stabilized at a plateau of just under $9 million in 1933, 1934 and 1935 before plummeting to less than $7 million in 1936. Finances were so bad that the utility was unable to even sell mortgage bonds in the spring of 1934.

Technology took its toll on the company's business. During the 1920s and early 1930s, the nation's railroad industry modernized passenger service, installing battery-operated electric lighting systems on the fleet of passenger rail cars. "Since there was no longer a market for Pintsch gas," Laclede Gas Light reported in its 1934 annual report, "the company has discontinued its manufacture, and the entire Pintsch gas plant and distribution system have been abandoned, which resulted in a write-off of $229,449."

The Arrival of Natural Gas

Technology also worked to the company's benefit during the Great Depression. In 1931, natural gas arrived just south of St. Louis.

Natural gas had been commercially available in certain regions of the country since the late 19th century. Indiana, Ohio and West Virginia had all enjoyed gas booms in the late 19th century. The gas fields of Kansas began major development early in the century, and the Hogshooter field in Oklahoma was opened up in 1910. Consumers across the state of Missouri in Kansas City and Joplin, as well as in Oklahoma City, Oklahoma, were the earliest customers of the Kansas and Oklahoma fields. The era was a time of rapid incorporation of natural gas utilities and pipeline companies. The Kansas Natural Gas Company, the Oklahoma Natural Gas Company and the Lone Star Gas Company were some of the earliest major companies formed in the Kansas and Oklahoma fields.

Natural gas may well have continued as a regional curiosity had it not been for the 1919 discovery of the Panhandle-Hugoton field on the Southern Plains. An immense supply of domestic gas, coupled with technological advances in pipeline construction and conditions favorable for capital formation, led to the development during the 1920s, 1930s and 1940s of the nation's natural gas pipeline industry.

The First Pipeline

Pipeline gas was delivered to St. Louis in 1931 by the Mississippi River Fuel Co., one of the early pipeline firms. Owned by Standard Oil Co. of New Jersey, Columbia Carbon Co. and United Carbon Co., Mississippi River Fuel built a 22-inch steel pipeline 431 miles from near Perryville, Louisiana to a point just south of St. Louis. Laclede Gas Light watched the arrival of gas in metropolitan St. Louis with great interest. But the company was not an immediate customer of the new pipeline, which had a daily capacity of 100 million cubic feet of gas.

The St. Louis gas utility quickly decided to be one of the pipeline's first customers. On March 1, 1932, Laclede Gas Light Company purchased the Missouri Industrial Gas Company for approximately $795,000. During that spring and summer, Laclede Gas Light changed from artificial gas with a BTU content of 650 to mixed artificial and natural gases with a BTU content of 800.

1931
Pipeline gas was delivered to St. Louis by the Mississippi River Fuel Co., one of the early pipeline firms.

During the mid-1930s, Laclede Gas Light sold coke for home furnaces as a way to reduce the smoke pollution that bedeviled St. Louis.

1932
Laclede Gas Light's introduction of natural gas was the first step in reducing the amount of smoke that plagued the river city from 1880 to 1950.

The company had to adjust or adapt in excess of 2 million burners on practically every gas appliance in its service territory to accommodate the higher heat content. Laclede Gas Light employed an additional 800 men during the changeover, a welcome boost to the region's economy that Depression summer. The total cost was approximately $500,000.

By 1936, Laclede Gas Light was distributing 5.7 billion cubic feet of mixed gas to customers in the form of natural gas and manufactured gas. The company was still burning more than 300,000 tons of coal each year to manufacture gas and coke for the home heating market, but the addition of natural gas to the gas stream meant that the amount of coal burned each year was far less than it had been in the past.

Laclede Gas Light's introduction of natural gas in 1932 was the first step in reducing the amount of smoke that plagued the river city from 1880 to 1950. The smoke problem, exacerbated by the city's location as a major rail center for the lower Midwest, got so bad in 1940 that Life Magazine called St. Louis "a city in decay."

Under Mayor Bernard F. Dickmann, St. Louis passed new smoke abatement regulations in 1937, creating a Division of Smoke Regulation as a separate unit in the city's Department of Public Safety. Laclede Gas Light's 15-year conversion of its fuel source from coal-based manufactured gas to all natural gas was an important first step in cleaning the city's dirty air.

Battles on Many Fronts

The 1930s were a contentious era when Laclede Gas Light fought battles with its critics over a host of issues. Utilities Power & Light Corp. was a target of the federal government concerning holding company control of Laclede Gas Light.

84   Laclede Gas Company

The company was at loggerheads with the city of St. Louis over taxes and municipalization efforts. Laclede Gas Light endured a bitter work stoppage in 1935, and for much of the decade, the utility's electric power subsidiary, Laclede Power & Light, was at war with Union Electric over electric service territories.

Things began going wrong for Harley Clarke, the flamboyant Chicagoan who headed Utilities Power & Light Corporation, early in the 1930s when Laclede Gas Light and Interstate Power Corp., his two major operating subsidiaries, started reporting lower revenues. By 1935, Utilities Power & Light Corporation was in the hands of the Reconstruction Finance Corp., a Depression-era lender of last resort.

The lack of St. Louis ownership of Laclede Gas Light had been an issue with the city government and the media since at least the onset of the Depression in 1930. In 1931, Clarke had replaced the likable, and local, Laclede Gas Light President G.B. Evans with E.P. Gosling. Evans, president from 1925 to 1931, had been employed with Laclede Gas Light since just after the turn of the 20th century.

Gosling spent much of his tenure in disputes with the city administration and the newspapers. The city charged that Laclede Gas Light refused to convert to all natural gas because it wanted to protect its investment in manufactured gas plants and coke distribution. The utility argued that it simply could not afford to make the conversion at a time when revenues and meter connections were both dropping.

The company and the city administration clashed again during the mid-1930s when the board of aldermen passed a 1936 ordinance to assess the company five percent of its gross receipts for the "use and occupation of the streets and other highways of the city." Judge Robert Otto, Laclede Gas Light's counsel, advised management that the ordinance was invalid.

An even more serious dispute between the company and its employees erupted in the spring of 1935 when members of the Gas House Workers Union walked off the job. The three-month strike over company recognition of the union and a closed shop was marked by intermittent violence, and it was only settled when the union dropped its demands that all employees be unionized.

In January 1936, the state arbitration board decided that wages should be increased 7 percent, retroactive to

Like many industries at the time, Laclede Gas Light experienced its share of labor problems.

July 12, 1935, instead of the 40 percent increase asked by the employees. The request for "seniority rule" submitted to the arbitration board was denied.

No dividends were paid during 1936 on either preferred or common stock.

The Holding Company Act

Franklin Delano Roosevelt's election as president in 1932 ushered in a number of sweeping changes for the nation's economy, including a restructuring of America's utility industry. FDR had run against Samuel Insull and the perceived abuses of the holding companies during his 1932 campaign for the White House. Once elected, he made good on his promises to change the way the utility industry operated.

The most sweeping change of the First New Deal was congressional passage of Roosevelt-sponsored legislation to break up the nation's electric and gas utility holding companies. The Public Utility Holding Company Act of 1935 required holding companies to divest non-contiguous operating utility subsidiaries. The act was challenged in court by the holding companies, but upheld by the U.S. Supreme Court in 1938.

By that time, Harley Clarke and the Utilities Power & Light Corporation were struggling to survive. Clarke was ousted as Laclede Gas Light's chairman in 1936, and Gosling was terminated as president at the same time.

P.B. Shaw, a holding company executive from Chicago, was named interim president while the board searched for a replacement for Gosling.

In the spring of 1937, the Laclede Gas Light board named J.B. Wilson, a holding company executive with years of experience operating utilities in Illinois and California. Wilson was what the 21st century media would call a workout specialist. From 1933 to 1937, Wilson had worked for the Middle West Utilities trustee in Chicago, managing the affairs of the Insull holding company operating utilities while receivers sorted out the firm's tangled financial affairs.

Wilson's tenure as president was not much longer than that of Shaw. During his year at the helm, he managed the St. Louis gas utility for New York-based Atlas Corp., which had purchased the operating utilities of Utilities Power & Light Corporation from the Reconstruction Finance Corp. in 1935.

Atlas was an investment conglomerate, and not strictly a holding company. The brainchild of Floyd Bostwick Odlum, Atlas was one of the nation's first investment trusts. Odlum stocked the trust with the devalued stocks and bonds of U.S. corporations during the Great Depression, including RKO Studios, Convair, Northeast Airlines and Bonwit-Teller.

To comply with the provisions of the Holding Company Act, Odlum folded his Utilities Power & Light Corporation stock into another investment trust, the Ogden Corp., and began selling operating utilities to the public. In 1939, the Missouri Public Service Commission approved the Ogden Corp. acquisition of Laclede Gas Light. In 1940, Ogden Corp. spun out to public control its biggest utility holding, Indianapolis Power &

1935
The Public Utility Holding Company Act of 1935 required holding companies to divest non-contiguous operating utility subsidiaries.

Light Corp. Odlum and Ogden Corp. were preparing to spin out to public control Laclede Gas Light when Japan attacked the U.S. Naval Base at Pearl Harbor.

Laclede At War

The war that had ravaged Europe and Asia for more than two years came home to American shores on the first Sunday in December 1941. The Japanese attack on the U.S. Navy anchorage at Pearl Harbor, Hawaii precipitated the nation into the global conflict. During the next 44 months, places that most Americans had never heard of — Midway, the Kasserine Pass, Guadalcanal, Ploesti, Peleiliu, Omaha Beach, Okinawa, Bastogne and Iwo Jima — were seared into a nation's consciousness.

Laclede Gas Light and its employees joined forces in a national effort to win World War II. "It will be some time before we all realize what war means," President L. Wade Childress, who had replaced Wilson in 1938, told employees in his annual Christmas message in 1941, just weeks after the Pearl Harbor attack. "It will mean sacrifices."

Childress noted that "we can't all go forth to do battle. For some of us that is impossible. But our support here at home can be manifested in many ways." He added that Laclede Gas Light was important to the war effort, especially in providing gas to the dozens of war industries in the region that depended on heat treating of metals for the production of armaments.

As it had during World War I, coke and coke gas played a key role in the nation's defense efforts. Already during the winter of 1942, Laclede Gas was shipping 500 tons of coke a day from the Catalan Street plant to Granite City Steel. The Illinois mill used the coke from Laclede Gas to produce more than 180,000 tons of molten iron a year for America's war industries.

Laclede Gas' longtime residential heating and cooking business began to be impacted in the spring of 1942 when the federal government stopped the direct sale of all gas and electric appliances. Increased demand for industrial gas, however, more than offset the potential loss of residential gas cooking customers during the war.

Laclede Gas workers quickly adopted the national conservation ethic, saving rubber bands, paper and paper clips at work and scrap metals, cotton and woolen rags at home. Employees grew victory gardens in vacant lots and on company property to help with food

1939
The Missouri Public Service Commission approved the Ogden Corp. acquisition of Laclede Gas Light.

Laclede Gas Light's home service department served as a clearinghouse for home front defense activities during World War II.

shortages. In September 1942, dozens of employees at the Central Service Building at 3950 Forest Park Avenue donated blood to help the St. Louis Red Cross Blood Donor Service raise its quota for emergency transfusions for men in the armed forces. By the end of 1942, more than 450 employees had completed civil defense training in the use of air raid shelters, blackout curtains and gas masks.

The Laclede Honor Roll

The "Win the War" spirit that permeated Laclede Gas during 1942 and 1943 was driven by one simple fact. The reality of the war was brought home to those left behind in Missouri by the large number of co-workers who had left St. Louis to fight on the war's far-flung fronts.

A framed plaque in the lobby of 1017 Olive Street emphasized the sacrifices of Laclede Gas employees. The Laclede Honor Roll listed the company's employees who had heeded the call to serve their country. By January 1943, there were 137 names on the honor roll. A year and a half later, in the summer of 1944, 209 Laclede Gas employees were serving or had served in the armed forces.

With a total work force of slightly more than 1,500 at the start of World War II, nearly one in seven Laclede Gas employees saw active duty military service during the war. More hundreds of sons and daughters, brothers and sisters, husbands and boyfriends of Laclede Gas employees were called to the colors during the conflict.

Laclede News, the employee communications vehicle that L. Wade Childress had instituted in 1937, became a means for employees to keep in touch with co-workers around the globe. In March 1944, the employee newspaper interviewed Lt. Harry Wachsler, home on leave from his dive bomber squadron in the South Pacific. Wachsler talked about the recent raid on the Japanese naval base at Truk and added that he had landed his float plane to rescue a fellow aviator. Laclede News pictured Wachsler and his plane, decorated with a "Gas House Liz" decal on the nose.

Staff Sgt. Elmer Duecker, the 19-year-old son of Elmer J. Duecker of the customer installation department, reported on his experiences as a radio-gunner in one of the new B-29 Superfortresses being employed to bomb Japan. Capt. John Adolphson wrote from occupied France in the summer of 1944 that he had survived the Allied landings at Normandy. "We are camped on one of the best cow pastures in France," he wrote. "My command post, where I am

Hundreds of Laclede employees participated in Red Cross blood drives during the war.

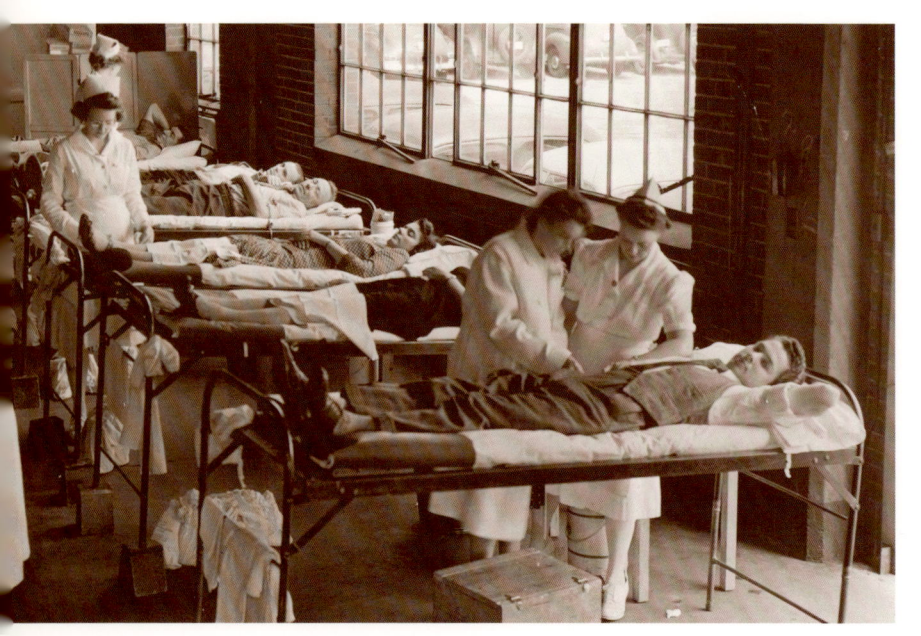

writing this letter, is a hole in the ground covered by 4 x 4 timber and sandbags."

Gold Stars

With so many employees in combat, it was inevitable that some wouldn't come back to Laclede Gas. In September 1944, employee Harry Weiland learned via the War Department that his 22-year-old son Harold had died of wounds sustained in the fighting in Italy. The Gold Star would be the first the War Department awarded to members of the Laclede Gas family. It would not be the last.

The next month, Jacob Kukuljan, an employee of the paving division of the street department, received word that his son, Staff Sgt. Richard L. Kukuljan, had been shot down and was a prisoner of the Germans.

Lt. Harry H. Dickason, a former employee, was reported missing after his plane was forced down by bad weather in the Adriatic Sea. Dickason was later reported dead. 1945 brought more bad news. In February, employees learned of the death of Philip Nachefski, a heater helper at the Coke Station. A paratrooper, Nachefski had been killed in fierce fighting during the German breakthrough at the Battle of the Bulge.

Employee Marie Renneck lost her husband, Capt. Eugene Renneck, when he was killed in action in the Pacific in the waning days of the war. Eddie Scott, a former coke plant employee, was declared dead in early 1945 after being reported missing in action in the Pacific Theater the previous fall. Lt. Robert V. Allyn, an employee of the customer accounting department since 1934, was killed on April 27 during heavy fighting on Okinawa. Lorraine Owens of the stores department lost her husband, and former Vice President B.F. Pickard lost his son.

For some, the end of the war brought closure. Andy Aubuchon, the company's paymaster, learned in the summer of 1945 that his brother, Tech. Sgt. Urvan Aubuchon, had died nearly two years previous at the hands of the Japanese. A member of the utility's collection department when he enlisted, Aubuchon had been shot down over Burma in November 1943 and had died in a Japanese prisoner-of-war camp.

The supreme sacrifice of the six Laclede Gas employees who gave their lives in the defense of their country was a sober reminder of the challenges that had been faced by the company and its employees since the onset of the Great Depression more than 15 years before. But the end of the war in the summer of 1945 saw employees returning to their workplaces, full of enthusiasm for what lie ahead.

Already in September 1945, 15 returning veterans were paving the way for the more than 125 ex-servicemen and women who would return to Laclede Gas during the fall of 1945 and the winter and spring of 1946. Company President L. Wade Childress welcomed "all servicemen who are returning to their former jobs. We are glad to have you back."

The two years following the end of World War II would constitute one of the most exciting times in the company's history. Between 1945 and 1947, Laclede Gas converted its entire system to clean-burning, efficient natural gas.

1945 to 1947
Laclede Gas converted its entire system to clean-burning, efficient natural gas.

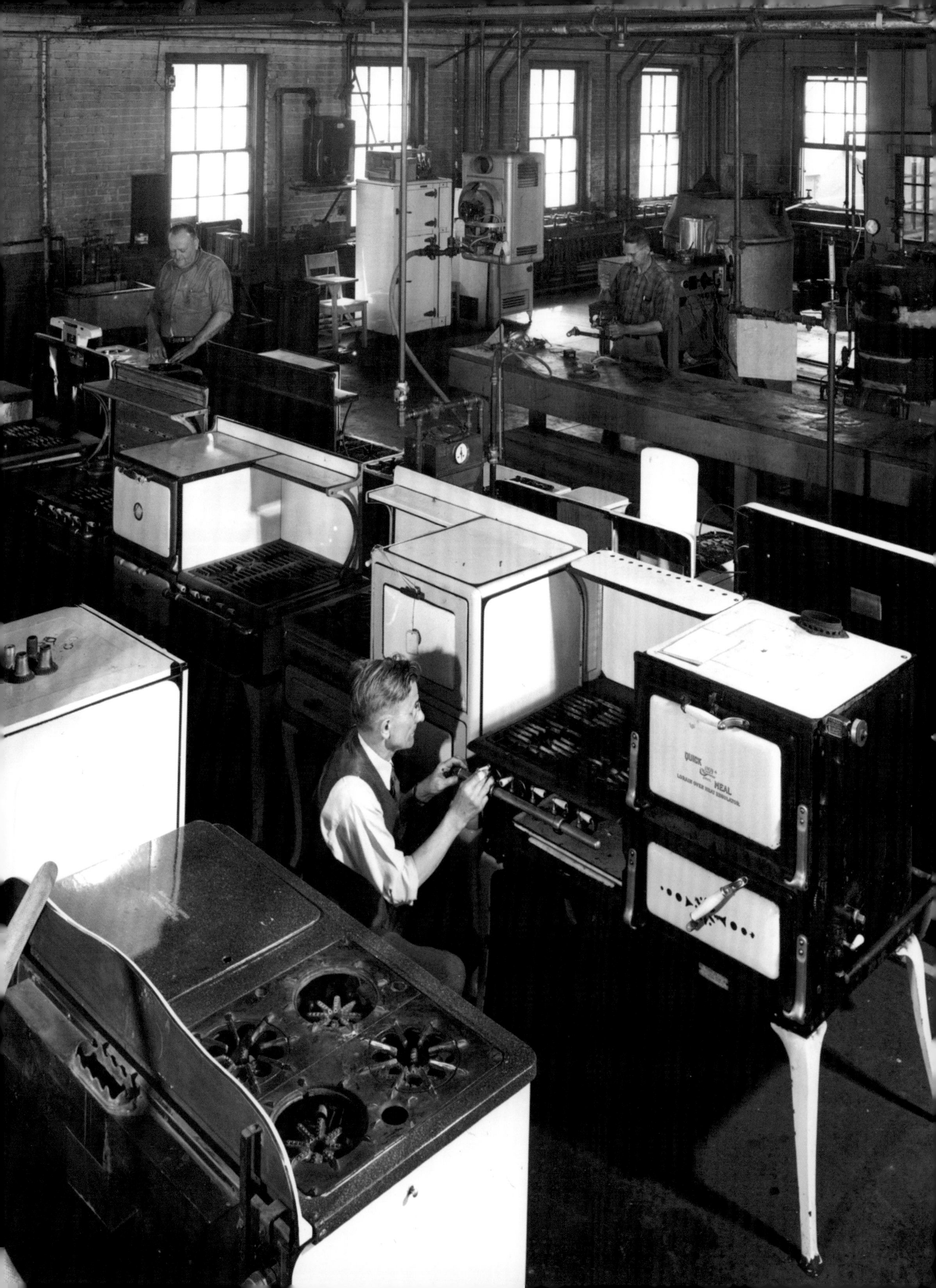
QUICK
MEAL
LORAIN OVEN HEAT REGULATOR

CHAPTER 8

The Conversion

Lee Liberman arrived at Laclede Gas in the fall of 1945, the first in a wave of returning veterans and newly-hired employees who would shape the fortunes of the company through almost the end of the 20th century.

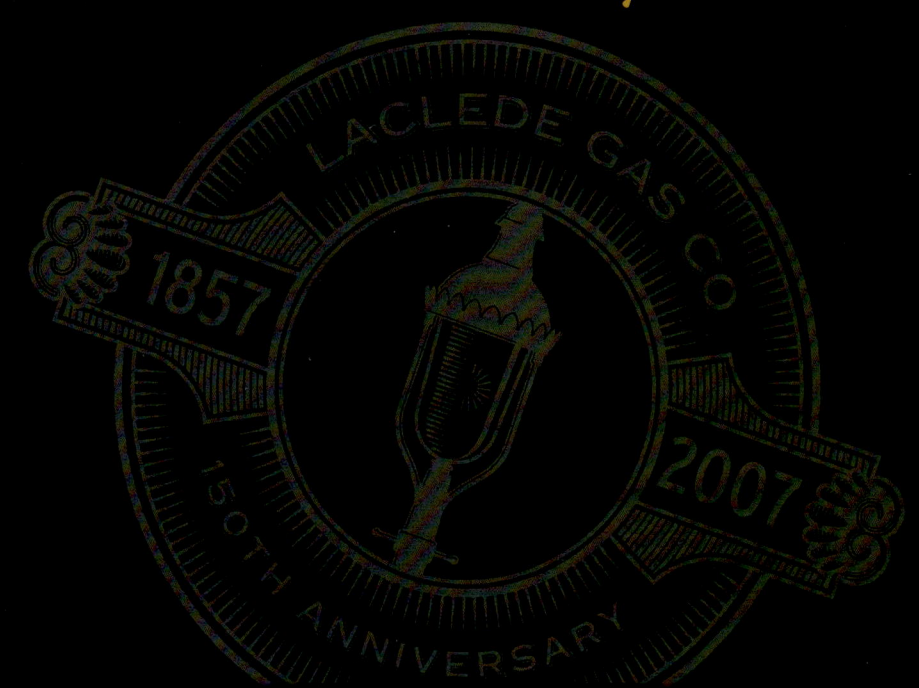

When Laclede Gas brought natural gas to St. Louis in 1949, more than 2 million burner tips in the metropolitan area had to be changed out to burn the higher-BTU gas. The utility repaired thousands of gas stoves to make them suitable for cooking with natural gas.

The 24-year-old Liberman returned to St. Louis from California, where he instructed Army Air Corps pilots in the operation of a sophisticated new autopilot system. Born in Salt Lake City, Liberman had moved to St. Louis with his parents when he was 10 years old. He graduated from Yale University in 1942 and then joined the Army Air Corps with hopes of becoming a pilot. But his eyes were too weak for flight school, and he was assigned to duty as an instructor at an air base near Los Angeles.

"I was discharged at Scott Army Air Corps Base," Liberman explained, "and I decided to go to law school. I couldn't start school until the second semester in January 1946, so I went down to the U.S. Employment Service looking for a job, and I got two referrals: Laclede and Union Electric. I went in to interview with Laclede and got hired. I was accepted at Stanford Law School, but I almost immediately met the girl who later became my first wife. I decided to remain awhile at Laclede, and ended up being there 47 years."

Liberman joined Laclede Gas Light as a cadet engineer and was quickly assigned to the coke plant on Catalan Street. In 1945, Laclede Gas was distributing a mixture of natural gas and manufactured gas to its customers, and its franchise only allowed the company to serve customers within the old city limits of St. Louis. The company was in the process of implementing recommendations that Stone & Webster had made in the spring of 1940. Laclede Gas President L. Wade Childress had hired the utility consulting engineering firm to advise him on efficiencies, but World War II had broken out before the utility was able to incorporate the Stone & Webster suggestions into standard operating procedure.

Stone & Webster had reported that the company's coke oven plant was economically operated, and that the firm's decision to outsource the sale of coke to residential heating customers was a smart move. The consultant suggested that Laclede Gas consider establishing "a department for the promotion of coke sales."

Stone & Webster was less enthusiastic about the company's record in gas heating sales. The sales department, it said, "has not been an effective tool for the purpose of promoting the more general use of gas."

Nor did Stone & Webster think that the contract Laclede Gas had signed with Mississippi River Fuel Co. for delivering pipeline natural gas to St. Louis would allow the company to expand its market for natural gas sales. Stone & Webster noted that "under the terms of the present natural gas purchase contract, involving both a demand and a commodity charge, a situation may arise in the not too distant future where additional house heating business can be carried only at an actual loss to your Company."

In 1945 and 1946, Laclede Gas was busy implementing the changes that Stone & Webster had suggested prior to the outbreak of war. During his first three years on the job, Liberman would witness the transformation of

1940
Laclede Gas President L. Wade Childress hired the utility consulting engineering firm, Stone & Webster, to advise him on efficiencies.

St. Louis in the immediate post-war years boasted a population of more than 850,000 people. The city was a transportation hub, and was a center of chemical and iron and steel manufacturing, as well as housing one of the nation's largest brewery complexes.

Laclede Gas as the utility shed its final holding company ties, exchanged the electric division with Union Electric for the St. Louis County Gas Co., and converted all of its customers to straight natural gas.

The Exchange

Throughout the 1930s and early 1940s, Laclede Gas Light and Union Electric had fought for electric utility customers. Union Electric was the city's electric utility, but Laclede Power & Light, the gas company's electric division, served customers on the city's north side. Declining revenues for both Laclede Gas and Union Electric during the Great Depression meant that the two utilities strenuously competed for new business along the boundaries of each company's franchise service territory.

Laclede Gas had upped the ante with Union Electric in 1937 when it brought in a veteran from Utilities Power & Light Corporation to head Laclede Power & Light. C.L. Harrod came from Indianapolis, where he had been operating executive of Indianapolis Power & Light Co. Harrod's assignment was simple. He was to oversee the installation of two mammoth Springfield high-pressure boilers in Laclede Power & Light's generating station. With the new boilers installed, Laclede Power & Light had sufficient capacity to serve a city of 150,000 people.

But the fight between the two St. Louis electric power companies

L. WADE CHILDRESS

L. Wade Childress was one of the more important presidents in the long history of Laclede Gas. Although his tenure at the helm of the St. Louis gas utility was less than a decade, Childress left a legacy that persists to this day.

When Childress arrived at 1017 Olive Street as president in 1938, Laclede Gas Light was reeling from nearly a decade of upheaval. The company was in the process of being reorganized by the Securities and Exchange Commission as a result of federal holding company legislation passed in 1935. Laclede Gas Light was still recovering from a bitter three-month strike in 1935, and the company's annual revenues had declined by one-third from their high in the late 1920s.

Childress' elevation to the top spot at Laclede Gas Light sent a message to the community that the era of absentee holding company ownership was finally over. Childress had spent practically his entire business life in St. Louis, moving to the city in 1893 from his birthplace of Murfreesboro, Tennessee. Childress was 19 at the time, and he came to St. Louis to begin work as a railroad clerk.

While working as a clerk, Childress took the opportunity to start a freight trucking concern to serve the city's railroads. He formed the Columbia Terminals Company in 1902, became president of the firm in 1905, and began his long career as a civic and industrial leader. Childress remained president of the transfer company until 1935, when he was named chairman of the board. By 1938, Columbia Terminals employed more than 2,000 people.

In 1929, Childress further expanded his business interests when he organized the Mississippi Valley Barge Line Company. He served as president of the river fleet until 1947, when he became board chairman. Childress also was on the board of directors of the Mercantile-Commerce Bank & Trust Company and the Mercantile-Commerce National Bank.

L. Wade Childress was elected a board member of Laclede Gas Light in 1937. The following year, he was elected president of the company by unanimous vote of the board, a position he held until he became chairman of the board in June 1947. Childress replaced Joseph B. Wilson, who resigned in March 1938, as president.

Childress infused a breath of fresh air into the affairs of Laclede Gas Light. In 1940, he hired Stone & Webster, one of the nation's premier utility engineering consultants, to examine ways in which the company could become more efficient and more profitable. He steered Laclede Gas Light through the difficult operating conditions that prevailed during World War II. Childress presided over the conversion to all natural gas in 1946 and 1947, and he laid the groundwork for the company's final emergence as an independent utility in 1948.

In civic affairs, Childress was founder of the Governmental Research Institute. When Dr. M. A. Goldstein founded the Central Institute for the Deaf, Childress was one of his earliest backers. He also was a member of the Metropolitan Board of the YMCA, as well as a member of the board of trustees of the YWCA. From 1942 to 1945, he also served on the executive board of the War Chest.

Childress died at his home in Richmond Heights on January 31, 1950.

---

came to an unequivocal halt in the late summer of 1941, when the Securities and Exchange Commission suggested a novel solution to the holding company divestiture problems faced by both Laclede Gas and Union Electric. Both were owned by holding or investment companies, Laclede Gas by Floyd Odlum's Atlas Corp., and Union Electric by North American Co., which had also owned Laclede Gas Light early in the 20th century.

In addition, the two St. Louis utilities were what the investment community termed combination companies. Laclede Gas served St. Louis with gas and parts of the city with electric power. Union Electric served St. Louis with electricity and surrounding areas of St. Louis County with gas through its St. Louis County Gas Co. subsidiary.

The Securities and Exchange Commission and the Missouri Public Service Commission were concerned that the two St. Louis utilities be divested as "integrated operations" as specified by the 1935 Holding Company Act. Accordingly, when the two utilities filed their proposed plans of reorganization with the state and federal regulatory agencies, they proposed to trade their respective utilities. Laclede Gas agreed to sell Laclede Power & Light to Union Electric, while Union Electric reciprocated by selling St. Louis County Gas Co. to Laclede Gas.

Laclede Gas closed on the sale of Laclede Power & Light in May 1942. Union Electric paid $8.6 million for the gas company's electric power subsidiary and began preparing St. Louis County Gas Co. for sale to Laclede Gas Light Co.

Due to wartime restrictions, Laclede Gas didn't take possession of St. Louis County Gas Co. until November 1946, about a year after World War II had ended. By then, the suburban gas property was valued at more than $10 million.

But because Laclede Gas was no longer identified with far-off holding companies, banks in St. Louis stepped up to finance the purchase. Northwestern Mutual Life Insurance Co. subscribed to a mortgage bond issue, while First National, Mercantile-Commerce, Mississippi Valley, Boatmen's National and Manufacturers Banks all participated in a 10-year loan that allowed Laclede Gas to acquire its suburban counterpart.

The integration of St. Louis County Gas in 1948 also brought a backup fuel supply for Laclede Gas' anticipated source of natural gas. In 1946, St. Louis County Gas began construction of a stand-by propane gas storage facility at its Shrewsbury Gas Plant. In later years, Laclede Gas would supplement its often meager supply of natural gas with propane from the Shrewsbury storage facility, as well as three propane storage facilities that Laclede developed at manufactured gas plants in the city of St. Louis. One was at the coke plant, and the others were at Station A and Station B. The two latter plants produced a combination of natural gas and coal gas, manufactured to help in winter peak demand periods.

The 1948 acquisition of St. Louis County Gas freed Laclede Gas from the constraints of serving customers located inside the old city boundaries of St. Louis. Already by 1945, the booming suburbs of St. Louis County were approaching a population of 250,000 people. As the automobile became the preferred means of transportation in the 1950s, and federal and state governments began the process of building a controlled access, interstate highway system across America, more and more St. Louisans moved to the suburbs. Thanks to the acquisition of St. Louis County Gas, Laclede Gas could grow along with metropolitan St. Louis and the suburbs in the decades immediately following World War II.

L. Wade Childress noted that the merger of the two gas companies was weighted with promise, the promise of a new horizon for St. Louis and the promise of a "single, rational gas service system — serving better because it serves all. Another part of the promise will be realized in a single policy for distribution of straight natural gas."

Straight Natural Gas

On April 15, 1946, Laclede Gas announced its decision to convert to straight natural gas immediately upon completion of a new interstate pipeline

1942
Laclede Gas closed on the sale of Laclede Power & Light in May.

1947

Mississippi River Fuel Co. began construction of what it called Main Line 2, a 24-inch line that paralleled the company's original 1931 pipeline.

Contract crews for Laclede Gas changed burner tips in more than 175,000 homes between April and November 1949.

being constructed by Mississippi River Fuel Company that would connect to Laclede's distribution system in St. Louis. In addition, Childress noted that Laclede Gas intended to reduce rates to customers as soon as Mississippi River Fuel Co. was able to begin delivering an adequate supply of natural gas to St. Louis from the Perryville Field in Louisiana.

In 1947 and 1948, the pipeline company was in the process of completing this pipeline to the St. Louis area. In 1947, Mississippi River Fuel Co. began construction of what it called Main Line 2, a 24-inch line that paralleled the company's original 1931 pipeline. The new pipeline would terminate on the east side of the Mississippi River in Columbia, Illinois. Built at a cost of nearly $34 million, Main Line 2 was completed in 1949. The pipeline was welded together in sections, compressor stations were added, and the system operated at pressures up to 720 pounds per square inch.

With straight natural gas flowing into its system through Mississippi River Fuel's Main Line 2, Laclede Gas began the mammoth task of converting all its customers to natural gas. Because natural gas has a much higher heating value (1000 BTU per cubic foot) than the mixture of natural gas and manufactured gas (800 BTU per cubic foot), every heater and appliance burner on the Laclede Gas system had to be converted to safely handle natural gas.

2 Million Burner Tips

Once the decision to convert to straight natural gas was made, Laclede Gas established a timetable for the conversion of its customers. Company engineers estimated that there were approximately 2,273,000 separate burners in the service area that would need to be adjusted so customers could take full advantage of the new fuel. The cost of the conversion was estimated at $3 million, and Laclede Gas announced from the first that the company would bear the entire burden of the costly procedure.

Although the initial start date of the conversion was set for early 1947, steel was in short supply immediately following World War II, and the strengthening of the nation's pipeline system delayed Mississippi River Fuel Co.'s completion of Main Line 2 until late 1948. By the spring of 1949, Laclede Gas finally was able to begin the arduous job of converting to straight natural gas.

In April 1949, Robert W. Otto, president of Laclede Gas, sent a letter to every customer informing them that the changeover would begin on May 16

96 Laclede Gas Company

Laclede crews "turned on" natural gas at the site of one of the utility's St. Louis gas holders. Mississippi River Fuel Company transported the gas by pipeline from northern Louisiana to St. Louis.

and would be completed by the end of November. The company published newspaper advertisements containing a map of every service district and their boundaries. Each district was numbered according to the order in which they were to be converted. Customers were asked to watch for the map and to note the dates that the servicemen would be in their district.

Each customer was given a four-page folder explaining the changeover to natural gas. The package contained instructions that were to be followed regarding the use of gas appliances from the time of the changeover until the appliances had been fully converted. The instructions encompassed customers' gas ranges, refrigerators, water heaters and other small appliances such as space heaters. The actual conversion work was performed by crews working for Conversion & Surveys, Inc., a contractor hired by Laclede Gas.

St. Louis' local newspapers were extremely cooperative, and Laclede Gas made every effort to provide the media full information on details of the conversion work. The publicity was of great importance in securing the cooperation of the more than 500,000 customers Laclede Gas served in metropolitan St. Louis.

Laclede Gas divided the franchise territory of St. Louis County Gas into 30 separate districts, each comprising about 2,500 customer households. Work on converting 175,000 appliances in the county began in May and was finished in August. The day after the last appliance in the county was converted, crews began converting appliances in the north part of the city.

By the end of November 1949, Laclede Gas had completed the conversion with little disruption in service. The introduction of straight natural gas enabled the company to

Because natural gas was delivered under higher pressure than manufactured gas, much of Laclede's distribution system had to be replaced or upgraded during the 1950s.

expand services and provided St. Louis and St. Louis County with a modern fuel for home and industrial customers.

More importantly, the switch to natural gas removed the source of much of the pollution that had made St. Louis one of the smokiest cities in North America. When St. Louisans traded their coal furnaces for natural gas heating systems, the air in the city became visibly cleaner within a decade. Coupled with the change in the 1950s from coal-fired steam locomotives to diesel engines, the arrival of natural gas heralded the end of smoke pollution in St. Louis.

Building a Bigger Backbone

With the natural gas supply in place early in 1950, Laclede Gas undertook a major strengthening of its gas transmission system. In May, the company began work on the construction of a 20-mile gas main from the Mississippi River across the entire St. Louis metropolitan area. The 30-inch diameter backbone line ran from the Laclede Gas coke plant at the confluence of the Mississippi and the River Des Peres to the St. Louis city limits, where the line turned northwest to its termination in the vicinity of Natural Bridge and Brown Road.

Part of the utility's $26 million improvement program to provide St. Louis with straight natural gas, the new backbone pipeline was built by crews from Frazier-Davis Construction Co. of St. Louis and engineered by Sverdrup & Parcel, Inc., also of St. Louis. Streets were blocked off all that summer as crews dug trenches to bury the huge pipeline, but most St. Louisans agreed with the company's assertion that any temporary inconvenience was more than offset by the contribution that ample supplies of natural gas would make to the residents and businesses of the city.

Bob Shulman, a staff writer for the St. Louis Star-Times, described the Laclede Gas pipeline construction project as "one of the more spectacular construction jobs local sidewalk superintendents have ogled in many a year." More than 400 construction workers operated 115 pieces of equipment, including 10 side-boom Caterpillar tractors, three high-lifts, two massive backhoes and two boring machines, in digging the trench and laying the pipeline across St. Louis.

A measure of just how much natural gas would change Laclede Gas came in June 1950 when the company announced the sale of the Catalan Street coke plant. One of the firm's major facilities since it was first opened in 1915, the coke plant produced 142 billion cubic feet of gas during its 35 years of operation. Laclede Gas sold the plant to Great Lakes Carbon Corporation, a New York-based supplier of coke to the iron and steel industry. Great Lakes Carbon paid Laclede Gas $700,000 for the St. Louis coke plant. A hearing instituted before the Missouri Public Service Commission requested Laclede to show cause as to why the plant shouldn't be sold for more than $700,000.

Lee Liberman testified that an auction had been held and there just were not many firms or individuals that wanted to own a coke plant. "We made the best deal we could," Liberman told the commissioners. They approved the sale.

More Changes Ahead

The introduction of natural gas to St. Louis changed Laclede Gas more than any other event in the company's history. It transformed the company from a manufacturer of gas and chemicals into a distributor of the most efficient heating and cooking fuel in the world. The introduction of natural gas also immediately increased the company's revenues.

Laclede Gas reported sales of more than $20 million in 1950, a 33 percent increase from the $15 million in revenues it had reported in 1948 and again in 1949. Laclede Gas reported 1950 profits of $2.4 million, the greatest in the company's long history.

The utility began marketing itself to the community as Laclede Gas Company in 1950 to reflect the introduction of natural gas. On November 24, 1950, Laclede Gas established a new peak day send-out of 246.2 million cubic feet of gas, almost 90 million cubic feet higher than the peak day send-out in the 1949-1950 winter.

But the popularity of natural gas in St. Louis was soon to be tested by the inability of the pipeline companies to deliver the amounts that a growing customer base demanded. Unless Laclede Gas could discover a way to store large volumes of gas during the spring and summer, the utility would likely be plagued by shortages on very cold days during each winter heating season.

1950

On November 24, Laclede Gas established a new peak day send-out of 246.2 million cubic feet of gas, almost 90 million cubic feet higher than the peak day send-out in the 1949-1950 winter.

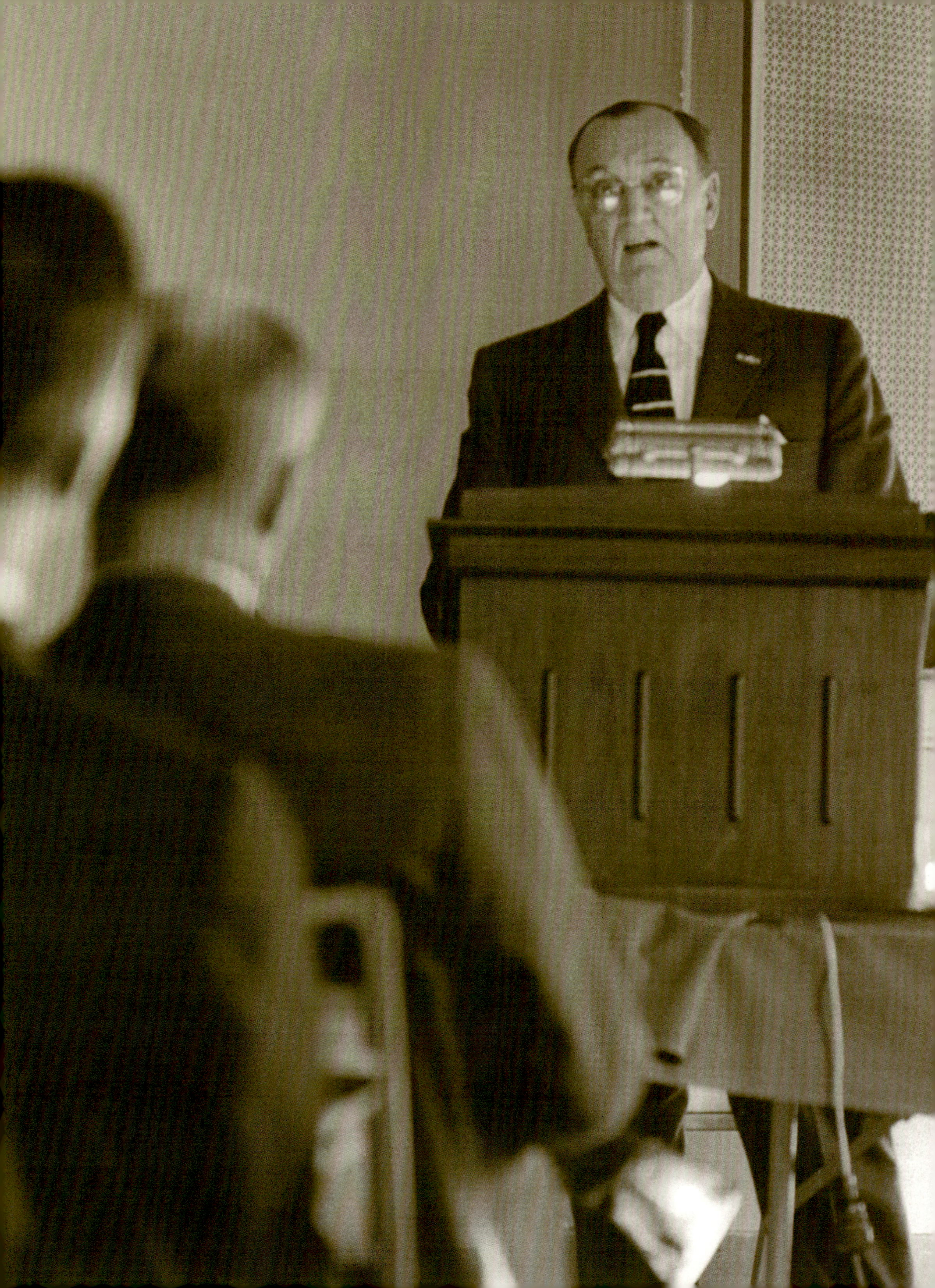

CHAPTER 9

The Judge Otto Years

Anybody who ever knew Robert W. Otto told stories about the man they called "The Judge."

Judge Robert Otto was as comfortable at a podium before a roomful of reporters as he was in the executive suite. Judge Otto was in charge of Laclede Gas for more than 20 years, from 1947 to 1968.

Judge Robert W. Otto was president of Laclede Gas during the period of rapid development and expansion immediately following World War II. As the company's attorney, he had presided over the acquisition of the St. Louis County Gas Co. As president, Otto oversaw the conversion from mixed gas to straight natural gas distribution and the development of the underground natural gas storage field in north St. Louis County. All three events were extremely important to the company's postwar growth. Judge Otto also defended the company against a hostile takeover attempt and guided Laclede Gas to some of the strongest growth in its history.

Lee Liberman, who worked directly for the Judge early in his career with Laclede Gas, recalled traveling to Jefferson City for a Missouri Public Service Commission hearing when the Judge was running late. When Liberman sped through a small town outside Jefferson City, an alert traffic patrolman wrote him a ticket.

The Judge told Liberman not to worry, that he could get the charges dropped. Judge Otto, however, was singularly unsuccessful in his attempts to find a local official with whom he could talk about the traffic ticket Liberman had received earlier in the day.

Finally, Liberman drove to the county seat of Union and stood in front of the traffic court judge. He expected the worst. "This thing reads like a novel," the traffic judge said, banging his gavel and assessing Liberman $50 and costs.

The judge then turned to Liberman and said, "When you get back to St. Louis, please tell Bob Otto to send me those papers I'm looking for."

The Judge guided Laclede through some of its most significant events, including the introduction of natural gas, the acquisition of the St. Louis County Gas Co., and the development of the company's first natural gas underground storage field.

'The Sunny Side of the Plane'

Judge Robert W. Otto was born on Christmas Day, 1892 in Washington, Missouri. He attended the University of Missouri and earned a law degree at Northwestern University. In 1916, Otto was elected prosecuting attorney of Franklin County and in 1921 was appointed assistant attorney general of Missouri. In 1924, he became attorney general of Missouri, the youngest man to ever hold the office. Just months into his term, Otto was appointed a justice of the Missouri Supreme Court.

When he later lost a bid for re-election, Otto joined Laclede Gas in 1932 as general counsel. He was elected president in 1947, a position he held until May of 1956 when he became chairman of the board.

Otto had a distinctive personality that left lasting memories with the people of the Laclede Gas family.

Kathy Westerheide started her career with Laclede Gas in 1961 as a mail messenger. Soon, she accepted a position in the travel department of the corporate secretary's office.

"Judge Otto went to Traverse City, Michigan for two or three weeks every summer," she said. "He also flew to Mexico City on vacation regularly. Judge Otto always wanted a seat on the sunny side of the plane! At 1017 Olive, prior to the installation of automatic elevators, Judge Otto would summon an elevator by kicking the elevator doors. The Judge also would fire Beatrice Schaeffer, his longtime secretary, about once a week."

Rex Bannister worked for Laclede for 33 years. One of his first duties when he joined the company was drilling wells to determine the size of the underground storage facility in Florissant.

"Judge Otto could remember your name forever," Bannister said. "I met the Judge early on. Once he invited us out to his home for dinner. His method of barbecue was to throw a whole pork tenderloin in the coals. He had a big rip in his pants, and when his wife came out to the barbecue pit to complain, he told her, 'They're old pants anyway.'"

Judge Otto stepped down as board chairman of Laclede Gas in 1968 and became director emeritus in 1974. He died in St. Louis on May 2, 1977 at the age of 84.

A Hostile Takeover Attempt

In the late 1940s and early 1950s, as Laclede Gas was undergoing some of the most rapid growth in its history, Judge Otto defended the company against a hostile takeover attempt that would have altered the future course of the utility's growth.

The attempt to corner the company's stock was engineered by William Marbury, the St. Louis attorney who headed Mississippi River Fuel Co., Laclede's natural gas supplier. At the time, Laclede was one of the fastest-growing natural gas utilities in North America, closing in on serving more than 100,000 residential gas customers in the city and its booming suburbs.

William Marbury, who styled himself "just a country lawyer," dominated Mississippi River Fuel Co.'s history from the 1930s to the 1960s. Wall Street analysts, however, considered Marbury

1968
Judge Otto stepped down as board chairman of Laclede Gas.

1948
After winning approval from the Missouri Public Service Commission, William Marbury, through Mississippi River Fuel Co., purchased 200,000 shares of Laclede common stock.

more a genius than a Missouri country lawyer. During the Great Depression, he earned his law degree from St. Louis University while working as a night dispatcher at Mississippi River Fuel. Marbury left the company after graduation in 1937 but returned in 1945 as assistant to the president. By 1949, he was president and chairman of the board of Mississippi River Fuel and immediately took the company public.

At the time, the Federal Power Commission (FPC) regulated the natural gas industry through the Natural Gas Act passed in 1942, including issuing certificates of convenience and necessity, allowing a proposed pipeline to enter the business. The FPC also had within its jurisdiction approval of regulating the rates pipelines could charge their customers and establishing the rate of return pipelines could earn, in effect setting profit margins. Marbury felt strangled by the mass of red tape and thought that the natural gas industry had exhausted its potential earning power in the sometimes difficult climate of regulation. He believed that if Mississippi River Fuel was to grow, it simply had to branch out.

The first step in the expansion plan was to try to gain some control of Laclede Gas. In 1948, after winning approval from the Missouri Public Service Commission, Marbury, through Mississippi River Fuel Co., purchased 200,000 shares of Laclede common stock that represented approximately 6½ percent of the outstanding common stock, by far the largest block of Laclede securities.

"In 1948, Bill Marbury tried to buy stock in Laclede and needed approval from the Missouri Public Service Commission who had to sign off on any owners of more than 10 percent," Lee Liberman explained. "Judge Otto sent me to Chicago to get proxies signed, and we prevailed in the proxy fight, although Marbury did manage to get one seat on the board."

Stupp Brothers Buys Laclede Stock

Marbury's hopes of purchasing control of Laclede Gas soon were dashed when both the Federal Power Commission and the Securities and Exchange Commission ruled that a natural gas transmission company could not own or control a distribution company customer. In late 1948, Marbury began to dump the Laclede stock Mississippi River Fuel had acquired. At a time when Laclede was just emerging as an independently owned public company, the dumping of large volumes of shares could have had a very bad effect on the stock's price.

Lovett "Pete" Peters, Laclede's longtime financial vice president, was concerned about Marbury's threat. "Pete told the story of calling Marbury and asking him not to sell all of his Laclede stock," recalled Bob Jaudes. "Marbury told Peters in no uncertain terms to mind his own business. That happened on a Friday, and shortly after, the Stupps stepped in."

Stupp Brothers Bridge & Iron Co. was one of the city's largest privately owned construction firms. The Stupp family business began in 1856 when Johann Stupp emigrated from Cologne,

Germany. He came to St. Louis at the suggestion of friends and opened a small iron shop. The founder of the family enterprise was an artistic forger and a worker of metals. Johann operated a forge, making intricate designs from iron and other metals. In 1857, Johann Stupp was joined by his brother, who also was named Johann, and the company prospered in the years following the Civil War.

Johann's grandson, Erwin, ultimately became president of the family firm, and he started to significantly grow the business during the 1940s. Stupp Brothers Bridge Co. began its expansion as a structural steel shop, constructing bridges, buildings and coal tipples, railroad car under-frames and Liberty ships for the Merchant Marine during World War II. In the years following the war, the company also developed a specialty in building large river crossing bridges and pipes for oil and gas line transmission. By the 21st century, Stupp Brothers led the nation in the manufacture of line pipe for gas transmission lines.

From 1946 through 1948, Stupp Brothers built compressor stations for Mississippi River Fuel Co. At the time, the construction company was owed a partial payment of $3 million for its work on the five compressor stations. One Sunday morning in 1948, Erwin Stupp received a telephone call from William Marbury, who offered to trade Mississippi River Fuel's shares in Laclede Gas to Stupp Brothers as partial payment for the compressor station debt.

1856
The Stupp family business began in 1856 when Johann Stupp emigrated from Cologne, Germany.

OIL!

One unforeseen result of Laclede's search for an underground storage structure was the company's discovery of oil a half-hour drive north of downtown St. Louis.

"We hired Max Ball, and we also hired Ralph E. Davis," Lee Liberman explained. "Davis was the industry's expert on reserves in the ground, and Ball had a national reputation. They drilled a shallow well and found that the structure did exist. The only problem was, we had discovered oil. We only had a lease to store gas, not leases to produce oil. It was the first oil ever discovered in Missouri."

The discovery of oil placed Laclede Gas management in somewhat of a quandary. Judge Otto immediately opted for informing the world that the utility had discovered oil in northern St. Louis County. Liberman recalled that Al Burgess, the company's vice president, had some previous experience with drilling and urged Judge Otto to proceed cautiously and judiciously.

"We've got to get a leasehound," Burgess told the Judge, who immediately asked, "What's a leasehound?" Burgess explained that it was a person who traveled around the area securing leases from landowners to allow Laclede Gas to drill for oil.

The news wasn't long in becoming public. On July 13, 1951, the St. Louis Globe-Democrat published a front-page article announcing that Laclede had discovered oil in St. Louis County. "By nine o'clock that morning," Liberman recalled, "some doctor was calling Judge Otto and asking how he could get in on the deal. 'First, you've got to find a leasehound,' the Judge told him."

There was enough oil in the sandstone formation beneath northern St. Louis County for production spanning a number of years, but the field wasn't a gusher by any stretch of the imagination. The discovery did keep Laclede in the headlines for several weeks during the summer of 1951. The assets of Laclede Development Company, which Laclede incorporated to drill for oil, eventually were sold in January 1954 to Rock Hill Oil Company for the amount that Laclede had invested.

1948

Stupp Brothers received 210,500 shares of Laclede common stock, plus $417,000 in cash for the five compressor stations it had installed.

Robert Stupp recalled that his father "told Marbury that he would think about the offer and let him know what the company decided in the week ahead. Marbury told him, 'No, you have to make a decision right now.' My dad thought for a few minutes, and said, 'OK, you've got a deal.' For our ownership, we received a seat on the board of Laclede Gas."

The next day, the St. Louis newspapers carried a story from Washington, D.C. reporting that the Federal Power Commission had ordered Marbury and Mississippi River Fuel to divest its investment in Laclede because of a recent ruling that transportation companies could not own stock in distribution companies.

Marbury had known for several weeks that the FPC wouldn't approve his ownership of Laclede Gas. Marbury's transaction with the Stupp family represented 6½ percent of the outstanding common stock of Laclede. Stupp Brothers received 210,500 shares of Laclede common stock, plus $417,000 in cash for the five compressor stations it had installed. At the time, Laclede common stock was selling for $9 a share.

The transaction rescued Laclede from the possibility of a hostile takeover, not to mention a potentially disastrous drop in the company's stock. The transaction also began a nearly 60-year relationship between Laclede and the Stupp family. As part of the purchase, the Stupp family was awarded the seat on the Laclede Gas board of directors that Marbury had controlled.

Erwin Stupp served on Laclede's board from 1948 to 1965. Robert Stupp's older brother, Jack, was on the board from 1965 through 1989. Robert Stupp served on the board from 1989 to 2004, when stock exchange rules governing retirement age necessitated his resignation. Robert Stupp's oldest nephew, John Stupp, Jr. has served on the Laclede board since 2004.

Marbury went on to diversify Mississippi River Fuel out of pipeline ownership. In the late 1950s, he formed Mississippi River Corp., a holding company based in St. Louis. Mississippi River Corp. expanded into the cement manufacturing business and in 1959 began buying stock in the Missouri Pacific Railway, long one of the Gateway City's major corporate citizens. MoPac, as it was known to several generations of local residents, had fallen on hard times during the Great Depression and was in receivership from 1933 to 1956.

Marbury gained control of MoPac in 1962 and immediately named Downing B. Jenks, the president of Rock Island Lines, as president of MoPac. Marbury and Jenks believed that only a handful of large, intercontinental railroads would be able to succeed in the future competitive era of intermodal transportation. In 1966, Marbury engineered an ultimately unsuccessful hostile takeover of the Santa Fe Railroad. Jenks succeeded Marbury as a president and chief executive officer of Mississippi River Corp. in 1971, just months before Marbury died.

Nearly 60 years after the events of 1948, Stupp Brothers owns 6.95 percent of the outstanding stock of Laclede Gas. Stupp is and has been Laclede's largest shareholder for the past half-century, and a member of the Stupp family has served continuously on the board of directors for almost 60 years.

Storing Gas Underground

Once Laclede Gas began to take delivery of natural gas, the St. Louis utility immediately faced a problem it had not anticipated. More heating customers wanted natural gas in the winter than could be accommodated by pipeline deliveries. By 1953, the utility had hooked up its 100,000th residential heating customer.

The solution was both simple and complex. If Laclede could take delivery of substantial quantities of natural gas during the summer off-season and store it for the winter peak season, the utility could solve the problem. But finding a place to store the huge volumes of gas needed to meet wintertime demand was easier said than done.

In the late 1940s, Judge Otto read an article in an American Gas Association publication describing the efforts of an Illinois natural gas utility to inject gas into an underground storage cavern named the Herrscher Dome, near Chicago.

Lee Liberman, who was an assistant to Judge Otto at the time, recalled that the Judge was fascinated by the concept of underground storage, "so he called in a geologist named Bill Clark and asked him to find a similar structure for Laclede and to report back in 30 days. Clark was very skeptical about the project, but Bob Otto was insistent. Clark came back 30 days later and said that he thought possibly we could find a suitable storage facility in the area near Florissant. We would need to drill shallow test holes, and we would have to do a core test."

1953
The utility had hooked up its 100,000th residential heating customer.

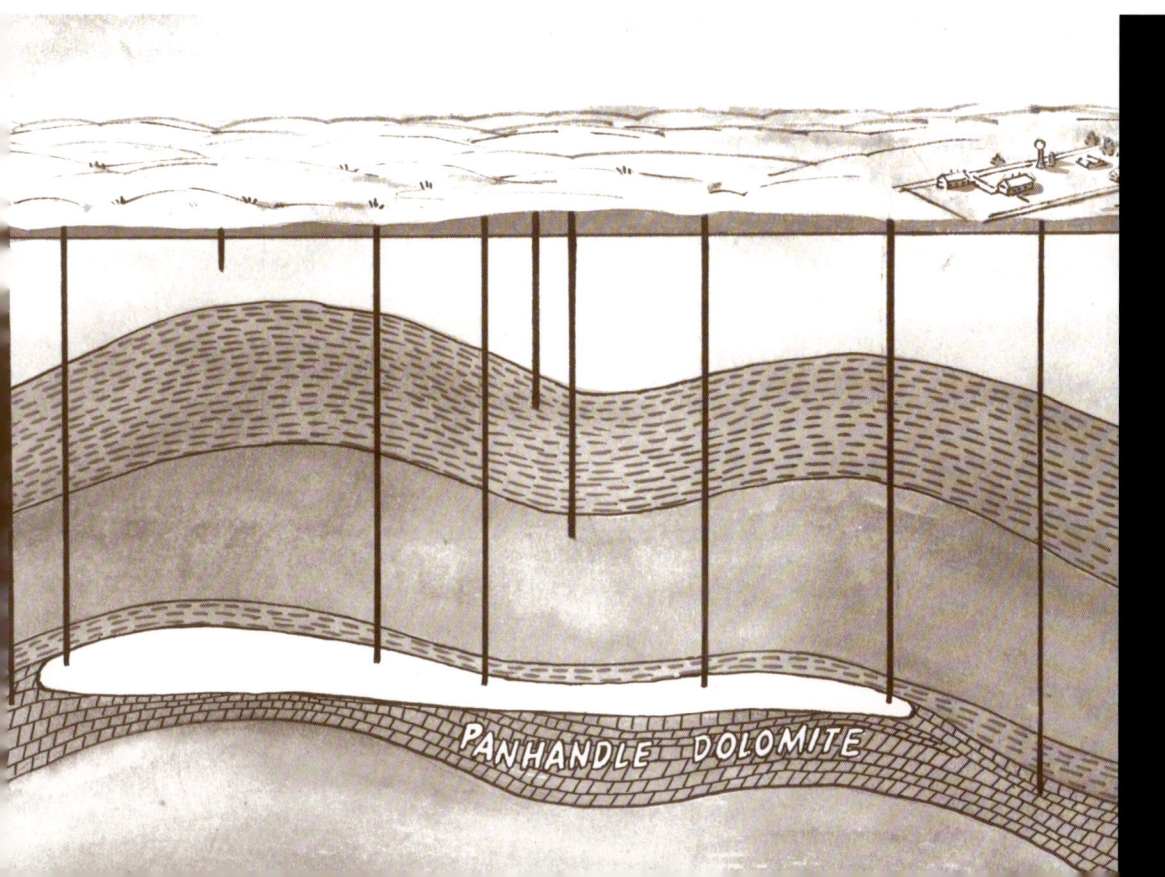

The St. Peter Sandstone formation underlying northern St. Louis County proved to be an excellent storage medium for natural gas. By 1960, Laclede was storing 11 billion cubic feet of gas in the underground field near Florissant.

Allen H. Burgess, Laclede's vice-president of operations, explains the workings of an observation well on the surface of the utility's underground storage facility to a group of gas company executives in town for the national convention of the American Gas Association in 1957.

In reality, three things were needed for underground storage to work. First, the company had to have a structure that was either an anticline — pushed up by geologic conditions against a very impermeable and non-porous rock formations — or, in lieu of that, a dome-like structure of a porous and permeable stratum, overlain and underlain by impermeable or plastic media that would contain the gas within the stratum. The discovery of a structure was determined by drilling down to the first clearly identifiable stratum and finding the shape of it.

Laclede drilled 42 shallow wells in the Florissant area, and geologists determined that a dome-like structure did, in fact, exist. The next step was to determine whether a porous and permeable stratum able to hold gas existed. The third step involved determining whether there was a stratum both above and below the gas-holding stratum, capable of sealing the gas within the permeable and porous stratum.

Under a Missouri law enacted in 1953, the company was given the right to condemn sub-surface strata for gas storage purposes, after first obtaining an order from the Missouri Public Service Commission.

On July 13, 1952, just one year after the first well was drilled, Laclede Gas sponsored a half-hour presentation on KSD-TV announcing the suitability of the Florissant Arch for the storage of vast quantities of natural gas. Judge Otto, Max Ball, the company's consulting geologist, and Dr. Edward L. Clark, Missouri state geologist, explained the importance of the St. Peter Sandstone as a vehicle for storing the city's annual gas supply.

The *Globe-Democrat* applauded Laclede's $10 million underground storage effort, noting in an editorial that "the company is to be commended for its initiative in attempting to provide additional gas storage for this community."

Serving an Additional 85,000 Customers

The initial injection of gas into the underground reservoir north of St. Louis began on December 2, 1955. By October 1956, 1.5 billion cubic feet of gas were in storage. During November 1956, a withdrawal test was conducted over a 24-hour period. The results indicated that the storage field was exceeding expectations. The company also built a compressor station capable of injecting more than 15 million cubic feet of gas per day into storage, as well as nine injection and withdrawal wells and the associated gathering lines and equipment.

In 1959, Laclede Gas enlarged the compressor station with an additional 880-horsepower compressor. The new equipment brought the total horsepower available for gas injection into storage to 2,900 horsepower. The enlarged compressor capacity enabled the company to more quickly replace withdrawals of storage gas, assisted in maintaining the stability of the underground cavern, and gave the company a higher utilization of available pipeline gas during the heating season.

By the fall of 1960, more than 11 billion cubic feet of gas were in storage in the St. Peter Sandstone. Laclede estimated that it could serve an additional 85,000 heating customers each season with the stored gas.

The location north of the city for the underground storage facility was ideal. Natural gas came to St. Louis from the south through the renamed Mississippi River Transmission's pipeline from the Monroe and Perryville Fields in Louisiana. All that was needed was to extend lines from the city distribution system north to the compressor station. When customer demand was below line capacity, the excess flowed on to the storage area. When demand exceeded pipeline capacity, gas could easily be fed to the city from both north and south.

Underground storage of natural gas was a major aid in easing the problem of peak loads caused by high requirements during the winter months. It allowed Laclede Gas to take on tens of thousands of additional heating customers. Underground storage also helped Laclede control the cost of gas purchases by acquiring large quantities of gas in the summer months, when supplies were cheaper.

Kathy Westerheide, Laclede's retired land manager, worked in the underground storage area during much of her career. Westerheide recalled that "the injected gas is contained underground in the pore space of the St. Peter Sandstone formation, which lies approximately 1,500 feet below the surface. Its cap rock, the Maquoketa Shale, is at a depth of 800 feet. It forms the impermeable seal for the gas in storage. Movement of the gas within the dome is controlled by pressure. Therefore, in addition to injection-withdrawal wells, we have a number of observation wells. Water displacement within the observation

1955
The initial injection of gas into the underground reservoir north of St. Louis began on December 2.

150 Year Anniversary   **109**

Utility billing and accounting functions in the 1950s and 1960s were still highly labor intensive. Introduction of automation and computerized billing systems in the late 1960s and 1970s would make administrative functions at Laclede far more efficient.

wells is one means used to determine the location of the stored gas. The gas extends under the Missouri River into a small portion of St. Charles County, thereby expanding our leasehold interests by 4,475 acres."

Management of the underground storage area, especially in the beginning, entailed an education process for customers. Westerheide recalled one landowner calling to complain that his rosebushes were dying and that he suspected the gas in storage of killing them. "Another homeowner called to inquire if he would puncture the dome by excavating for an in-ground swimming pool," Westerheide said.

More than a half-century later, Liberman pointed to the success of Laclede's underground storage program. "We found that the St. Peter sandstone had all the ability we needed to hold natural gas," he said. "It was one of the greatest things that ever happened to Laclede because it finally gave us great capacity to expand the business."

Aggressive Optimism

In the spring of 1956, Judge Otto relinquished the presidency of Laclede Gas to H. Reid Derrick, his longtime associate, and stepped up to chairman of the board of the St. Louis gas utility. The nine years he had spent at the helm of Laclede had been among the most eventful in the company's long history.

In 1957, Laclede celebrated its centennial anniversary. Chairman Otto told employees that the company faced the future "with aggressive optimism."

The growth during Otto's tenure as president had been little short of phenomenal. Operating revenue had nearly tripled, from $16 million in 1948 to $45 million in 1957. Sales of gas increased from 172 million therms in 1948 to 619 million therms in the winter of 1956-1957. The number of heating customers had risen 600 percent, from 27,000 in 1948 to 163,000 in 1957.

In nine years, Laclede had added nearly 1,000 employees. The 2,700 people working for the company in 1957 was one of the largest work forces in St. Louis; Laclede's payroll rippled through the St. Louis economy each week. Construction requirements were budgeted at nearly $12 million a year for 1957 and 1958, a sum equivalent to what the company's annual revenues had been just 10 years before.

The company was conservatively financed, with capitalization of $92 million. Laclede Gas had issued $15 million in first mortgage bonds in 1954 and had used part of the proceeds the next year to eliminate $4 million in gas plant acquisition debt stemming from the 1947 acquisition of St. Louis County Gas Co.

New President Derrick was bullish on Laclede's future. "We look forward to a period of continuous growth," he told *Gas Age Magazine* in the fall of 1957, "and we are anticipating it with a program of continued plant expansion and sound financing."

What neither Derrick nor *Gas Age* could anticipate was the tremendous growth that St. Louis and Laclede Gas would experience during the 1960s.

1957
The number of heating customers rose 600 percent from 27,000 in 1948 to 163,000.

INTERLUDE 3

The Natural Gas Era

The quarter-century between the end of World War II and the Arab Oil Embargo of 1973 was a golden era for America's natural gas industry. Gas was in plentiful supply and the industry benefited from several factors in the immediate postwar era.

America was wracked by labor strife in the soft coal industry — a major energy producer during the first half of the century — during the late 1940s. While coal in the immediate postwar era still captured a significant portion of the home heating market, labor problems in the industry helped make the introduction of clean, efficient natural gas to America's homes all the easier.

The lifting of rationing of consumer appliances and industrial steel in late 1946 and early 1947 created a market for natural gas producers and provided the raw material for a boom in pipeline construction.

The opening up of the Carthage Gas Field in east Texas, the Permian Basin Gas Fields in west Texas and adjacent New Mexico, the vast new gas fields along and just offshore the Texas and Louisiana Gulf Coasts, and the San Juan Basin Gas Fields in northwestern Colorado and New Mexico added trillions of cubic feet of natural gas reserves to America's supply during the 1950s and 1960s.

More Pipeline Construction

Pipeline companies were quick to take advantage of the new supplies. Between 1950 and 1956 alone, five pipelines were built from the Gulf Coast gas fields to the Southeast, Mid-Atlantic and Northeast. Each of the five pipelines was more than 1,000 miles in length.

Transcontinental Gas Pipeline Co., a new entry in the industry, built a 1,840-mile pipeline in 1950 from the Gulf Coast to New York. Natural Gas Pipeline Co. of America built a 1,300-mile pipeline from the Texas Gulf Coast to Chicago in 1951, and a subsidiary of Panhandle Eastern built a 1,300-mile line later that year from the Louisiana Gulf Coast to St. Louis and central Illinois. Gulf Interstate Co., a part of the Columbia Gas System, and Michigan-Wisconsin Pipeline Co. both built 1,200-mile pipelines during the immediate postwar period.

The boom in gas exploration and pipeline construction was accompanied by major new discoveries in Canada and Mexico. In 1957, gas from the Peace River Gas Fields in northern British Columbia and Alberta reached the Pacific Northwest via a 700-mile pipeline. Canadian companies built 2,300 miles of pipelines across southern Canada between 1955 and 1965, and Canadian gas began flowing to U.S. consumers as far east as New York state.

To the south, immense new gas fields along the Mexican Gulf Coast began development in the mid-1950s. In 1955, the United States imported negligible amounts of natural gas from Mexico. Five years later, Mexico shipped 47 billion cubic feet of gas north to the United States, and by 1965, the figure was 52 billion cubic feet of gas a year.

Development of massive new fields off the Texas and Louisiana Gulf Coasts helped fuel America's growing demand for natural gas in the 1950s.

Between 1945 and 1982, pipeline and local distribution companies constructed 172,000 miles of natural gas pipelines, which represented an investment of $33 billion and provided gas for 40 million homes and businesses. Coal for the home heating market all but disappeared during the period.

Between 1945 and 1954 alone, natural gas companies doubled their marketed production and captured 22 percent of America's total energy market. During that period, residential, commercial and industrial consumption of natural gas skyrocketed. Industrial consumption of natural gas more than doubled, from 3.1 billion cubic feet in 1946 to 6.9 billion cubic feet in 1956. Residential consumption nearly quadrupled, from 660 million cubic feet in 1946 to 2.4 billion cubic feet in 1956. By 1966, natural gas was available to consumers in all 48 contiguous states.

The Role of Technology

Technological advancements had a great deal to do with the expansion of natural gas in the postwar period. Two advancements in particular — cathodic protection of pipelines and underground storage of gas — made the postwar expansion possible.

Corrosion has always been a problem for the gas pipeline industry. The thin-wall steel pipe used to transmit gas across the country is susceptible to rust, which in turn causes leaks and a resulting loss of pressure. In the early days, pipeline crews applied coatings to the pipe, primarily coal tar that was then wrapped with asbestos felt. Starting in 1940, pipelines that were joined by Dresser Couplings were all coated with coal tar and wrapped with felt.

Still, expansion and contraction of the pipe sometimes caused the coating around the Dressers to crack and develop gas leaks. In other places, hundreds of pinhole leaks caused by rust and corrosion necessitated digging up hundreds of feet of pipeline for repairs.

By the early 1950s, the industry was just beginning to investigate the feasibility of cathodic protection of gas pipelines. The concept went back to 1824 when Sir Humphrey Davy ran an electric current along the sheathing of ships' hulls to protect them from saltwater corrosion.

There were basically two ways to provide cathodic protection. Crews applied zinc and later magnesium anodes, essentially a positively charged electrode, to hot spots on the pipe. For protection of a longer section of pipe, the method called for running direct electric current to the pipeline from a rectifier. Rectifiers protected many of the older, poorly coated pipelines. In 1957, one pipeline company in the Great Plains states reported 180 rectifier installations in operation on the company's pipeline system.

Getting electricity for the rectifiers often was a problem, especially for pipelines that passed through uninhabited regions of the American West. Rural Electrification Administration distribution cooperatives, for example, were late in coming to places like the high plains of eastern Montana and northeastern Wyoming.

The solution, one that served ranchers in the area for generations, was to build wind-powered generators and site them on hilltops across the region. The "windchargers," as they were known to the pipeline crews, were three-bladed affairs that produced direct current electricity.

Laclede Pipeline Co., a wholly-owned subsidiary of Laclede Gas, was created to own and operate a propane pipeline across the utility's service territory in the St. Louis metropolitan area.

David Price, later president of the Williston Basin Interstate Pipeline Company, recalled the fight to get pipeline crews to apply the then newly introduced cathodic protection to pipelines.

"In the early 1950s, it took a great deal of work to convince the old pipeliners that cathodic protection was not a pseudoscience," Price recalled. "In those days, there were no Department of Transportation rules and regulations requiring pipelines to be coated and cathodically protected. It just made good sense from an economic and safety standpoint. The evaluation of the results was probably more empirical in nature than scientific."

Cathodic protection was the standard for pipeline construction after 1955. Pipeline companies applied cathodic protection to many existing pipelines during a lull in construction during the mid-to-late-1960s.

Another technique that became widespread during the 1960s was the injection of mercaptans into pipelines and local distribution mains. Natural gas is lighter than air and odorless. The addition of the chemical odorant mercaptans — which give natural gas its distinctive rotten egg smell — was a safety precaution that increased the acceptance of natural gas in residential markets and assisted crews in locating gas leaks. Without mercaptans, natural gas markets might have taken years longer to develop.

Underground Storage

The second technological advance of the postwar years that spurred the development of North America's natural gas economy was the progress made in establishing underground storage. The underground storage capacity that Laclede Gas developed at Florissant in the mid-1950s was duplicated by gas distribution utilities across North America during the 1950s and 1960s.

Since it is used in residential markets as a heating fuel, natural gas consumption and demand rises dramatically in the winter and drops off during the summer.

Local distribution companies lived with that fact of life for much of the 20th century. During the manufactured gas era, when gas was used primarily for cooking, it could be stored in collapsible, telescopic gas holders such as those Laclede maintained at a number of locations in metropolitan St. Louis. But the development of home heating markets after World War II meant that the industry had to find ways to store gas during the summer for use during the winter heating season.

The solution was to inject gas into underground storage chambers for retrieval during peak demand months. Gas company geologists called the concept "gas wells in reverse." The first usage of underground storage of natural gas was in Ontario in 1915. By 1955, the gas utility industry in the United States and Canada had invested nearly $350 million to construct 172 underground storage caverns in some 17 states and provinces.

By the mid-1950s, underground storage was capable of holding more than 1.8 trillion cubic feet of natural gas and plans were to spend another $65 million building an additional 12 underground caverns capable of storing another 180.5 billion cubic feet of gas.

If a proper site could be found, storing gas underground was an economical method for local distribution companies. The technology was particularly attractive to gas utilities in the Midwest, where winter peak demand could be severe.

When a storage field was discovered, the first step was to test it to ensure the ability to hold gas under pressure. Gas available during low demand periods was injected underground into the storage field. When gas was needed during the winter, it could be withdrawn and introduced into the distribution system. Natural gas could reach Laclede Gas via pipeline during the summer, be stored underground and be made available for distribution during the winter heating season.

H. Reid Derrick, the courtly Alabamian who headed Laclede Gas from 1956 to 1970, addresses shareholders during an annual meeting in the 1960s. Derrick presided over non-stop growth during his tenure.

CHAPTER 10

The H. Reid Derrick Years

Laclede Gas reported to shareholders that 1957 was "a solid base of accomplishment" to position the utility for future expansion in the 1960s.

1957
With more than 350,000 residential customers, Laclede operated the second largest gas distribution utility system in the Midwest.

During his first year as president of Laclede Gas, H. Reid Derrick presided over a continuation of the tremendous growth his predecessor, Judge Robert W. Otto, had guided during the early 1950s. Despite a warm winter, Laclede's 1957 fiscal year was the second best in the utility's history. That year, Laclede celebrated its centennial with operating revenues of $45.6 million, net income of nearly $4 million, and earnings per share of common stock of $1.16.

The utility reported 5 billion cubic feet of gas in storage at the underground facility near Florissant, a capacity that allowed it to add 40,000 additional heating customers during the year. With more than 350,000 residential customers, Laclede operated the second largest gas distribution utility system in the Midwest, behind Chicago's People's Gas. Nearly half of Laclede's residential customers used gas for heating in 1957.

Laclede made changes to two of its oldest facilities during its centennial year. In the summer, the utility retired Station B, the smallest and oldest manufacturing plant on the Laclede system. First opened in 1873 following the utility's execution of the Tripartite Agreement, Station B produced gas for more than 75 years and was maintained as a backup facility following the introduction of straight natural gas in 1949. The old plant was expensive to operate and maintain, and company accountants estimated that the retirement would result in an annual savings of more than $150,000.

While crews were dismantling the Station B equipment, other employees were modernizing the Catalan Street Station, the coke plant that Laclede had built before the outbreak of World War I. Between 1955 and 1957, Laclede installed nearly four dozen propane storage tanks at Catalan Street. The big white tanks were capable of storing 1.5 million gallons of propane, more than enough to provide the equivalent of 50 million cubic feet of natural gas a day during winter peak periods.

For Bob Davis, those propane tanks still represent some vivid memories. "Before we had underground storage, we used propane to augment natural gas in extreme cold weather conditions," Davis, then a junior engineer, recalled a half-century later. "We had 30,000-gallon tanks at Catalan Street, maybe 15 or 20 of them. I remember the cold nights in the early 1950s when Bill Donnelly and I had to climb up on the tanks to open the safety valves that had closed due to the excess flow of propane. On several occasions, either Bill's wife or my wife came down with coffee and blankets. The tops of the tanks were 20 feet up. They had ice on them, and that made them very slick. Oh, they were slick."

During the late 1950s, Laclede was growing at the same pace as St. Louis. From 1940 to 1956, the population of St. Louis and surrounding St. Louis County increased by nearly one-third to 1.4 million. Jobs were plentiful in 1957 and St. Louis was aggressively courting Fortune 500 corporations to relocate to the Gateway City. Laclede was intimately involved with the community's industrial development efforts, which resulted in more than $107 million of new industrial and commercial construction in just the first six months of 1957.

When Chrysler Corp. built a major Plymouth assembly plant southwest of St. Louis in 1958, the automaker became one of Laclede's biggest customers.

Shrewsbury

By the late 1950s, the more than 2,600 Laclede employees were spread out from one end of the metropolitan area to the other. About a third of the work force commuted downtown each day to 1017 Olive Street, the corporate office. Another third of the operating employees worked out of Laclede's complex on Forest Park Avenue. With growth focused to the south of St. Louis, an increasing number of employees reported to work at the company's Shrewsbury facility.

Half of that total was attributed to Chrysler Corporation's decision to build a major automotive assembly plant on 200 acres of ground 20 miles southwest of downtown St. Louis. The $50 million plant, scheduled to begin assembling Plymouths for the 1959 model year, was the largest industrial development project announced for St. Louis since the end of World War II.

Laclede Gas provided natural gas for a number of other major industrial expansions during the year, including the McDonnell Aircraft Corporation's engineering campus and the Monsanto Chemical Company's new headquarters on Olive Road at Lindbergh Boulevard.

Laclede capped its string of 1957 successes in October with the American Gas Association's 39th annual convention at the St. Louis Civic Center, culminating with the election of Judge Robert W. Otto, Laclede's chairman, as 1957-1958 president of the association. It was the third time in 11 years that the national association had met in the Gateway City.

After the acquisition of St. Louis County Gas Co. in 1948, Laclede gradually began to see the need for decentralization to more readily serve customers in the outlying sections of its distribution area. As early as 1954, Laclede's Service & Installation Department began operations at the Shrewsbury office located in the city-county border area of St. Louis County. Shrewsbury, as it quickly became known to Laclede Gas employees, was a part of the gas plant installation that was purchased from St. Louis County Gas.

The decentralization plan consisted of dividing the city and county gas service areas into three districts — the South District, Central District and the North District — as a better means of rendering efficient service to Laclede's many customers during the 1950s and 1960s. By 1959, the Laclede Gas customer service area had increased from 116 square miles served in 1949 to an area totaling

1959
By 1959, the Laclede Gas service area increased from 116 square miles served in 1949 to 227 square miles, nearly double the area served ten years earlier.

227 square miles, or nearly double the sales area served ten years earlier.

Included in the construction budget for 1959 was a new operating center at Shrewsbury for the South District. Plans for the center included offices and work space as well as necessary storeroom facilities. In addition, Shrewsbury included a new laboratory. The center opened in April 1960.

John Moten Jr., who later retired from Laclede as senior vice president of operations and marketing, joined the utility as an assistant chemist in November 1962 at the Shrewsbury lab.

"We had all straight natural gas in 1962," Moten said. "We did material testing at the lab and also tested to make sure we had the required amount of odorant in the gas. Odorants are sulphur-based chemicals used to give natural gas its distinctive odor. We also tested pipe-fittings, residential meters, large-volume meter flow rates and pipe thread sealant compounds. We also did extensive testing of gas for heat content." Moten added that "the lab also provided support services. We developed a simple method to sample and test the air in underground conduits and sewers for natural gas and sewer gas."

Moten noted that "Laclede was the only company in the country to use straight propane and add it to natural gas. Most companies only used a propane and air mix. It was an exciting time to be in the lab because it was a center of a lot of activity."

A 1963 Milestone

Laclede's growth continued unabated through the late 1950s and early 1960s. By 1963, the company had more than doubled its service area, increased its investment in gas distribution lines 300 percent, and nearly quadrupled gas sales to 800 million therms a year, all in the short space of 13 years.

Laclede Gas marked a milestone in 1963 when it hooked up the company's 400,000th meter. The company spent $2 million on underground storage and $1.2 million on propane storage during the year. Its gross plant investment stood at $172 million, an increase of about $9 million a year in each of the previous 13 years.

The company's payroll was approaching $19 million a year in 1963, and Laclede was making major investments in new equipment. The utility completely

John Moten Jr. got his start with Laclede Gas in 1962 analyzing chemical samples at the Shrewsbury Lab.

H. REID DERRICK

H. Reid Derrick, president of Laclede Gas from 1956 to 1970, and chairman until his death in 1976, was a leading figure in the nation's gas industry from 1953 when he was elected president of the Alabama Gas Corporation at the age of 42.

Prior to beginning his career with Alabama Gas during the Great Depression, Derrick earned a degree from Virginia Polytechnic Institute in 1931. His career was interrupted by service in the U.S. Navy during World War II, where he attained the rank of lieutenant. Following the war, he returned to the gas industry and became vice president and general manager of Chattanooga Gas Company.

Derrick was with Chattanooga Gas until 1948, when he decided to go back to Birmingham as vice president of operations at Alabama Gas Corporation. He was elected president in 1953. In May 1956, Derrick succeeded Robert W. Otto as Laclede Gas Company's president. In October 1968, he was elected chairman of the board, succeeding Otto.

During Derrick's tenure with Laclede Gas, the company experienced tremendous expansion in both service area and the number of customers. In 1963, Laclede Gas completed the purchase of St. Charles Gas Company. The agreement with St. Charles Gas opened the way for future market development. Derrick felt that "Laclede, through its new subsidiary, will be able to participate more fully in the future urban growth of Greater St. Louis."

Another milestone was reached in the summer of 1963 when Laclede passed the 400,000 mark in number of customers. As late as 1950, there were 315,000 meters on Laclede's lines. During the next 13 years the company added as many customers as it had in the preceding 50 years.

In June 1967, Derrick announced that Laclede Gas would move to a new 30-story office building to be erected at 720 Olive Street. Laclede had outgrown its old headquarters building at 1017 Olive Street, and the relocation served notice that the company required larger facilities to continue expanding.

Derrick told employees that the company "looked on the new Laclede Gas Building as an expression of faith in downtown St. Louis, and we are glad to be a part of this stimulating renewal which is bringing new life, new business, new vigor and new beauty to the downtown area."

On September 25, 1970, Derrick announced that he would relinquish the office of president effective October 1, and that Executive Vice President Lee M. Liberman would be named president and chief operating officer. Derrick served as chairman of the board until the spring of 1976.

During his 20 years with Laclede, Derrick was active in many civic and charitable endeavors in St. Louis. He was a member of the boards of Boatmen's National Bank of St. Louis, the Alabama Gas Corporation and the American Investment Company. He also served as a member of Civic Progress, the United Fund's executive committee and board of directors, and the board of control of the St. Louis Art Museum.

---

refurbished its load dispatching center at the Forest Park Center, opened new service sub-centers and remodeled the customer telephone contact department at Forest Park.

Laclede's 1963 business plan also envisioned growth through the acquisition of neighboring gas systems.

Acquiring St. Charles Gas

Laclede Gas made a significant purchase in the fall of 1963 when it acquired the St. Charles Gas Company.

The proposed acquisition was Laclede Gas' first venture outside its franchised area. St. Charles Gas served 4,300 customers in rapidly growing St. Charles County, immediately north and west of Laclede's service area in St. Louis County. Laclede Gas would soon participate in the growth of an area that was rapidly becoming an integral part of metropolitan St. Louis.

With shareholder approval in hand, Laclede Gas Executive Vice President Lee Liberman began serious negotiations with the owners of St. Charles Gas Company. In October 1963, Laclede exchanged 48,000 shares of its stock for an 80 percent interest in St. Charles Gas, with an option to acquire the remaining 20 percent during the next ten years.

1965
Joseph H. Grand, the well-respected owner of MONAT, sold his controlling interest in the company to Laclede Gas.

Christian Peper, St. Charles Gas president, had headed the utility since 1953 when he acquired control of the company for a small group of local investors from Bill Marbury. A St. Louis native, Peper earned his LLB degree from Washington University in 1935 and an LLM from Yale University in 1937. In the fall of 1941, he was an organizer of the firm of Martin, Peper & Martin. Partner William McChesney Martin Sr. was an attorney who had retired after serving as president of the Federal Reserve Bank of St. Louis. Peper also was one of the original limited partners in the St. Louis brokerage firm AG Edwards & Sons.

In an interview in 2006, Peper remembered that "Laclede had acquired an 80 percent interest in 1963. We were competing with Laclede to secure gas from the Mississippi River Pipeline. We had talks with Lee Liberman, and we made an agreement to have Laclede buy the remaining shares in 1972. It was a complete joining of St. Charles and Laclede, with St. Charles Gas being merged into Laclede."

Laclede's foray into expansion outside of St. Louis quickly was followed by acquisition of another small-town gas utility that provided service to customers in the rapidly growing communities south and west of the metropolitan area.

Expansion South of St. Louis

In 1964, shortly after closing on the acquisition of St. Charles Gas, Laclede Gas took the initial step for expansion south of St. Louis into Jefferson County when it joined Missouri Natural Gas (MONAT) in acquiring the assets of Midwest Missouri Gas Company. While Midwest Missouri only served about 1,100 residential customers in one small section of Jefferson County, the discussions with MONAT led to a company offer the next year to purchase the much larger Missouri Natural Gas.

In 1965, Joseph H. Grand, the well-respected owner of MONAT, sold his controlling interest in the company to Laclede Gas. The acquisition provided Laclede the opportunity to serve more than 10,000 additional residential and commercial customers in St. Francois County.

Most of those customers were already familiar with the efficiency of natural gas for cooking and heating. "There is a complete line of gas-burning appliances on the Missouri Natural showroom and general offices in nearby Farmington, Missouri," Laclede explained in a press release. "All of the latest, modern high-efficiency equipment is available to customers, with installation if they desire."

Missouri Natural's home service department was soon integrated into the larger Laclede organization.

Lois Ann Meyer, a Bonne Terre native, joined MONAT in 1960, fresh out of the University of Missouri journalism program. At the time, MONAT's operations in Bonne Terre, Farmington, Festus, DeSoto, Flat River, Fredericktown, Poplar Bluff and Ste. Genevieve were predominantly rural.

"As Home Service Director," she said, "I took care of radio advertising and newspaper advertising. We actually did a radio show and gave out recipes. We did a lot of school demonstrations and some

122   Laclede Gas Company

Laclede sponsored gas cooking classes for St. Louis high school home economics classes during the 1960s.

adult demonstrations on cooking with gas. We had a 'blue flame' room. When cable came to the area, we did a television show and just wheeled the cameras up the street. The office was always in Farmington. We had tremendous sales of gas ranges. At that time, we had Roper gas ranges, and later the Caloric gas range. Now we have Premier, Amana and Crosley. We also used a dealer relations man."

The two gas companies quickly developed a cooperative relationship. "The Missouri Natural Gas people were not real happy about the acquisition," Meyer explained. "The companies had two entirely different territories, and there was no competition between them. There was fear of the unknown and of going into a bigger company. It ended up to be the best thing that ever happened to us."

While Laclede digested the St. Charles Gas and MONAT acquisitions during the mid-1960s, all eyes were turned to the St. Louis riverfront.

The Gateway Arch

When it was built during the 1960s, the Gateway Arch symbolized St. Louis' role as the "Gateway to the West." During the 19th century, thousands of immigrants and settlers from the eastern United States passed through St. Louis on their way to find new homes in the vast territory between the Mississippi River and the Pacific Ocean.

The Arch was conceived as an elegant monument to westward expansion, a symbol of a time when the country was young and eager to explore the vast territory that Lewis and Clark had described during their 1804-1806 journey through

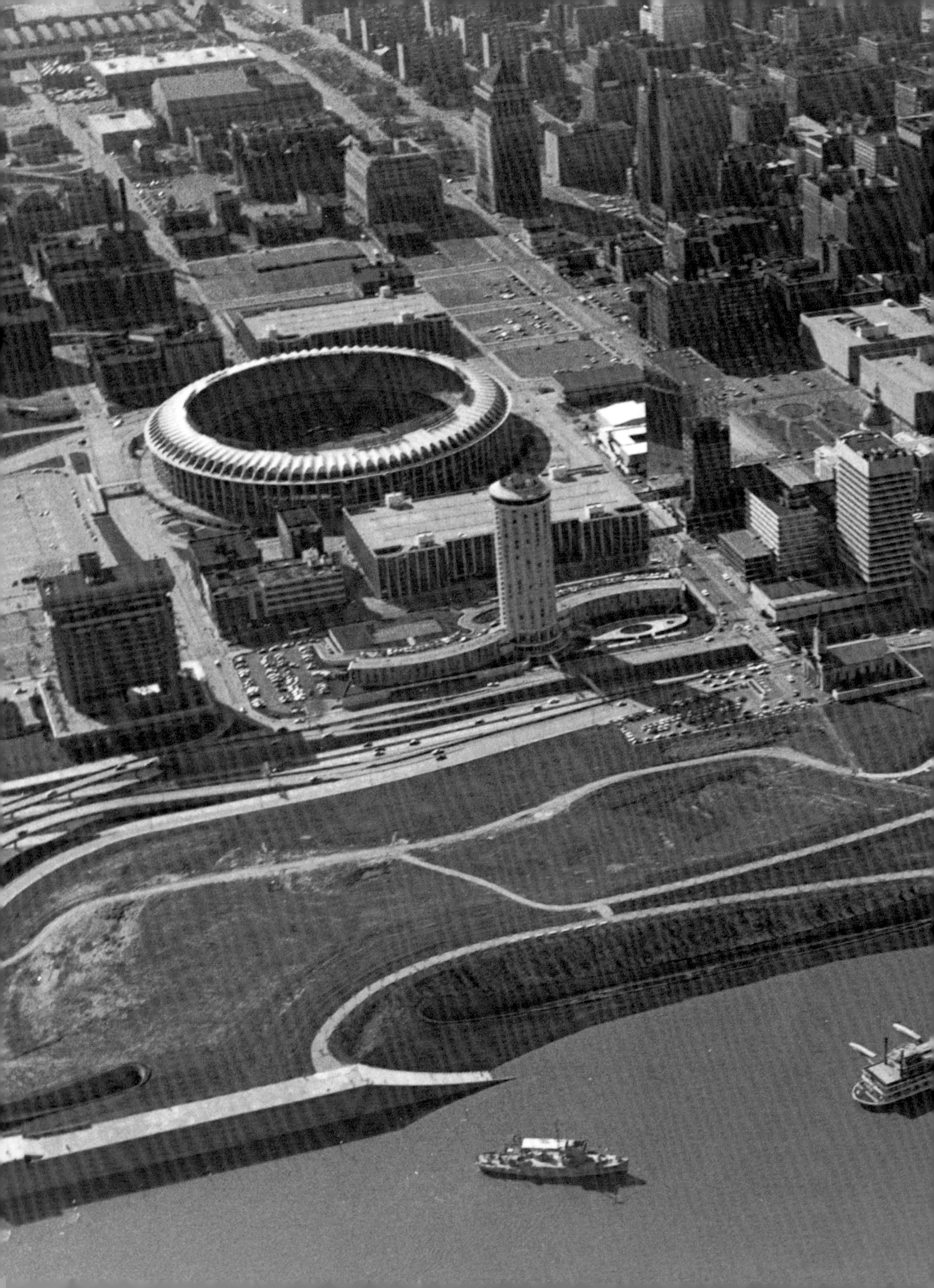

Erected on the St. Louis riverfront from 1963 to 1965, the Gateway Arch became the city's enduring symbol over the next four decades.

1967
At 630 feet in height and 630 feet wide at the base, the Arch is taller than the Statue of Liberty but shorter than the Eiffel Tower.

the Louisiana Purchase. Reports of vast empty plains, soaring mountain ranges and streams rich in beaver and other fur-bearing animals served to ignite the westward migrations of the early 1800s. St. Louis was the starting point for these journeys and adventures.

The idea for a national monument was first proposed during the Depression year of 1933 by a St. Louis attorney. Luther Ely Smith envisioned a memorial dedicated to the wisdom and influence of Thomas Jefferson. He also thought that the monument should be located on the St. Louis riverfront. Beginning in 1935, the Works Progress Administration (WPA) appropriated $9 million to acquire riverfront properties and raze the existing buildings.

Following site selection and acquisition, a St. Louis committee sponsored a nationwide design competition in 1947. Award-winning Finnish architect Eero Saarinen won the competition with his Arch design in 1948. Plans lay idle for almost 20 years. Construction of the Arch was started in 1963 and finished on October 28, 1965. The Arch finally opened to the public in the summer of 1967.

At 630 feet in height and 630 feet wide at the base, the Arch is taller than the Statue of Liberty but shorter than the Eiffel Tower. Each leg of the Arch is an equilateral triangle. The Arch assumes the shape of an inverted catenary curve, the shape formed by a heavy chain hanging freely between two supports.

The Arch was constructed of double-steel walls consisting of a stainless steel skin and an inner wall of carbon steel. The space between the walls — 3 feet at the bottom and 7¾ inches above the 400-foot level — is filled with steel-reinforced concrete to the 300-foot level. Above that, steel stiffeners are used.

The total cost of the project was almost $13 million.

In the 40 years since its opening, the St. Louis Gateway Arch, visited by more than 1 million people a year, has become one of the most durable icons of St. Louis and its pioneering spirit. Along with the Museum of Westward Expansion and the Old Courthouse, the Arch forms the Jefferson National Expansion Memorial, a tribute to the early days of westward expansion, America's love of adventure, and the vision of the country's third president, Thomas Jefferson. It is an enduring symbol of the city that Laclede Gas has served since pioneer days.

Shortly after the Arch opened, Charles Guggenheim, an educational television producer in St. Louis, approached Laclede Gas with the opportunity to sponsor a video presentation on the building of the Arch. Laclede partnered with the American Iron & Steel Institute (AISI) to produce "Monument to a Dream," an award-winning film presentation on the construction of the Gateway Arch.

About the time that the Gateway Arch was rising over the St. Louis skyline, Laclede Gas was taking part in the modernization of the city's downtown profile. Company engineers quietly began investigating the replacement of its 1017 Olive Street general office building.

720 Olive Street

The 10-story building at 1017 Olive Street had served as the headquarters of Laclede Gas since the building's completion in July 1913. Officially known as the Gas Exchange Building, it was constructed at a cost of $650,000. As Laclede Gas continued to grow, especially in the era following World War II, the once spacious quarters grew too small.

Adele Follmer went to work for Laclede Gas as a secretary in 1968. She recalled that the quarters were cramped. "In 1968, the Legal Department was on the 9th floor of 1017 Olive," Follmer said. "It was the same floor as the Purchasing Department. The Executive Offices were on the 10th floor. You could actually open windows at 1017 Olive, and the pigeons sat on the sills. I parked at 10th & Walnut for 85 cents a day, and I thought that was outrageous."

The utility's headquarters originally accommodated other tenants besides Laclede, but the last of these, Mississippi River Barge Line, moved out in 1957. In the spring of 1964, Laclede's Sales Department was moved to the nearby Locust Building because of space limitations.

With the anticipated continued growth of Laclede Gas, the utility's management in 1967 recommended the construction of a new headquarters structure at 720 Olive Street in downtown St. Louis. The new building would be a 30-story office tower of bronze-tinted aluminum and glass that would rise

The 1967 groundbreaking for 720 Olive Street was a red-letter day for redevelopment efforts in downtown St. Louis.

more than 400 feet above the city. When finished, it would be the tallest building in downtown St. Louis and would give tenants an excellent view of the Gateway Arch from the upper floors. Laclede Gas planned to occupy seven floors and a customer service area in the lobby.

With more than 450,000 square feet of office space, the new facility would demonstrate the viability of downtown St. Louis.

The Computer Revolution

Another development that would be as significant for Laclede Gas during the next 40 years as the construction and occupation of 720 Olive was the computerization of the company's operations. In July 1967, the company's Data Processing Department converted to an IBM System/360, the fastest and most reliable computer available at the time. The third-generation System/360 was more than five times faster than its predecessor, the IBM 1410 System.

The company had installed its first computerized IBM punch card system in 1951. By 1967, the System/360 allowed data processors to run more than 1,000 punch cards a minute. During the early and mid-1960s, Laclede also significantly upgraded its laboratory facility, ordering and installing sophisticated new equipment, including an atomic absorption spectophotometer, a gas chromatograph and an infrared spectophotometer.

Still, it would be years before computerization became a way of life at Laclede. Adele Follmer recalled that the Legal Department in the late 1960s was just learning how to maintain its new copier.

"We had a very small library and a bigger office with a Xerox Copier," Follmer said. "We had to maintain it and clean the drum. We shared the department with Claims. I had an IBM Executive electric typewriter. It was a big machine, and all the letters were spaced differently. You learned not to make mistakes. We went to self-correcting IBM Selectric machines later on. We still had them when I retired. We used them for typing index cards. We also had old mechanical Comptometer adding machines."

A New Building is Born

Meanwhile, plans for the new building proceeded smoothly. The developer of the $24 million structure was Arlen-St. Louis Company, a joint

Computerization at Laclede got its start in 1967 when the company purchased its first IBM System/360.

venture of Arlen Properties, Inc. of New York and Myron Moss, a St. Louis real estate developer. Arlen Properties, Inc. was one of the nation's leading real estate developers, and Moss had been active in downtown St. Louis redevelopment for about 10 years. He owned the property at 720 Olive, which housed a Woolworth's "dimestore" during the the 1960s. Moss' original partner had pulled out of the project, and he had then asked Arlen to join the development team. The New York-based architectural firm of Emery Roth & Sons designed the new building. Richard Roth Jr., a third-generation design specialist and principal of the firm, headed the design team for the Laclede Gas Building.

First National Bank of St. Louis provided construction financing to the developers. Upon the project's completion, the construction loan was converted to permanent financing of $17 million by the John Hancock Mutual Insurance Company. Lee Liberman negotiated the lease with the developers, a lease that kept Laclede rental rates low.

Groundbreaking took place on September 18, 1967. Mayor Alfonso J. Cervantes was the principal speaker, and others at the podium included Laclede Gas President H. Reid Derrick; R. Ray Shockley, president of Downtown St. Louis, Inc.; and Arthur G. Cohen, president of Arlen Properties. A full-scale floor plan of the tower's ground floor, including entrances, elevator banks and other features, was painted on the pavement of the parking lot adjacent to the site.

Construction of the building took slightly more than two years. The project was completed at the end of January 1970. At that time, Laclede announced that the company would move into the new headquarters during the weekend of February 20-22. Mrazek Van & Storage Co., Inc. moved all property from 1017 Olive and the sales department at 1015 Locust to the new building. More than 50 movers and 10 vans hauling approximately 140 loads accomplished one of the biggest moves in downtown St. Louis history.

Employees had been preparing for the move since mid-January. All furniture, equipment and supplies were color-coded to make the move to the various floors of 720 Olive as smooth as possible. An elite unit of Mrazek moved the delicate IBM equipment to the new data processing department. Sections of Olive and Locust Streets were sealed off to normal traffic so that an uninterrupted flow of material and equipment could move to the new Laclede Building. Laclede Gas opened on Monday morning, February 23, at its new location.

Laclede's old building, which had been a St. Louis landmark, would be rented out as office space and rehabilitated in the 1990s. The new Laclede Building would house the utility through the tumultuous 1970s and beyond.

1970
More than 50 movers and 10 vans hauling approximately 140 loads accomplished one of the biggest moves in downtown St. Louis history.

During the late 1960s and early 1970s, Laclede Gas upgraded its transmission and distribution system by laying new pipe across the service area.

CHAPTER 11

Energy Crisis

For Laclede Gas and the rest of the nation's utility industry, the 1970s were a sober reminder of the cyclical nature of the American economy. Since the end of World War II in 1945, the nation had enjoyed boom times. America's Big Three automotive companies produced cars and trucks at a record pace, the nation's integrated steel industry was the biggest and most profitable on earth, and jobs were plentiful in all sectors of the economy.

The period from 1945 to 1973 was the last sustained era in American history in which one wage earner could support a family. Mortgage interest rates remained stable in the 5 to 6 percent range for a quarter-century, making home ownership affordable for millions of Americans. Inflation was all but non-existent for much of the immediate post-World War II era, and with the exception of short-lived corrections in the mid-1950s and in 1961, the stock market was remarkably bullish for much of the period.

But by the late 1960s, there were cracks in the bedrock foundation underpinning the American economy. President Lyndon Johnson attempted to operate a "guns and butter" economy when he fought the Vietnam War from 1964 to 1968. The resulting inflation began whipsawing consumers and industry at the end of the decade.

More significantly, the U.S. economy depended on inexpensive hydrocarbons to continue flourishing and expanding. Americans had a love affair with the V-8 engine, and that infatuation required 20-cent gasoline at the pump to continue. A homeowner in 1970 could heat a three-bedroom home in St. Louis with efficient natural gas for the winter at a cost of no more than a couple of hundred dollars.

Inexpensive oil and natural gas had been a stable of the American economy for decades. Our allies in the Middle East, such as Saudi Arabia and Iran, possessed seemingly inexhaustible petroleum reserves that were at America's disposal. And geologists suspected that the Gulf of Mexico off coastal Texas and Louisiana was a veritable lake of natural gas.

As it turned out, both assumptions were only partially correct. The wake-up call came in the fall of 1973.

Embargo

Laclede Gas and energy companies across the United States discovered the fragility of the nation's oil and gas supplies in mid-October 1973.

Led by Saudi Arabia, the Organization of Petroleum Exporting Countries (OPEC) announced in mid-October that the Arab members of OPEC were cutting production and placing an embargo on shipments of crude oil to Western countries. The United States and the Netherlands were singled out for punishment because of their support of Israel during the Yom Kippur War that had begun in early October.

The oil industry had no choice but to cooperate with the embargo. As a result, world oil prices rose to previously unheard of levels. The economies of the industrialized countries across the globe were soon impacted. By early 1974, most of the world was hit by the worst economic slump since the Great Depression.

The crisis was further exacerbated by government price controls in the United States. The controls limited the price of already discovered "old oil" while allowing newly discovered "new oil" to be sold at a higher price, which soon resulted in scarcity. The price controls were intended to promote oil exploration.

Many felt that the resulting scarcity would be dealt with by a government rationing program. For the first time

1970
A homeowner could heat a three-bedroom home in St. Louis with efficient natural gas for the winter at a cost of no more than a couple of hundred dollars.

since World War II, motorists faced the prospect of long lines at gas stations in St. Louis and across the United States.

Since oil demand decreased only slightly with price increases, prices had to rise dramatically to reduce demand to the new, lower level of supply. The market price for oil immediately rose substantially. The world financial system was marked by recession, high inflation, and elevated oil prices that would persist until the early to mid-1980s.

Laclede and other gas distribution utilities were faced with a dilemma. The embargo affected only petroleum imports. The United States bought almost no natural gas from the Middle East. But the reality was that natural gas also was in short supply, and that quickly led to a dramatic turnaround in the company's bottom line.

Laclede experienced a decline in sales and earnings in 1974, its first substantial reduction in net income since the late 1930s. Sales declined precipitously after President Richard Nixon's early November 1973 appeal to the nation to cut energy use in the wake of the Arab oil embargo. Laclede's customers responded to the president's request and reduced their usage of gas by thermostat cutbacks. Coupled with other conservation measures, this produced a sudden and unanticipated reduction of about 8 percent consumption for the winter of 1973-1974.

But the reality was that domestic supplies of natural gas actually had been running perilously short since the early 1970s. The severity of the natural gas shortages became apparent during the hard winter of 1976-1977. The threat of a natural gas supply shortage had been building for years because the then Federal Power Commission (FPC) had kept the regulated price of natural gas at the wellhead artificially low. Regulated prices, in turn, increased demand and discouraged the development of new supplies.

Prior to the winter of 1976-1977, many in the industry had speculated whether there really was an energy shortage. But the cold weather across the Midwest that winter and the following winter of 1977-1978 demonstrated beyond any doubt that the shortage was indeed real and that new sources of supply needed to be developed along with a coherent national energy program.

The winter of 1977-1978 was one of the coldest ever experienced in Laclede's service area. Temperatures were 23 percent colder than normal and 6 percent colder than those experienced in the severe winter of 1976-1977. The weather in 1978 exhibited a pattern of consistently cold temperatures but without the sub-zero temperatures of the previous winter. Laclede was able to maintain full service to customers, thanks to its exploration program and natural gas and propane storage programs.

Bob Jaudes, who ultimately would become Laclede's chairman, recalled just how difficult it was to keep gas flowing to customers during the difficult winters of 1976, 1977 and 1978. Then Laclede's senior vice president responsible for gas supply, Jaudes noted that "we had researched weather records and designed our gas supply model on the winter of

1974

Laclede experienced a decline in sales and earnings, its first substantial reduction in net income since the late 1930s.

1935-36. By late January of 1977, we were in the toughest supply situation that I've ever been in. The weather had been colder than our design winter, and many were forecasting that a disaster might be coming. Lee Liberman was bombarded with constant gloomy forecasts. He said he was tired of a constant barrage of bad news with no proposed remedies. So I told Lee that I wouldn't bother him every day with negative reports, but when I did come see him, the situation would be really bad."

By the last week of January, the supply outlook was very bad. "The board meeting was on a Thursday," Jaudes recalled, "and we needed to meet no later than Friday so I could tell Lee that we had to start shutting things down no later than the following Monday. But the weather moderated on Sunday and Monday, and our gas storage started to fill up again. That was the most intense period we ever had in all the years I can remember."

On October 15, 1978, President Jimmy Carter signed into law, as part of the National Energy Acts, the Natural Gas Policy Act of 1978 (NGPA). This legislation addressed the problem of gas shortages by creating a complex, vintage-based system for gradually deregulating producer prices for natural gas. The incremental pricing provisions of Title II of the NLGPA required higher cost natural to be allocated to industrial customers served directly by interstate pipelines. Another one of the National Energy Acts — the Powerplant and Industrial Fuel Use Act of 1978 — restricted the use of natural gas as a fuel for new electrical generation and other industrial uses. This legislation increased additions to gas reserves and contributed to limited industrial demand growth over the next four years which, coupled with higher natural gas prices and demand destruction, resulted in the "gas bubble" of the 1980s.

The NGPA raised the specter of an increased dependence on foreign oil because gas prices would inevitably rise above the government-controlled price of oil, thereby increasing imports.

The decade of the 1970s ended with the nation reeling from energy shortages and dealing with a newly formed Department of Energy that saddled oil companies with a number of regulations that didn't necessarily solve the problems they were intended to address. The United States would experience another round of price increases when

Shortages of natural gas in the 1970s were driven by regulated, artificially low wellhead prices for newly-discovered gas.

The nation's gas industry built thousands of miles of new pipeline transmission capacity during the 1970s.

a revolution in Iran in 1979 contributed to a second doubling of oil prices and to rampant inflation in the early 1980s.

For Laclede, the message was clear. If the company wanted to ensure customers an adequate supply of natural gas, the utility would have to go find it.

Exploration and Development

By 1971, the decline in the nation's proven reserves of natural gas began to receive tremendous amounts of public attention. The cause of the decrease was generally attributed to inadequate incentives for producers in the form of

---

THE STRIKE

The overthrow of the Shah of Iran in 1979 set in motion an economic firestorm that scorched consumers nationwide. For the second time in the 1970s, oil prices doubled almost overnight. Crude oil that had been selling for $14.60 per barrel since 1976 increased to $29 per barrel by the end of the decade. Inflation, which had been kept under control since the mid-1970s, skyrocketed, fueled by the doubling of energy costs.

President Jimmy Carter aggravated the economic problems when he promulgated a voluntary wage-price guideline of 7 percent. This meant that the president wanted wages and prices to increase by no more than 7 percent annually in any given industry. While the guidelines were completely voluntary, most companies fell in line and indicated a willingness to support the president in his fight against inflation.

Labor contracts form many utilities in the gas industry were up for negotiation, and Laclede Gas was no exception. The company's two-year contract with the Oil, Chemical & Atomic Workers of America (OCAW) expired on July 31, 1979. The company announced that in line with President Carter's request, it would abide by the wage-price guidelines set by the president. Laclede Gas then offered a new contract containing 7 percent wage and benefit increases each year for the next three years. The major bone of contention in the negotiations was the union's demand for a cost-of-living clause in the new contract.

Union negotiators argued vehemently that rank-and-file members were losing ground, even at the 7 percent increase allowed under President Carter's guidelines. Home mortgage rates in the St. Louis area had jumped to 12 percent and more, and inflation was taking huge chunks out of workers' paychecks. Union locals across the nation were on strike during the spring and summer of 1979, mostly in reaction to the unsettled economic conditions.

Laclede Gas was adamantly opposed to the insertion of the cost-of-living clause in the contract because it would take labor costs out of the company's control. The company argued that cost-of-living clauses were highly inflationary and were not in any way related to an increase in productivity. Laclede Gas negotiators felt that increased productivity was the only practical barometer by which increases in real wages could occur. In addition, under Missouri law, there was no way for Laclede Gas to recoup in a timely fashion through increased rates the regular periodic increase in costs which would occur under a cost-of-living clause in the contract.

Negotiations had been ongoing since July 10, 1979, but because of the major obstacle of cost-of-living increases, they broke off on September 12 when the union went on strike.

During the strike, management employees maintained operation of the system, working long hours and doing whatever had to be done to keep the delivery of essential services running smoothly.

On February 12, 1980, the strike finally ended. It was brought to a conclusion as a result of the intense efforts of the U.S. Federal Mediation & Conciliation Service. Federal mediators found common ground that the company accepted and that the union agreed to take to its membership. Shortly after, OCAW rank and file ratified the agreement.

The three-year settlement provided increases in wages and benefits of 10.5 percent in the year ending July 31, 1980, 8 percent in the year ending July 31, 1981 and 9 percent in the final year of the contract. The Mediation Service also recommended that the company form a Labor-Management Committee to improve relations between management and the union.

The five-month strike proved the hard truth of President Lee Liberman's maxim. "Nobody ever wins a strike," he said in his comment on the settlement in his column in *Laclede News*.

the price that they were allowed to charge for gas sold in interstate commerce. Lower market prices meant that there was less incentive to drill for hydrocarbons, and the gas that was discovered was sold within the unregulated market.

During the summer of 1970, the Federal Power Commission allowed producers to increase the price for gas from the fields of northern Louisiana. The area, centered around Monroe, was the source of most of the gas purchased by Laclede Gas at that time.

Laclede had taken several steps to help solve and ease its gas supply problems, steps that enabled the utility both to grow moderately and at the same time to continue to supply existing markets. The utility's efforts included restricting the addition of large industrial loads, improvement of winter gas availability through expanded underground natural gas storage, and increased storage capacity

Offshore rigs helped tap the awesome gas potential beneath the Gulf of Mexico.

Laclede Gas was able to supply a significant portion of its gas needs during the 1970s from exploration wells the company drilled in Texas, Oklahoma and Louisiana.

of propane gas to meet winter season peak needs.

But because of the ongoing supply problem and a desire to control a portion of its source of gas, Laclede entered into an agreement with Mississippi River Transmission Corporation (MRT) and Freeport Oil Company to drill a deep exploratory well in an area of the Texas Panhandle known as the Mills Ranch Prospect. Mills Ranch consisted of an estimated 11,000 contiguous acres suitable for both exploratory and developmental wells.

Rex Bannister, a geological engineer who had spent the early part of his career with Laclede developing the underground storage facility at Florissant, was assigned to work with MRT in starting and expanding the exploration program.

Born and raised in Clinton County, Oklahoma, Bannister served in the South Pacific during World War II, flying 38 missions in a B-25 with the 5th Air Force. After the war, he entered the University of Oklahoma at Norman, graduating with a Bachelor of Science degree in geological engineering. He joined Laclede Gas in 1953 and worked with Al Burgess to develop the underground storage program.

"We first started injecting gas in 1955 after we had drilled all the wells necessary to establish the capacity of the underground cavern," Bannister explained. "We had finished drilling all the exploratory wells around 1964."

Bannister then transferred to the company's Marketing Department. When Laclede became interested in exploration in early 1970, the board of directors formed the Exploration Department. Bannister was named to head the company's gas exploration efforts.

Laclede's first major gas discovery was an exploratory well in Wheeler County, Texas, named the Fabian No. 1. Drilled to a depth of 21,000 feet in the Hunton limestone formation, it was completed in November 1972 as a producing well with an estimated daily production capacity of approximately 20 million cubic feet of gas. Laclede's Exploration Department had enjoyed a dose of beginner's luck.

Fabian No. 1 was the largest producing well discovered in North America that year. Other wells, including the the Daberry No.1, soon followed as the field was further developed. Laclede Gas also participated in wells located in Beckham County, Oklahoma, just across the state line from Wheeler County. All of the prospects were part of the huge Anadarko Basin that had been a prolific source of gas since its initial discovery in 1918.

For its efforts, Laclede received various percentages of the production from each successful well. Mississippi River Transmission had the right to purchase all of the gas produced, except the volume that was owned outright by Laclede. In addition, MRT was obligated to deliver Laclede's gas to the St. Louis area.

By 1974, the exploration program was expanded to include more projects in Beckham and Roger Mills Counties in Oklahoma. In addition, two other prospects, the East Vixen and Onion Bayou fields in Louisiana, were then being developed. Laclede owned a 50 percent interest in the North Converse Field in Sabine Parish, Louisiana, which

1972
Fabian No. 1 was the largest producing well discovered in North America that year.

1982
Laclede had participated in drilling 87 wells through the exploration and development program.

had five wells completed in the mid-1970s. At the time, Laclede owned 37 billion cubic feet of new gas from its exploration activities. The discoveries greatly improved the gas supply picture for Laclede and its customers.

Laclede's success ratio was little short of phenomenal. By 1982, Laclede had participated in drilling 87 wells through the exploration and development program, and 43 of them were commercially successful. Most drillers considered a 20 percent success ratio outstanding.

Moving the gas to metropolitan St. Louis proved to be more expensive than originally anticipated, however. Laclede argued that its own gas reserves should be transported to the market area by interstate pipelines on a fair and non-discriminatory basis. Laclede typically had to sell some of the gas to the transporting pipeline in order to obtain the transportation service. In one instance, only 34 percent of Laclede's wellhead production reached the St. Louis area, with the balance being sold to Mississippi River Transmission Company and other transporting pipelines.

In 1981, Laclede Energy Resources, a wholly owned subsidiary of Laclede Gas Company formed in the early 1970s to find coal reserves, was tasked with a new assignment: to undertake all new exploration and development efforts. But as gas supplies expanded in the early 1980s, prices went down, nullifying most of the advantages of the exploration program.

In 1982, the company posted a loss of $1.6 million in non-utility exploration and development income. As a result, Laclede began limiting its activity to development of proven fields.

With the advent of even more plentiful supplies in the early 1990s, the drilling programs came to a close. By then, the company had not participated in any exploration activity for several years. In May 1997, Laclede completed the sale of all of its oil and gas production properties.

Diversification

The energy crises of the 1970s convinced Laclede Gas management that it needed to investigate other sources of income if the company hoped to protect customers and shareholders from the shock of supply disruptions in the future. In addition to entering the natural gas exploration business in 1970, Laclede embarked on a program of diversification in fields unrelated to the sale and distribution of gas and gas appliances. The new activities would be an attempt to broaden the earnings base of Laclede.

In late 1969, the board of directors formed Laclede Development Corporation to participate in joint ventures with real estate developers in the St. Louis area. The diversification subsidiary's first acquisition was a 50 percent interest in a joint venture to build the Sierra Vista Apartments on 60 acres of land in northwest St. Louis County.

Shortly afterward, Laclede formed another subsidiary, Laclede Investment Corporation. The new entity began selling fire and burglary alarms through the purchase of a 95 percent interest in Empire Alarms, Inc. The name of Empire

Alarms Inc. was later changed to Laclede Gas Security Systems, Inc.

In 1970, Laclede incorporated another new subsidiary, Laclede Gas Family Services, Inc., to offer hospital indemnity insurance to Laclede's customers and others in the area. The company obtained insurance through an arrangement with ITT-Hamilton Life Insurance Company. Laclede named the program the Blue Flame Family Protection Plan.

At the same time, Laclede Development began broadening its investment base with construction of Laclede Airport Park, a 50-acre commercial and light industrial property at St. Louis Lambert Airport.

In 1973, Laclede Gas formed Laclede Communication Services, Inc. to establish a studio for the creation of video commercials and other video productions. The studio also provided facilities for telecasting of St. Louis sporting and entertainment events. Laclede Communications Services began operations in 1974, specializing in the telecasts of baseball, hockey and football games.

Laclede Gas was philosophical about the success of its diversification efforts. If an initiative did not prove profitable, the company didn't hesitate to get out of the investment. In late May 1977, Laclede sold the major assets of Laclede Gas Security Systems, Inc. at a small loss. In October 1985, Laclede sold Laclede Communication Services because the subsidiary had not grown as quickly as expected.

Laclede Venture Corporation was established as a wholly owned, non-utility subsidiary of Laclede in June 1985. It immediately entered into a general partnership with C.P.I. Corporation and Gateway Mid-America Partners. The partnership engaged in research and development of light beam technology and its application to the production of high-quality and low-cost human sculpture.

Except for a failed investment in the city's Germania Bank in 1987, Laclede did not make any more diversified acquisitions until the 21st century. Laclede did, however, remain active in real estate development, realizing substantial profits from that sector.

The End of an Era

The fall of the Shah of Iran in 1979 and the election of Ronald Reagan as president the next year finally brought an end to the upheavals of the 1970s. The energy crises that characterized the decade brought with them unprecedented inflation that would plague the American economy well into the 1980s.

Laclede's revenues increased $100 million to nearly $400 million between 1977 and 1979 alone. But expenses increased at an even faster rate. By 1980, the company was paying interest rates of 10 percent. Everything the company purchased, from pipes to vehicles to insurance, was increasing at double-digit annual rates.

But the 1980s would bring new challenges. Laclede would have to learn how to buy and sell gas in the new climate of deregulation.

1979
Laclede's revenues increased $100 million to nearly $400 million between 1977 and 1979.

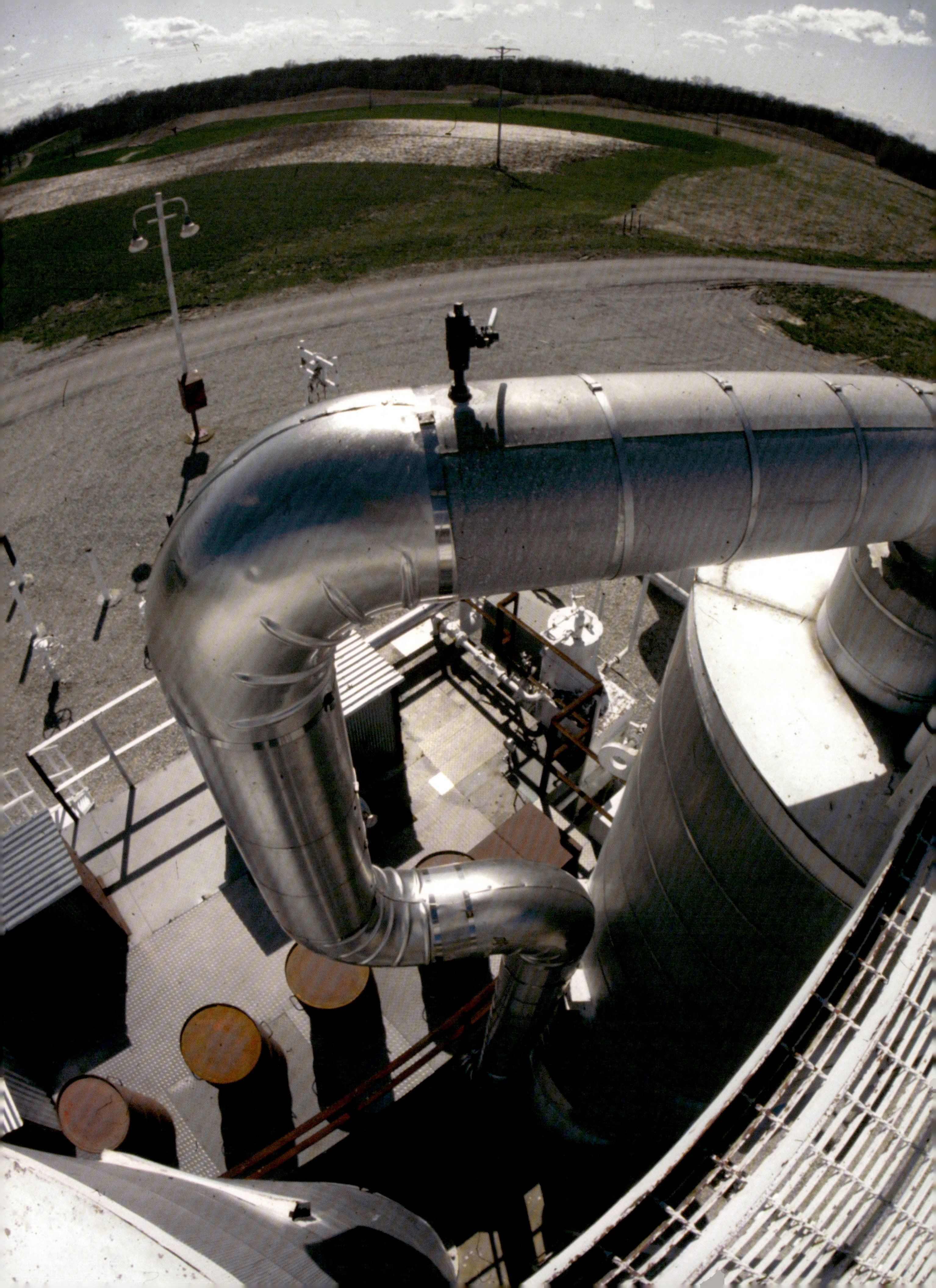

CHAPTER 12

Dealing with the Bubble

Perhaps no era in the long history of America's relationship with natural gas was more unsettled than the 1980s.

Laclede's propane underground storage facility in North St. Louis County helped the utility weather the natural gas shortages of the 1970s and supplement the growing supply of more expensive, deregulated gas during the 1980s.

Natural gas went from a climate of persistent shortage at the beginning of the decade to an abundance never before experienced in less than 10 years. The over-supply was the result of government policies that began a 20-year deregulation of the production and wholesale sectors and encouraged a wave of exploration and drilling unprecedented in the history of the natural gas industry.

Between 1980 and 1985, the development of a gas "bubble" transformed the delivery and distribution of natural gas, ultimately leading to dramatic cutbacks in rates and corresponding increases in consumption by residential, industrial and commercial customers. Laclede Gas, and other distribution utilities, reaped the benefits of plentiful supplies of natural gas and became adept at marketing gas to end-use customers.

Although the 1980s were not a particularly profitable era for distribution utilities such as Laclede, the St. Louis utility learned valuable lessons about its customers that the company would put to good use during the 1990s and the 21st century. Laclede also put into place during the 1980s mechanisms to take advantage of the greater flexibility afforded distribution utilities under deregulation policies promulgated by the Federal Energy Regulatory Commission (FERC).

In 1980, hard on the heels of the energy upheaval occasioned by the overthrow of the Shah of Iran and the taking of American embassy hostages in Teheran, few would have predicted that natural gas would be in plentiful supply before the decade was half over.

The Gas Bubble

In the early years, the Natural Gas Policy Act (NGPA) of 1978 achieved its intended results. Higher prices at the wellhead quickly began to stimulate exploration activity, and drillers were brought back to the gas market. With the advent of a higher rig count engaged in gas exploration, more gas came on stream as a result of development drilling and exploratory drilling. With the enactment of the NGPA, the federal government moved toward a complete deregulation of the gas industry.

While deregulation was being accomplished, gas continued to build up in the production pipeline. By 1983, the American Gas Association was reporting that for the third year in a row, U.S. natural gas reserve additions exceeded production; the aggregate for the period 1981-1983 was 7 percent per year.

Sharply escalating prices for natural gas closely followed the supply shortages of the late 1970s. By the early 1980s, prices had reached their level of resistance. Natural gas consumers in St. Louis and across the nation began conserving. Industrial and large commercial customers registered their displeasure with price increases by fuel switching to propane, fuel oil, coal or electric power. Propane and fuel oil were particularly suited to fuel switching, since most industrial natural gas boilers were capable of running on alternate fuels.

Nature conspired to worsen the situation. The winter of 1982-1983 was one of the warmest on record across the Midwest. By late March 1983, the heating season was 15 percent warmer than normal in most of Missouri, Illinois, Indiana and Ohio, and 21 percent warmer than the preceding winter. Meanwhile, because of price decontrols at the wellhead, natural gas rates for the average residential customer in the region had climbed some 60 percent in just one year.

Suddenly in the early 1980s, natural gas pipelines and local distribution companies had more gas and fewer markets. The so-called natural gas "bubble" had been born. And in the second half of the decade, the weather continued to work in favor of a supply build-up. In fact, the temperatures in the latter half of the 1980s were dramatically warmer than they had been during the previous five years.

The trend continued until the mid-1990s across much of Mid-America. Even in a deregulated industry, natural gas remained as sensitive to winter weather conditions as it had since the beginnings of the modern industry in the 1920s and 1930s.

Because the natural gas bubble in the United States continued to grow — and was estimated at upward of 2.5 trillion cubic feet by 1988 — making money in the gas business continued to be difficult for local distribution companies. On November 1, 1993, the Federal Energy Regulatory Commission issued Order No. 636, in which interstate pipelines became common carriers of interstate natural gas supplies.

What Order 636 basically said was that pipeline companies could no longer take title to natural gas and resell it to local distribution companies. Instead, local distribution companies were free to buy gas directly from natural gas suppliers and marketers. (Industrial customers also could buy gas directly from natural gas suppliers and use the gas systems of the local distribution companies to transport the gas.)

Doug Yaeger, Laclede chairman of the board, president and CEO, recalled that "in 1992, Order 636 took the pipelines

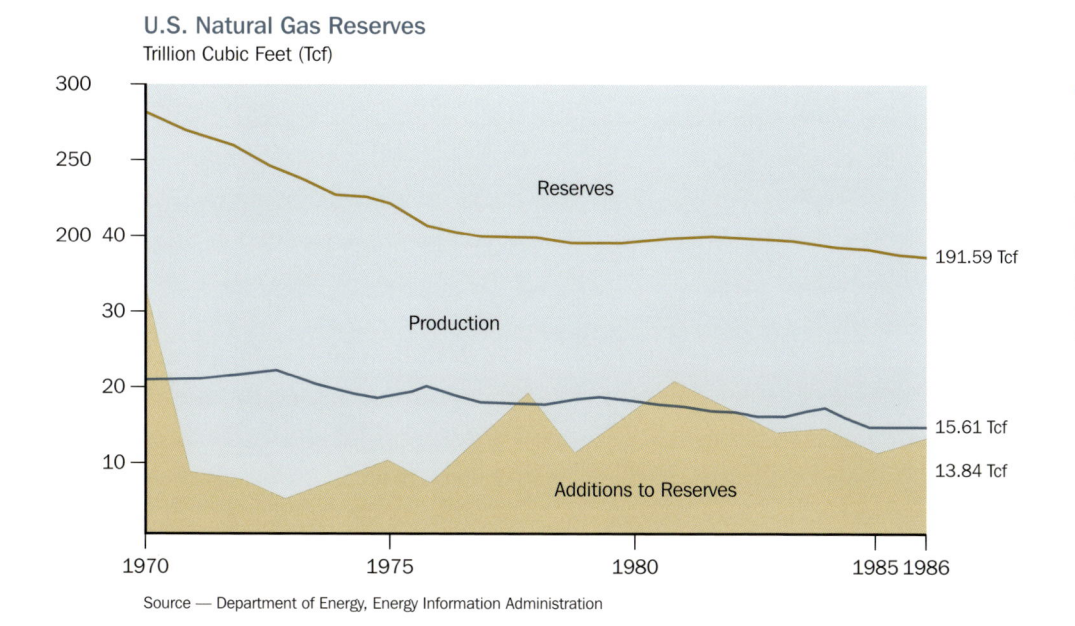

U.S. Natural Gas Reserves
Trillion Cubic Feet (Tcf)

Reserves — 191.59 Tcf
Production — 15.61 Tcf
Additions to Reserves — 13.84 Tcf

Source — Department of Energy, Energy Information Administration

By 1983
The American Gas Association was reporting that U.S. natural gas reserve additions exceeded production for the third year in a row.

150 Year Anniversary 145

1981
In December, Laclede promoted a new project it called the Residential Insulation Financing Program to provide low-interest loans to customers who wanted to make energy-saving home improvements.

out of the merchant function of gas supply. They could no longer buy and resell gas. Laclede now had to buy gas directly from producers and arrange for its own pipeline transportation. This now meant that we had to decide to sell or store any gas that we had to buy, and this necessitated setting up a whole new gas supply department."

For some distribution companies, a scramble ensued to find experienced people to perform these new duties. Yaeger noted that Laclede and its longtime exclusive supplier were able to smoothly make the transition from regulation to deregulation.

"Mississippi River Transmission Co. performed this service for two years on a "contracted out" basis," Yaeger explained, "and then Laclede took the function over and placed it in-house. We took on the task of managing our own gas supply portfolio, nominating the gas for delivery, making sure it was delivered and finding supplies to purchase on the open market."

Complying with FERC Order 636 had gone smoothly for the natural gas industry. By the 21st century, natural gas had put much of the upheaval associated with deregulation behind it.

Home Energy Audits

With the doubling of energy costs in the late 1970s and early 1980s, conservation became paramount for gas and electric utility customers who wanted to keep their energy bills as reasonable as possible. State governments also stepped in, offering tax credits for new insulation, storm windows and energy efficient furnaces and air conditioners. Laclede Gas focused its efforts on helping customers conserve energy. Laclede expanded the initiatives it had undertaken during the 1970s to educate customers about the benefits of energy conservation.

In December 1981, Laclede promoted a new project it called the Residential Insulation Financing Program to provide low-interest loans to customers who wanted to make energy-saving home improvements. In 1984, Laclede Gas made another new program available to customers, the Residential Conservation Service, or RCS. The new service offered home energy audits and arranged for energy-related contracting and lending services for Laclede customers.

Laclede used the services of Enercom, a company that employed state-certified auditors, to perform the audits. Each audit involved a thorough check of a customer's home, including caulking, storm windows, insulation, furnace, windows and exterior doors. Customer participation was voluntary and the charge for a residential energy audit was $15.

Following the audit, the customer received a report that outlined the improvements to be made and the savings expected. If the customer chose to make the improvements, he was given a list of contractors and suppliers who could carry out the recommended tasks. The customer also was provided a list of lenders if he needed to finance the improvements. If the customer used a state-authorized lender, he could pay back the loan through monthly installments on his gas bill.

John Moten Jr., then director of conservation services, headed the RCS program.

LEE M. LIBERMAN

Lee M. Liberman, retired chairman of the board, president and chief executive officer of Laclede Gas, defined the St. Louis utility's management culture for a generation. Liberman was born in 1921 in Salt Lake City, Utah, the son of an attorney. He lived in the Mormon Commonwealth until 1931 when the family moved to St. Louis. His father, originally from St. Joseph, Missouri, earned a degree from Yale University and graduated from the University of Missouri School of Law in 1912.

Lee Liberman attended the Field School in St. Louis through the 8th grade and then moved on to Soldan High School. He followed his father to Yale University, graduating with a degree in engineering in 1942. After serving in the Army Air Corps during World War II, Liberman was discharged in October 1945.

Jobs were hard to come by in the early post-war years, so he went to the U.S. Employment Service to look for work, and he got two referrals: Laclede Gas and Union Electric. Although he also had been accepted at Stanford University School of Law, Liberman decided to take Laclede's offer of employment. It proved to be a long and memorable relationship, because he remained at the St. Louis utility for 47 years.

In 1945, Laclede Gas had just emerged from a complicated reorganization, weaker financially and far smaller than it is today. Liberman started as a cadet engineer and worked as a chemist at the coke plant and at Station A on Rutger Street. In 1948, he was appointed superintendent of Station A. Transferred to the engineering department in 1949, Liberman served as a design engineer and as an assistant to various operations executives for the next five years.

In December 1954, Liberman was appointed assistant superintendent of distribution in charge of construction and maintenance, a post he held until his 1962 election as vice president of operations.

During the early part of Liberman's career, Laclede Gas was undergoing significant changes in its operational structure with the acquisition of the St. Louis County Gas Co. in 1948 and the conversion to straight natural gas in November 1949. But the greatest change of all, and the one that would really expand Laclede's core business, was the construction of the underground storage reservoir in Florissant, just north of St. Louis. It enabled the company to control the cost of its natural gas purchases and to maintain gas deliveries during the coldest winter weather.

Liberman, who was working as an assistant to Judge Robert W. Otto in the early 1950s, recalled that Laclede's president became fascinated with the concept of underground storage after reading about an Illinois natural gas company that was already using underground storage near Chicago. Today, Liberman recalls that development of the underground storage program was one of the most significant events in Laclede's history because it gave the company the ability to greatly expand its business during the growth years of the 1960s and 1970s.

Liberman held key positions in management, including vice president – marketing (1964), executive vice-president (1969), and president and chief operating officer (1970). In 1974, the board gave him the additional title of chief executive officer. In April 1976, Laclede's board of directors elected Liberman chairman of the board.

Throughout his career, Liberman focused on the importance of continuous access to adequate, dependable supplies of reasonably priced gas. Assurance of a competitively priced supply enabled Laclede to meet customer needs during the coldest winters, to support expansion into new service areas, and to actively promote new uses for gas.

A Strong Advocate

Liberman was a strong advocate of a national energy policy that would ensure the most efficient uses of the nation's fossil fuels. When Congress enacted the Natural Gas Policy Act of 1978, Liberman was one of the few executives of a gas distribution company to oppose its passage. Liberman told federal regulators that the act opened the way for huge increases in the wholesale price of gas in the early 1980s, without providing any economic incentives to expand the nation's existing gas reserves. Liberman argued that the act also fostered the continued waste of natural gas as a fuel for electric power generation.

During his tenure at Laclede, Liberman maintained an active role in the St. Louis civic community, serving as chairman of the St. Louis Symphony Society, the Washington University Board of Trustees, and the St. Louis Regional Commerce & Growth Association. He was named St. Louis Man of the Year in 1986, and his many civic honors included the Regional Commerce & Growth Right Arm of St. Louis Award, the Saint Louis Ambassadors Spirit of St. Louis Award and the Healthcare Leadership Award from the Hospital Association of St. Louis.

Liberman retired as chairman of the board in 1994.

"Bob Jaudes brought me downtown to set up the energy conservation program," Moten recalled. "At first I resisted because I was afraid that I could no longer be a chemist. Bob said that there are no more promotions out here in the lab at Shrewsbury. So I went downtown and worked on the 14th floor."

As part of RCS, Moten launched the budget-billing program. "I did a series of energy conservation commercials," he said, "and later, I was our spokesperson on energy issues and high gas prices. I also appeared before the city's board of aldermen. Truly, I was no longer a chemist. But it allowed me to use my technical background and apply it to consumer situations."

Along with the services already available to Laclede's customers, the RCS program readily demonstrated that the company was serious about educating customers on the ways and benefits of conserving natural gas.

'So Long, Sarah'

Those were words heard around the Laclede organization in the fall of 1984 when the Sarah Street Warehouse was demolished. Located at 220 Sarah Street next door to the Forest Park Service Center, Sarah Street was one of the oldest and best known Laclede facilities in St. Louis.

The 80-year-old warehouse, built during the St. Louis World's Fair, was one of the company's links to the past.

By 1984, the building was in need of extensive repairs and modernization. During the 1980s, the warehouse was costly to heat and cool. Laclede wanted to avoid a costly rehabilitation of the existing building, and the decision was made to demolish the old structure.

The Sarah Street facility had served as a storeroom for stationery products used at the company and for gas appliances sold through Laclede's sales group. The warehouse also housed a tool repair section.

According to Russ Eckrich, then assistant manager of material and supply, the building originally was a shoe factory. "Laclede moved its warehouse from 3615 Forest Park to the Sarah Street location in 1952," Eckrich told the Laclede News in 1984. "We were into appliance sales and service in a big way back then, including the sale and service of gas refrigerators, which aren't around anymore. I worked on an appliance truck — one of five trucks that worked out of Sarah Street. We'd even go pick up refrigerators and paint them for customers."

John McHale, former district superintendent of material and supplies at Forest Park, remembered the early days, too. "It used to be that every gas refrigerator ever sold in the city was warehoused at Sarah Street and delivered by Laclede Gas," McHale said.

The tool repair operation was moved to the east end of the garage at 4000 Forest Park, and the stationery storeroom, which handled all of Laclede's office supply needs, was moved to the Globe-Democrat Building at 710 N. Tucker. Laclede had an ownership interest in the building through its real estate subsidiary.

Don Westphale, a 32-year veteran of Laclede Gas and district superintendent

Gas chemistry became even more sophisticated during the 1980s and 1990s.

An equipment operator helps extend a main to service the Barrington Downs subdivision in North St. Louis County.

of the Sarah Street operation from 1971 through 1984, explained that the building was getting harder to care for each year. "It was cold, the roof leaked and the old elevator was having problems," Westphale said. "It was time to go."

Following the building's demolition, the Sarah Street lot was paved and designated as a parking lot for Laclede employees at the Forest Park Service Center.

Sharpening Marketing Efforts

The passage of the Natural Gas Policy Act of 1978 created wholesale price increases in the early 1980s that quickly made inroads into Laclede's competitive price advantage. But the company continued to advertise the superiority of gas as a fuel for customers. With gas reserves decreasing and producer gas prices increasing, a typical Laclede residential heating customer, who had an annual bill of $406 in 1979, saw that same bill more than double to $815 by 1983. As gas bills soared, Laclede faced increasing competition from Union Electric, which built its load and market share by marketing electric heat pumps.

Despite the intense effort on the part of the local electric utility to sell heat pumps, Laclede's 1984 marketing program focused on shoring up the gas utility's heating market. Laclede continued to advertise the fact that the heat pump required back-up assistance from another source of fuel.

Laclede Gas also pointed out the longevity of a gas furnace as opposed to a heat pump. Gas furnaces typically had a warranty of 20 years on the heat exchanger, wherein a heat pump could not match that.

Laclede Gas noted that other residential and commercial applications of natural gas for cooking, water heating and clothes drying provided greater efficiency at significant cost savings when compared to electricity.

In 1985, Laclede's rates declined significantly because Mississippi River Transmission Co. acquired increasingly plentiful pipeline gas at lower costs. At the same time, Laclede's electric utility competitor, Union Electric, was introducing a series of substantial rate increases that would double the cost of electric heating over the next five years.

In addition, Laclede benefited from a substantial increase in construction activity in both the city of St. Louis and St. Louis County, a surge that was driven by falling interest rates. In the single-family home market, Laclede installed gas heating in approximately 98 percent of all new construction. Meanwhile, in downtown St. Louis, Union Station and St. Louis Centre opened in 1985. Both facilities were important natural gas customers at the time.

Laclede also targeted the apartment and multi-family housing market. In 1985, the company began an advertising campaign directed at apartment renters, pointing out that the annual cost of electricity for a two-bedroom apartment was almost 50 percent higher than comparable amounts of natural gas for heating, hot water and cooking.

By 1986, Laclede was maintaining a strong competitive position in the residential, commercial and industrial

1980s
In the single-family home market, Laclede installed gas heating in approximately 98 percent of all new construction.

1982-1983
In its first year of operation, Dollar-Help raised more than $240,000 to help subsidize heating bills for elderly and low-income residents.

markets, thanks to its successful advertising and marketing campaigns and the continued downward trend in wholesale gas costs. The company was the dominant force in the home-heating field in metropolitan St. Louis, supplying gas for heating to more than 90 percent of the single-family residential market in its service area. The turnaround in gas costs and Laclede's increasing sophistication at marketing natural gas allowed the utility to pass along savings to customers.

With the decrease in natural gas prices, Laclede Gas passed along those savings to customers when it filed for a major rate increase in 1986.

Helping the Community

In line with its decades-old philosophy of helping the community it calls home, Laclede Gas instituted a number of programs during the 1980s that benefited St. Louis' low-income residents. When gas prices peaked in the early 1980s, Laclede moved quickly to ensure that its customers on fixed incomes would be protected from some of the more dramatic price increases.

In the fall of 1982, Laclede helped form Dollar-Help, Inc., which was established to help elderly and low-income people pay their heating bills. It was one of the first programs of its kind in the nation. Laclede's customers could contribute to Dollar-Help by overpaying their gas bills by as little as $1, or by asking Laclede to routinely over-bill their accounts by $1 or more. Dollar-Help was an independent organization headed by three St. Louisans known for their efforts to ease the plight of the poor, including Sister Patricia Ann Kelley, the Reverend Robert L. Huston and the Reverend Larry Rice. In its first year of operation, Dollar-Help raised more than $240,000 to help subsidize heating bills for elderly and less affluent residents.

In February 1984, Laclede increased the authorized common stock to 20 million shares and authorized a 2-for-1 stock split. Since the company's employees and retirees, as well as a large number of St. Louis residents, were shareholders, the split helped them increase their holdings of company common stock. Many small shareholders in the St. Louis metropolitan area used the company's popular Dividend Reinvestment Program (DRIP), which allowed them to purchase additional stock without a broker by investing dividends directly with the company.

Laclede and its management team were leaders in the commercial and industrial renaissance that St. Louis experienced during the 1980s. Downtown St. Louis was transformed during the decade. Southwestern Bell built a 44-story headquarters building in 1984, less than a year after the 30-story Centerre Plaza opened. St. Louis Union Station was rehabilitated into a thriving retail center and St. Louis Centre opened as the largest downtown shopping center in the United States. Both projects opened in 1985.

St. Louis emerged during the decade as one of the nation's major automotive assembly centers outside the Detroit metropolitan area. Laclede Gas worked closely with the nation's Big 3 automakers to ensure a supply of inexpensive natural gas for their St. Louis assembly operations.

In late 1983, General Motors opened its Wentzville plant to produce several models of Buicks and Oldsmobiles. Chrysler expanded the Fenton assembly plant in 1986 to add minivans to the production mix, and Ford nearly doubled the size of its Aerostar minivan plant in Hazelwood the same year.

The decade of the 1980s had started on a negative note, with gas in short supply and prices on an upward trend. But supplies and costs were in balance by mid-decade, leading to a stable period of plentiful supplies and falling prices by decade's end which extended into the early 1990s. Laclede Gas used that breathing period during the early 1990s to learn all it could about operating in a sharply deregulated wholesale environment.

Laclede's support of Dollar-Help assisted elderly and low-income people in paying their winter heating bills.

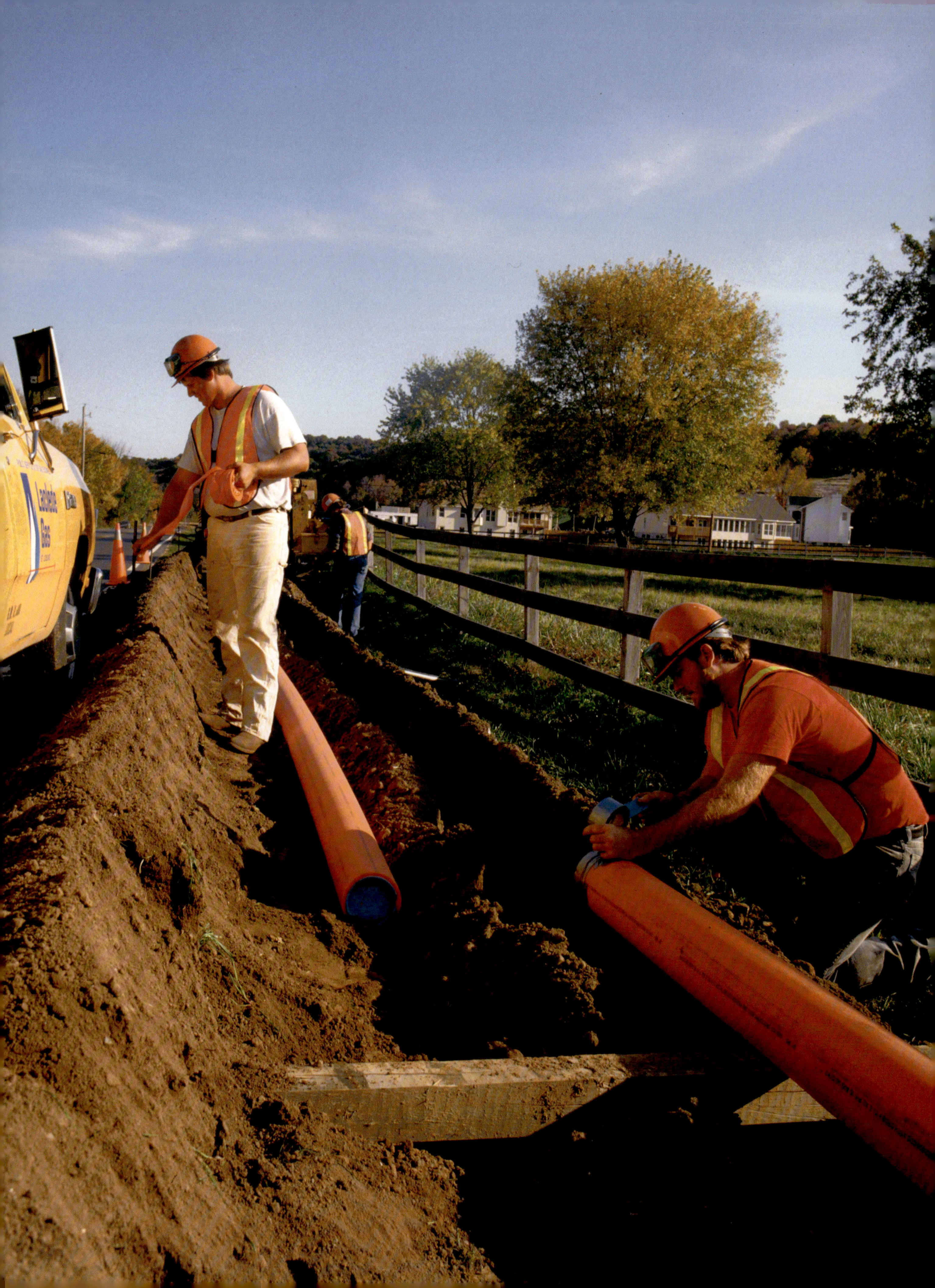
Laclede Gas

CHAPTER 13

Suburban Growth

After the upheavals of the 1970s and 1980s, Laclede Gas was a resilient organization that had been tested by adversity. Nearly 20 years of energy crises, gas shortages, high prices and other economic and societal turmoil had prepared Laclede and its employees to expect the worst.

Construction and Maintenance crews install a main pipeline in St. Charles County, one of the fastest growing counties in Missouri during the 1990s.

But as the 1990s dawned, the natural gas industry embarked on a new course. Flush with abundant amounts of natural gas, distributors such as Laclede expanded marketing efforts to residential and commercial customers. Stable gas pricing throughout the 1990s coincided with a boom in suburban population. For much of the decade, Laclede Gas enjoyed the kind of growth it had not experienced since the 1960s.

Beneath the Wide Missouri

By 1990, St. Charles County had been the fastest growing county in Missouri for more than a decade, its population increasing almost 48 percent since 1979. St. Charles Gas, the company acquired by Laclede Gas in the summer of 1963 and operated as a division of the St. Louis utility, had 4,000 customers when Laclede took operational control. By the 1980s, St. Charles Gas served more than 49,000 customers in St. Charles County and needed to increase both capacity and source of gas supply.

To solve the problem of inadequate distribution capacity, Laclede installed a new 16-inch feeder line that ran beneath the Missouri River. Crews threaded the mammoth pipe through a 2,000-foot-long hole that was drilled horizontally approximately 60 feet beneath the riverbed, just south of an old highway bridge that connected St. Charles and St. Louis counties.

Laclede solved the second problem, increasing gas supply, in January 1990 by making two connections in St. Charles County to a 12-inch intrastate pipeline operated by the Missouri Pipeline Company. Missouri Pipeline extended about 85 miles northwest of St. Louis to a connection with Panhandle Eastern Pipeline Company's interstate system. Gas from Missouri Pipeline was back-fed into the system to supply all of St. Charles County's needs, while the line beneath the river was tied into the Laclede system.

The Missouri River crossing utilized directional horizontal drilling technology in which equipment similar to that used for vertical drilling was employed to drill and ream a hole beneath the riverbed. During the 1980s, drilling beneath riverbeds had become a common river-crossing technique and was considered environmentally and economically superior to the older system of dredging a trench in the river bottom.

The procedure involved drilling a pilot hole and then reaming back and forth beneath the river using larger and larger reamers until the hole was 28 inches in diameter. Laclede's first two attempts were unsuccessful. But on June 15, 1990, crews completed an 8½-inch pilot hole to the St. Louis County side of the river, and then reamed back and forth until the required width of 28 inches was achieved on August 7.

The accompanying steel supply feeder pipe was welded to a length of 2,200 feet, put on rollers and prepared for the pull-back operation. The pipe was protected with a fusion-bonded epoxy coating. It then was hydrostatically tested for structural integrity for 12 hours. When the tests were completed, the pipe was ready for installation.

1980s
St. Charles Gas served more than 49,000 customers in St. Charles County and needed to increase both capacity and source of gas supply.

During the drilling and reaming of the underground hole, drilling mud was used to carry cuttings from the tunnel. A mixture of Bentonite clay and water, the drilling mud remained in the hole after drilling was over. When the new pipe was pulled through, the slurry acted as a lubricant to help the pipe slide through the hole. It also helped protect the pipe coating.

The entire operation took 16 hours to complete. At 8 a.m. on August 14, the pipe emerged on the St. Charles side of the river. After more hydrostatic testing of the line, the drilling and pullback operations were completed three days later. Laclede construction and maintenance crews then moved in to begin tying the new line into the utility's distribution system. The tie-in was accomplished on September 10 when the line was made fully operational.

With the conclusion of the vital new link in Laclede's distribution system, the St. Charles Gas Division was assured it had the gas supply to expand service during the 1990s in one of Missouri's fastest growing counties.

The Fulton Gas Shortage

Although it rarely happens, an accidental gas outage can quickly turn into a crisis situation. On October 12, 1992, the city of Fulton, Missouri was left without gas service due to a construction accident. An 8-inch pipeline into Fulton was ruptured during excavation work on U.S. Highway 54, leaving all 3,700 customers in the community without service. Shortly after the incident occurred, the general manager of Fulton's municipally owned gas system asked Laclede to assist the utility.

"For the most part, utilities have sort of an unwritten code among themselves," said Doug Yaeger, then Laclede's vice president for operations, gas supply and technical services. "Fortunately, it doesn't happen very often, but if another utility is in trouble and we are asked for assistance, Laclede will do what it can to help. In situations like this, vehicles and equipment are needed as much as manpower. Fulton was close enough that we could have our people and our equipment there within several hours."

In addition, crews from Laclede, employees from Union Electric and several Missouri cities in the area also offered help.

The city of Fulton already had taken necessary safety steps by having its crews shut off the line into the city after the break, which was repaired shortly after the accident. But there remained the additional step of turning off each customer's gas meter before the system's pressure could be brought back up to normal. With gas flowing back into the distribution system, each individual home and business would have gas appliances that would need to be relit. Crews also would have to check the gas service line and appliances for safe operation. If the appliances were not 100 percent safe, Laclede employees tagged them and closed all their valves as a safety precaution.

Staffers from Laclede's Service and Installation Department (S.A.I.D.)-North department assembled a 10-person work force and sent them to Fulton, where they were briefed on Fulton's service

1992
An 8-inch pipeline into Fulton was ruptured during excavation work on U.S. Highway 54, leaving all 3,700 customers in the community without service.

department procedures. The Laclede crews were then given routes to inspect. Laclede crews worked side-by-side with Fulton gas division service crews. The shared duties at each home involved turning the gas on, spot checking the meter and doing a leak check on the service lines.

Ronald Abernathy, a foreman from S.A.I.D.-North told Laclede News that "we were gratefully welcomed in all of the homes." The teams worked a full Friday until midnight and finished up late Saturday afternoon, when they returned to St. Louis.

Robert E. Fisher Jr., Fulton's mayor, wrote a letter to Laclede expressing his and the city council's appreciation for the assistance that was rendered in the city's time of need. As it had for all of its long history, Laclede once again demonstrated that good corporate citizenship involved cooperating with others to help when a crisis needed to be addressed.

In 1990, Laclede expanded its distribution system into neighboring Franklin and Jefferson counties, which are served by its sister company, Missouri Natural Gas.

Expansion Toward Eureka

When Laclede expanded its distribution system into neighboring Franklin County in 1990, the extension positioned the St. Louis utility as the principal supplier of natural gas in three of the fastest-growing counties in Missouri: St. Charles, Jefferson and Franklin counties. Expansion also allowed Laclede to serve an area of expanding population adjacent to its extended distribution system.

Customers in the area had been served by central propane distribution systems that were put in place by Laclede during the 1970s in anticipation of natural gas being available in the future. In 1993, Eureka and nearby residential developments finally were converted to natural gas service.

In June 1992, the Eureka Board of Aldermen unanimously approved an extension of the city's franchise agreement with Laclede. During the winter of 1993, Laclede completed construction of a 5.7-mile extension of an 8-inch pipeline into Eureka to connect the utility's first natural gas customers in that area. After the connecting pipeline construction phase was completed in January 1994, crews began installation of the distribution lines in the spring and completed them later that year.

Laclede already had converted several propane customers and potential new customers to natural gas at The Legends resort community in November 1993. The utility then began contacting current propane customers in two other residential subdivisions to explain the benefits of converting to natural gas. During the expansion, Laclede made

THE GREAT FLOOD OF 1993

Because of the permanent nature of the utility infrastructure, companies such as Laclede Gas are indelibly identified with the communities they serve. When natural disaster strikes, the utility work force is there to make sure that the gas continues to be available, and when that primary task has been accomplished, their attention is turned to helping neighbors in need. Such was the case with Laclede and its employees during the flooding of a large area of metropolitan St. Louis in the summer of 1993.

The 1993 flood was one of the most severe ever recorded in the Mississippi Valley, exceeded only by the massive flooding on the Lower River in the spring of 1927. The Great Flood of 1993 caused tremendous damage in the upper Midwest, although relatively few lives were lost due to the slow-developing nature of the flood…which allowed adequate warning and emergency preparation. The immediate cause of the flood was unusually high precipitation in Iowa, Missouri and Kansas beginning in late spring and peaking in June. Tributaries of the Mississippi River began to flood in June, and the water steadily moved south and east into the main channels.

In mid to late July, heavy rains began farther north and west in North Dakota, Nebraska, Kansas and Missouri, and record flooding started on rivers in all of those states. The Missouri River crested at 48.9 feet at Kansas City on July 27, breaking by 2.7 feet the previous record crest set in 1951. The crest pushed on down the Missouri River, setting new records at Boonville, Jefferson City, Hermann, St. Charles and other Missouri locations.

The record flow joined the already full Mississippi River just north of St. Louis and pushed the Mississippi to a record crest of 49.47 feet at St. Louis on August 1. In all, 92 locations set new record crests during the Great Flood of 1993. At its height, the flood covered nine states and inundated nearly 400,000 square miles.

The flood event was so big it simply overwhelmed everything in its path. As Mark Twain said 100 years ago, the Mississippi River "cannot be tamed, curbed or confined; you cannot bar its path with an obstruction which it will not tear down, dance over and laugh at."

Many Laclede employees volunteered their time, serving on the front lines of the fight against the rising rivers during the Great Flood of 1993. Flood duties involved sandbagging, helping to establish Salvation Army relief centers, collecting cash and canned goods, and cleaning up flooded homes. Many employees helped out during their off-duty hours to lend a hand to friends and strangers in need.

Greg Mee, who worked at Laclede's underground storage facility, asked the Salvation Army how he could help after driving by a riverside location where staffers were setting up a canteen. Mee volunteered and helped establish the Salvation Army canteen at Highways 367 and 94 in St. Charles County, and he also assisted with a variety of other tasks assigned by Salvation Army organizers.

Bill Cown, superintendent, materials and supplies, spent part of his vacation sandbagging. He gave up his annual fishing trip in order to sandbag for three days along the River Des Peres in South St. Louis County.

Don Leong, area supervisor, customer service, took his son and daughter with him to fill in sandbags for the River Des Peres levee in South St. Louis. He thought the experience would help his children realize the value of helping others.

Laclede employees also helped flood victims by contributing cash and other needed items to various relief agencies and to individuals. Laclede Gas matched employee contributions to help support the work of the Salvation Army and other flood relief efforts.

Although the Great Flood of 1993 was an extraordinary event, it showed the courage and resourcefulness of people helping others cope during a time of enormous stress. Laclede employees were no exception. Once they had ensured the city's gas supply was safe, they began their significant contributions to the flood effort. Laclede employees' response to the crisis was something the community had come to expect.

---

natural gas service available to several new subdivisions then under construction in the Eureka community. Laclede also began providing natural gas service to the new Times Beach dioxin incinerator in February 1994.

Robert M. Lee, vice president of marketing, told Laclede News that the utility "had long intended to some day bring natural gas service to Eureka. We already had several propane installations there — at The Legends, Stonebridge Mobile Home Court and the Shaw's Gardens Apartments. We were bringing service to nearby communities, such as Pacific. Now, the timing is right and Laclede is bringing service through the city of Eureka and to the site at Times Beach."

Natural gas desiccant systems, like the one used by the Schnucks retail grocery chain, save on cooling costs, as well as improving the attractiveness of the displays by eliminating frost on product.

In continuing the expansion into St. Charles, Jefferson and Franklin Counties, Laclede continually demonstrated its ability to deliver natural gas as the most efficient fuel for potential customers in the fast-growing counties surrounding the St. Louis metropolitan core.

Utilizing New Technologies

Laclede's rapid penetration of the new home and office construction market in the quickly growing suburbs of St. Louis during the 1990s was due as much to new technology as it was to marketing.

In order to appreciate the benefits of a natural gas desiccant system, one only had to experience the heat and humidity of a St. Louis summer. It has long been known that the higher the humidity, the hotter the air feels. When the humidity decreases, such as following prolonged rainstorms, the heat feels more tolerable even though the temperature may still be the same. The same principle applies to the heating and cooling of a commercial, industrial or office building. If the inside humidity decreases, it takes less energy to cool the building because the inside air has already become more comfortable.

Laclede's vigorous pursuit of the emerging air conditioning, refrigeration and dehumidification markets won the utility national recognition. In May 1998, at the Gas Cooling Technology Conference and Exposition in Philadelphia, Laclede won the prestigious Rising Star Award.

The key to Laclede's Rising Star Award was the superior dehumidification properties inherent to gas desiccant systems. Laclede began helping commercial and industrial customers reduce indoor humidity through the use of natural gas desiccant systems during the mid-1990s. Laclede and manufacturer crews installed new systems in selected Schnucks and Wal-Mart stores, Anheuser-Busch Breweries and Sigma Chemical facilities.

A desiccant attracts and removes moisture from the surrounding air and thus lowers the humidity. A common type of desiccant familiar to the typical consumer is the small packet of silica gel enclosed in the box with new cameras or placed inside some new leather purses. Salt also is a natural desiccant.

Desiccants used to remove moisture or humidity from the air save on cooling costs, keep the air healthy, prevent mold and mildew damage, and help to stabilize air temperature and humidity in the manufacture of sensitive products like computer chips and pharmaceuticals.

The customer transition to natural gas desiccant systems allowed Laclede to sell more natural gas during the summer, when demand was low, to industrial and large commercial customers. This allowed them to raise their thermostats

1998
In May, at the Gas Cooling Technology Conference and Exposition in Philadelphia, Laclede won the prestigious Rising Star Award.

and thus lower their use of electricity as required for the operation of electric air conditioning systems.

Supermarkets such as Schnucks particularly liked the concept because desiccant chillers allowed the stores to raise their electric cooling thermostats from 70 to 75 degrees. The lower humidity levels also reduced the cost of cooling frozen food. In addition the drier air made the frozen food displays look more attractive, because individual items no longer were covered with frost.

Laclede engineers continued to look for new markets that could benefit from low humidity, better air quality, lower electrical costs and a quick payback on installation. This newest technology showed that natural gas remained the preferred choice for many of Laclede's commercial customers.

Abundant Gas for Business

Dating from the time of conversion to straight natural gas, Laclede had been growing to be the dominant force in space heating and water heating. By 1998, 98 percent of new single houses being built were equipped with gas heating, and in the multi-family market, Laclede installed gas service for heating and other purposes in 88 percent more units in 1985 than it did in 1984. As part of Laclede's marketing efforts, the utility also looked at the impressive program of new construction and urban renewal taking place in downtown St. Louis.

When the St. Louis Centre opened in 1985, Laclede Gas was at the forefront of the expansion, supplying new retail and commercial customers with gas service.

At that time, St. Louis Centre was the largest enclosed downtown shopping center in the United States. The next year, Laclede supplied several key customers with natural gas at St. Louis Union Station, including the new Omni Hotel.

Supplying the renovated Union Station with gas service required the installation of new main facilities in the area, as well as a new pressure reduction regulator station on the site. The new gas facilities also enabled Laclede to

1998
Ninety eight percent of new single houses being built were equipped with gas heating.

150 Year Anniversary **161**

ROBERT C. JAUDES

Much of Laclede's progress in the 1990s happened on the watch of Bob Jaudes. As the 1980s wound to a close, the St. Louis native assumed he would wrap up his career at Laclede as the capable second-in-command to Donald Novatny, who had succeeded Lee Liberman as president and CEO in 1989. But Novatny's decision to retire the next year elevated Jaudes to the utility's top position. Jaudes would ably guide Laclede through one of its most spectacular periods of growth between 1990 and 1999.

Robert C. Jaudes was a native St. Louisan, born in 1933. He attended McKinley High School in south St. Louis, graduating in 1951. Jaudes joined the company in 1955 following graduation from Washington University with a Bachelor of Science degree in chemical engineering. Jaudes recalled going "to work in the Laclede lab located at Station A on Rutger Street, and I ended up working as a district design engineer at 3950 Forest Park Avenue, where I worked until March 1956 when I went into the U.S. Army."

Jaudes rejoined Laclede following his military service, serving as a standards engineer and then as a construction standards engineer in the engineering department. "My goal was to be chief engineer," Jaudes said, "and I worked in the engineering department until about 1960. Then I went to work for Delmer Hassenridder, Laclede's assistant vice president of operations, who had been a longtime executive of St. Louis County Gas. I worked for him from 1959 until 1962. We were considered the standards group, because we looked at everything the company did operationally, including how we dug holes, how we installed meters and laid pipelines."

In the early 1960s, Jaudes' work brought him to the attention of Liberman, who was then vice president of planning. In 1963 and 1964, Jaudes performed several special assignment projects for Liberman, including work on the regulatory treatment of company costs such as depreciation and utility plan valuation.

"I was asked to come down to 1017 Olive to work as a rate engineer," Jaudes said. "Lee Liberman had been performing those functions, and I was told to go and work for Lee for six months because it would be good experience."

In 1964, Jaudes became assistant superintendent of construction and maintenance. In 1966, he again was tapped by Liberman to serve as his staff assistant, where he worked on rates, gas supply and general regulatory matters.

"In 1966 I came back downtown for the last time to work for Lee Liberman. The rest of my career continued in one capacity or another with Lee until he retired," Jaudes said.

In 1973, when Liberman was named president, Jaudes filled the newly created position of assistant to the president. He was elected vice president of administration in 1975, senior vice president of operations and marketing in 1977, and in 1983 was elected to the company's board of directors.

Jaudes remembered the 1970s as a challenging time for Laclede Gas. When the nation struggled with a pervasive shortage of natural gas, Jaudes served as a principal architect of Laclede's successful efforts to keep the St. Louis area fully supplied. This activity included the expansion of the company's underground storage and propane peak-shaving capabilities and the protection of Laclede's pipeline gas supplies during federal regulatory proceedings. Jaudes worked closely with Rex Bannister, the vice president of marketing who was in charge of Laclede's exploration program.

Throughout the late 1970s and early 1980s, Jaudes worked alongside Liberman to develop Laclede's positions on key industry issues, such as gas supply, deregulation and gas pricing. He testified extensively before the Missouri Public Service Commission, the Federal Power Commission and its successor, the Federal Energy Regulatory Commission. After Congress enacted the Natural Gas Policy Act of 1978, Jaudes again worked with Liberman to ensure the utility's compliance with deregulation initiatives.

In 1986, Jaudes was promoted to executive vice president-finance, and in 1989 became executive vice president-operations and marketing. In 1990, he was elected the 14th president of Laclede Gas. In 1991, he assumed the additional title of chief executive officer. At Laclede Gas Company's annual meeting on January 24, 1994, Jaudes was elected chairman of the board.

During his 43 years with Laclede Gas, Jaudes was active in the community, serving on the board of directors of the Missouri Historical Society, the YMCA of Greater St. Louis, general chairman of the St. Louis United Way Campaign that raised nearly $60 million, and as chairman of the Salvation Army's 1993-1994 Tree of Lights Campaign, which raised $3.6 million.

Jaudes retired in January 1999 at the age of 65, and he continued to serve on the board of directors until 2004.

economically install additional services in the vicinity of Union Station that would be needed in the future.

The availability of abundant gas supplies carried over into the 1990s, and Laclede continued to court in an aggressive manner potential new retail and commercial customers. When the St. Louis Science Center and the Galleria Shopping Center opened in the late 1980s and early 1990s, both specified gas for heating and cooling.

In 1997, the Riverport Casino Center opened in Maryland Heights as a Laclede customer. The new development included four casinos floating on barges in a man-made basin fed by the Missouri River. In addition, the land-based portion of the complex included a 300-room hotel, two restaurants and other amenities. A development of this size is equivalent in natural gas sales to the addition of 750 residential gas customers. Laclede worked closely with the casino architects for more than a year in planning for the construction of gas service in the area.

The Promise of Natural Gas Vehicles

In the fall of 1992, Laclede added to its fleet two GMC Sierra pickup trucks and five Dodge 350 vans that were manufactured to be fueled by natural gas. For the first time, American automobile manufacturers produced dedicated natural gas vehicles, not vehicles converted from the use of other types of fuel such as gasoline or diesel.

During the 1970s and early 1980s, Laclede had operated its own fleet of 300 dual-fuel cars, trucks and vans for more than ten years. The company ceased their use when they were gradually made obsolete by advancements in fuel injection and computer-controlled automobile engine technology.

By 1992, Laclede was in the process of sampling new natural gas vehicles plus a variety of modern alternative fuel equipment. Laclede planned to offer customers guidance to meet emissions limits mandated by 1990 amendments to the Federal Clean Air Act.

The increase in the cost of reformulated clean diesel and gasoline provided a strong incentive for the development of natural gas vehicles. In addition, the Clean Air Act amendments also mandated a national vapor recovery system for service stations, vehicle emissions tests and the use of clean vehicle fuels.

Other agencies such as the Missouri Highway & Transportation Department and the Missouri Department of Natural Resources were either converting existing vehicles to run on natural gas or starting test programs to evaluate the use of natural gas vehicles (NGVs). State agencies used operation and maintenance data made available by Laclede to make informed decisions regarding the alternative fuel vehicles.

The use of natural gas in vehicles was not new. Compressed natural gas (CNG) was used as a transportation fuel in a number of countries beginning in the 1930s. In a CNG vehicle, natural gas is compressed and stored in cylinders mounted in or recessed beneath the trunk or undercarriage. The compressed gas passes through a shut-off valve and a regulator to lower its pressure as it enters

1997
During the first phase of the four-phase project, Bi-State could fill 50 compressed natural gas buses in 4.6 hours.

in the engine compartment. It enters the carburetor and is mixed with air; it then flows into the engine's combustion chamber and is ignited to create power. Special valves prevent the gas from entering the engine when the engine is turned off.

Crews at Laclede's Shrewsbury Service Center modified and upgraded a CNG compressor to supply company vehicles with natural gas at the necessary pressure. By the fall of 1995, Laclede was using 34 CNG vehicles, including 27 vans, two trucks, three cars and two forklifts. Sixteen of the CNG vehicles were conversions, while the remaining vehicles were purchased directly from the manufacturer.

Laclede also opened St. Louis' first public CNG fueling station in 1995 at the Shrewsbury facility. Public agencies such as the U.S. Postal Service and the St. Louis City Police Department fueled their fleet of vehicles at the facility. The city of Shrewsbury allowed Laclede to refuel 40 public agency CNG vehicles at the Shrewsbury station, in addition to Laclede's own fleet of 34 CNG vans and trucks. The number of public CNG vehicles served increased after a year following approval by the city of Shrewsbury.

Laclede demonstrated that it was offering a solution to the ongoing air emissions problem in St. Louis. In the years to come, the utility would remain committed to the development of clean-fuel natural gas vehicles.

A Big Step Forward

Laclede's efforts to encourage the acceptance of natural gas vehicles in St. Louis took a big step forward in July 1996 when the utility concluded an agreement with the Bi-State Development Agency to finance, construct and maintain a fast-fill compressed natural gas fueling station at Bi-State's Brentwood garage. Bi-State operated a fleet of buses in the Missouri and Illinois counties that made up the St. Louis metropolitan area. Laclede Venture Corporation, a non-utility subsidiary, was assigned the lead role in NGV development work.

For some time, because of its membership in the St. Louis Regional Clean Air Partnership, Laclede had been touting the benefits of CNG as a clean alternative to diesel fuel in Bi-State's fleet of buses. The U.S. Department of Energy also encouraged the use of alternate fuels to help improve air quality. The desire for cleaner air brought Laclede and Bi-State together.

Two years before Laclede and Bi-State reached the agreement, they had conducted a three-year pilot program in which Bi-State successfully tested two CNG-fueled buses on various routes throughout its system, which spanned the metropolitan region. Agency officials decided that CNG was an attractive option that would help meet increasingly stringent environmental regulations.

In 1997, during the first phase of the four-phase project, Bi-State could fill 50 compressed natural gas buses in 4.6 hours. Each of the 50 buses used the equivalent of the annual natural gas consumption of 13 typical homes.

Even though there had been cooperative CNG efforts between public utilities and transit agencies in other parts of the country, the St. Louis partnership was significantly different because of Laclede's level of direct participation in financing, construction and maintenance of the Brentwood fueling station. Through its participation in the project, Laclede helped Bi-State avoid many of the pitfalls and logistical problems that fleet owners typically experienced when they began operating their own fueling facility.

The benefits of the partnership for Laclede and Bi-State were obvious. Vehicles powered by clean-burning natural gas regularly showed a decrease in fuel and maintenance costs. For Laclede, the sale of natural gas for vehicles represented a significant new market not influenced by weather conditions, and constant throughout the year.

July 1997 marked a milestone in Laclede's decade-long effort to encourage the development of a larger market for CNG vehicles. After Phase One of the Bi-State project was completed, Bi-State had the capability of fueling nearly 200 CNG buses.

A Growing Environmental Consciousness

Laclede's work with CNG was just one facet of a new environmental reality that was making its presence felt in American society. As St. Louis and the nation grew more environmentally conscious in the 1980s and 1990s, Laclede reflected the environmentalism that was rapidly becoming essential to the maintenance

Laclede Gas and Bi-State Development Agency jointly conducted a three-year pilot program by testing CNG-fueled buses throughout the metropolitan region.

150 Year Anniversary

of the American economy, known in the 20th Century as "the green movement."

Burning natural gas for heating and cooking was far preferable to the consumption of other fossil fuels, such as coal and oil. Air emissions dropped dramatically when burning natural gas instead of coal, thereby making the environment cleaner. One glaring historical example was the massive smoke problem that St. Louis experienced during the 1930s, brought on by the burning of soft, bituminous coal for both industrial and residential use. The problem was largely eliminated during the late 1940s when Laclede converted its system to straight natural gas.

Laclede Gas promoted other environmental programs to enhance the quality of life of employees and customers. By 1995, Laclede was in the midst of a 10-year program to monitor and control asbestos in order to ensure the safety of its employees. Asbestos had long been used as a fireproofing material, but by the 1970s, the metallic fibers had been identified as a potential carcinogen. Suspected asbestos-containing materials in Laclede facilities built before the 1950s were identified and marked with new labels and signs. The labels were intended to warn people not to disturb certain materials without proper safeguards and permission.

Under Laclede's building work permit program, any employee who was performing work that might disturb building materials or insulation in an area that was suspected of containing asbestos first was required to obtain permission from one of Laclede's designated asbestos compliance staff.

Asbestos programs and associated awareness training were designed to ensure that Laclede employees did not improperly handle asbestos-containing materials.

Laclede also was a co-sponsor of the U.S. Department of Energy's first conference for its Clean Cities Program, held in St. Louis during the fall of 1995. The company demonstrated its interest in addressing the real-life challenges of increasing the use of alternative transportation fuels in America's major metropolitan areas.

By August 1997, 10 companies in the St. Louis area including Laclede, were operating CNG powered vehicles. Additionally, a number of public agencies and companies, such as Procter & Gamble and Boeing, had converted their fleets of forklifts to CNG. In 1997, Shell Oil opened the first service station that made CNG fueling capability available to be used directly by the public.

Laclede's environmental initiatives demonstrated that the utility regarded its commitment to clean air as an investment in the future of St. Louis.

As that future entered a new millennium, Laclede Gas could look back on the 1990s as a decade of growth and accomplishment. The 21st century would bring new challenges, including rising gas prices and competitive business pressures. But Laclede, as it had demonstrated so many times before, would be equal to the new challenges.

1997
Shell Oil opened the first service station that made CNG fueling capability available to be used directly by the public.

INTERLUDE 4

The Era of Deregulation

After the near catastrophic collapse of natural gas markets during the late 1970s, pipeline and local distribution company executives might have been forgiven for thinking that the industry had survived the brunt of the regulatory storm. Instead, the natural gas industry was whipsawed during the 1980s by two perhaps unforeseen results of passage of the Natural Gas Policy Act of 1978.

Gas supplies rebounded sharply after the 1979-1980 heating season, placing the industry in a surplus position that it did not emerge from until mid-decade. And a deregulation mandate laid down by the 1978 legislation transformed the industry during the 1980s, creating a model by 1990 for other segments of the nation's utility industry.

Far from proposing new legislation to regulate natural gas supplies and prices, the federal government began moving toward a complete deregulation of the industry, a process put in motion by the passage of the Natural Gas Policy Act of 1978.

Initially, the Natural Gas Policy Act operated in much the way it was designed. Sharply higher wellhead prices stimulated exploration and attracted drillers back into the natural gas market. From the late 1970s and early 1980s on, a great deal of new gas came on stream as a result of development drilling and new exploration drilling. Local distribution companies had to contract for as much gas as they could reasonably purchase.

Local distribution companies across the eastern half of the United States wanted to replenish the storage system so that when gas started to become available, they could acquire as much gas as possible. Replenishing gas storage was an expensive proposition. By 1982, most local distribution companies estimated that purchasing the gas they needed to supply customers accounted for 75 percent or more of the utility's costs.

In addition, the sharply escalating prices of natural gas after 1978 reached a level of price resistance by the mid-1980s. Natural gas consumers began conserving. Industrial and large commercial customers registered dissatisfaction with price increases by fuel switching to propane, fuel oil, coal and electric power. Propane and fuel oil were particularly suited to fuel switching, since most industrial natural gas boilers were fully capable of burning the alternate fuels.

Nature conspired to worsen the situation for the local distribution utilities. The winter of 1982-1983 was one of the warmest on record across the Midwest. By late March 1983, the heating season was 15 percent warmer than normal across Missouri, Illinois, Indiana and Ohio, and 21 percent warmer than the preceding winter. Meanwhile, because of price decontrols at the wellhead, natural gas rates to the average residential customer in the region had climbed some 60 percent in just one year.

For most local distribution companies, the collapse of the gas markets in the early 1980s required painfully unprecedented steps. Many of the gas contracts negotiated during the shortage of 1978-1979 had to be renegotiated because local

In today's deregulated, highly competitive energy environment, the availability of a reliable, economic supply of natural gas cannot be taken for granted. In the photo below, Laclede's Construction and Maintenance crews oversee the installation of the regulator station for the interconnect with the Southern Star (Williams) pipeline in St. Charles County.

distribution companies could no longer use the volumes of gas contracted for. The 1981-1983 period in particular was characterized by numerous lawsuits and countersuits alleging breach of contract between and among producers, pipelines and local distribution companies.

"I spent a lot of my time in D.C. before the Federal Energy Regulatory Commission testifying on take-or-pay contracts," Doug Yaeger recalled of his duties with pipeline supplier MRT during the early 1980s. "The gas bubble started when supplies were more plentiful, and more marketing was needed. Pipelines would try to bypass suppliers such as Laclede and hook up customers directly."

For producers, pipeline firms and distribution companies, the 1978-1985 period was an era of supply instability and price volatility similar to the situation that existed in the early 1930s. The deregulation of natural gas effective January 1, 1985 also meant that producers, pipeline companies and local distribution utilities had to learn how to operate an entirely new way.

The deregulation of the natural gas industry set into motion by the Natural Gas Policy Act of 1978 continued unabated into the early 1990s. The Federal Energy Regulatory Commission (FERC) 1990 Notice of Proposed Regulation (NOPR) set the stage for the next level of deregulation of the industry. Known to gas industry observers as the Mega-NOPR, the proposal was designed to accomplish several objectives, according to its backers.

The Mega-NOPR, also known as FERC Orders 436 and 500, ordered pipelines to provide equal access to their lines for the transportation of natural gas. According to FERC, this step essentially allowed utility or industrial customers to buy gas at the wellhead and transport the gas via the natural gas pipeline to either a community or an industrial consumer.

The onset of the FERC Mega-NOPR marked a new era in the natural gas industry. After 1990, it became advantageous for pipeline companies to have a subsidiary that could deal in aggregating supplies and transporting the gas via the pipeline to the end-user.

"In 1992, Order 636 took the pipelines out of the merchant functions of gas supply," Yaeger explained. "They could no longer buy and resell gas. Laclede now had to buy gas directly from producers and arrange for its own pipeline transportation. This now meant that we had to decide to sell or store any gas that we had to buy. This necessitated setting up a whole new gas supply department."

To take advantage of the new marketing freedom, Laclede Gas established a gas marketing subsidiary, Laclede Energy Resources (LER). A non-regulated marketer of natural gas that marketed to both large retail and wholesale customers in the Midwestern United States, the majority of LER's retail customers were large commercial and industrial customers located in the St. Louis metropolitan area. In addition, LER served a number of large retail customers located elsewhere in Missouri, Iowa, Illinois, Arkansas and Louisiana. LER also offered customers a variety of flexible pricing alternatives.

Just 10 weeks before the nation's natural gas business was tested in the crucible of the coldest weather to ever hit the eastern half of North America, the gas industry began dealing with the most wide-ranging deregulation scenario experienced by utilities in the 20th century. On November 1, 1993, FERC's Order 636 went into effect nationwide.

Not since before passage of the federal Natural Gas Act had the industry had to contend with such a sweeping lack of regulation. For the first time in more than half a century, natural gas pipeline companies were free to engage in unfettered competition.

Prior to the implementation of Order 636, local distribution companies signed long-term contracts with pipeline companies for up to 20 years of natural gas supply. Even before Order 636 was promulgated, local distribution companies had begun gaining experience dealing with independent brokers and marketers during the winter heating seasons of the early 1990s.

Under the terms of Order 636, a local distribution company nominated its daily natural gas needs from suppliers. If demand exceeded supply, the company was required to use storage gas and propane plant production capacity to supplement natural gas flowing through the utility's lines.

Pipeline companies could no longer sell gas directly to local distribution companies. Instead, the local distribution companies could buy gas directly from natural gas suppliers and marketers. Industrial customers also could buy gas from natural gas suppliers and use the gas system of the pipeline company and the local distribution companies to transport the gas.

Prior to Order 636, Laclede Gas purchased the majority of its gas supply from Mississippi River Transmission Corporation (MRT). When MRT was removed from the merchant function and could no longer market gas to customers, Laclede was left to line up its own suppliers, as well as perform pipeline nominations to ensure shipment of the gas to its marketing area.

For the first two years after the Order went into effect, MRT assisted Laclede in establishing a gas supply and transportation department, since Laclede had no experience in this area. Laclede then was able to bring those functions in-house, eventually expanding its supply slate to include a variety of different suppliers to set up transportation and storage arrangements accordingly.

The gas supply process changed dramatically in the 1990s. The federal deregulation of producer prices created an open and highly competitive market. The price of natural gas supplies was established by the economic balancing of nationwide supply and demand, along with all the other vagaries that traditionally influenced a commodity market. With the complete unbundling of the pipeline transmission process, local distribution companies such as Laclede were forced to make their own supply, storage and transportation arrangements, assuming both greater responsibility and greater risk at the local distribution company level.

By the early part of the 21st century, Laclede had made great strides in addressing challenges within the company's natural gas distribution business through internal improvements and innovative rate structures. But Laclede also discovered that external challenges needed to be addressed.

The lack of a meaningful, comprehensive national energy policy focused on improving accessibility to on-shore and offshore domestic natural gas reserves continued to cloud the future of supply and pricing during the early 2000s. The impact of natural disasters such as Hurricane Katrina in 2005 exposed the fragility of domestic natural gas supplies, which remained tight, resulting in upward pricing pressure in the increasingly competitive 21st century national market for natural gas.

Around the clock, System Control monitors pressure and flow rates through the more than 16,000 miles of Laclede's pipelines. During an average winter month, the company distributes 600 million cubic feet of natural gas per day.

CHAPTER 14

The Laclede Group

For most Americans, the dawn of the 21st century was a time of uncertainty. Software experts worried that Y2K would require months of writing new code language to keep computer networks from crashing on January 1, 2000. They did not, but it took weeks for America to determine who was elected president in November 2000 when the race for the White House turned on some disputed ballots in Florida.

Less than a year after George W. Bush was inaugurated, America was devastated when Islamic fundamentalists flew airplanes into New York's World Trade Center and the Pentagon in Washington, D.C. The carnage of 9/11 united a nation in a crusade against terror and served notice that the world had inexorably changed that bright, but catastrophic, September Tuesday morning.

For Laclede, the upheavals of the 21st century were more subtle. Deregulation of the utility's core distribution business changed the way Laclede bought and delivered gas to customers. Growth in the core business was restricted, however, by the long-term population decline of St. Louis service territory and by the inevitable price destabilization brought about by potential shortages of natural gas. To plan for continued growth in the 21st century, Laclede had to investigate creative ways to grow outside of its core distribution business.

The Importance of Strategic Planning

At the start of the new millennium, Laclede embarked upon a strategic planning initiative to chart a future course for the company and to plan for continued growth. Laclede was seeking flexibility as a means of expanding its business, as well as a blueprint for the new direction the company would pursue in the coming years.

In the summer of 2000, Laclede launched a major planning initiative. Employees across the company were involved in the review so that the company could assess where it had been, where it was going, where it needed to go and how best to get there. Following the review, Laclede developed a strategic

Doug Yaeger discusses the strategic planning and continued growth of the company with members of the executive council. The corporate structure was reorganized in the form of a holding company, The Laclede Group in 2001.

plan. In Laclede's core utility business, management would work to stabilize core earnings. At the same time, Laclede would strive to improve operational performance and customer service. Shareholder return was to be enhanced by adding growth components to the core business income.

As a critical step in the process, the board of directors unanimously approved the strategic planning team's recommendation that Laclede's corporate structure should be reorganized in the form of a holding company. Unlike the holding company concept of the 1930s, the holding company would be subject to local control. Under the plan, Laclede Gas would become a wholly owned subsidiary of The Laclede Group, as the new holding company was known. Each of the other separate operating companies within the organization also would become subsidiaries of The Laclede Group.

Doug Yaeger, Laclede's chairman of the board, president and CEO, recalled that "we set up The Laclede Group as a holding company concept in order to give us more flexibility to look at any new business ventures that made sense. Laclede Gas has 85 percent of the gas market and more than 90 percent of any new construction in the St. Louis metropolitan area. In a stagnant market, we can look at other ventures that will make us money. Laclede Gas is so heavily regulated that the concept of the holding company gives us room to maneuver in looking at different businesses."

As a utility, Laclede Gas remained regulated and would continue as the core business. But The Laclede Group was to be unregulated and free to pursue other business ventures that made sense from both a profit and an operational standpoint. Growth through acquisitions was an important part of the expansion strategy, but only if the acquisitions demonstrated a strategic fit and provided an appropriate return on investment with minimal risk.

After receiving approval from the Missouri Public Service Commission in the summer of 2001, The Laclede Group became operational effective October 1, 2001, the start of the company's fiscal year.

A year later, the board reaffirmed that the company's strategic direction was sound. Laclede also launched a business planning process in which department managers were charged with defining their department's business objectives for a three-year planning horizon by identifying the needs of four primary stakeholders: customers, the community, employees and shareholders.

Laclede's new form of planning involved an innovative way of thinking and working. The company continued to provide safe, reliable natural gas service to the community, but the plan also created a road map that allowed Laclede to improve upon things it could do better.

The plan established a more solid business foundation within the utility arena. It also gave Laclede the ability to leverage its knowledge of the gas industry so that the company could expand into non-regulated areas that had a higher growth potential than had traditionally been achieved during the post-World War II era of regulated gas distribution.

2001
The Laclede Group became operational effective October 1, the start of the company's fiscal year.

As home construction expands into fast-growing Franklin County, Missouri Natural Gas expands the company's distribution system by installing fuel runs in a new development in Washington, Missouri.

2004
Laclede added 2,533 new residential customers in St. Charles County, representing nearly half of the metropolitan area's total residential customer connections.

The Shift to the Suburbs

Laclede's core business had been healthy and profitable during the early years of the 21st century, but residential gas growth lagged other components of the utility's business. St. Louis County operations actually lost a small number of customers during the first five years of the 2000s. Meanwhile, however, the suburban counties north and west of the old city of St. Louis were growing at a rate of 5-10 percent during the period.

By 2004, Laclede was gaining new natural gas customers because of strong growth throughout the St. Louis metropolitan area. In fact, Laclede had seen close to a 7 percent increase overall in new residential customers, which included single-family detached and attached homes, and multi-family homes. The major focus of that growth was in St. Charles County, thanks to several massive residential developments and an abundance of available land for new construction. In 2004 alone, Laclede added 2,533 new residential customers in St. Charles County, representing nearly half of the metropolitan area's total residential customer connections.

To prepare for the expansion into St. Charles County, Laclede had carried out a consolidation two years earlier, in September 2002. The company consolidated St. Charles Gas Company into Laclede Gas and Midwest Missouri Gas Company into the utility's Missouri Natural Gas Division. The consolidation streamlined operations in both St. Charles and Jefferson counties.

The increase in new connections outside of St. Louis County in the first years of the 21st century were explained by a number of factors, including improvements in existing sewer, water and highway infrastructure plus the abundance of large parcels of undeveloped land that made Jefferson County, in particular, attractive for residential and small commercial development. Several builders who had previously limited their construction efforts to St. Louis and St. Charles counties began building projects in Missouri Natural's service area.

Jefferson County became a hotbed of commercial development, with a total of 150 new commercial customers added in 2004. The greatest area of increase was in the Missouri Natural Gas service area where 128 new customers were added, a 49 percent gain over commercial additions in 2003. The reason for the growth was quite simple.

Tom Reitz, superintendent of service and division operations at Laclede, summed it up well when he noted that a growing number of people were "seeking more spacious lots, while for others it was a more affordable home that attracted them to the Jefferson County area. Before now, there were only a limited number of builders and developers that targeted these areas. So while the growth had been steady, it was still somewhat slow." Reitz also pointed out that "once the larger builders became involved, the residential market began increasing at a more rapid pace."

During fiscal 2005, Laclede continued to expand its customer base with the addition of 6,000 new residential connections. The strongest growth continued to be St. Charles and Jefferson counties

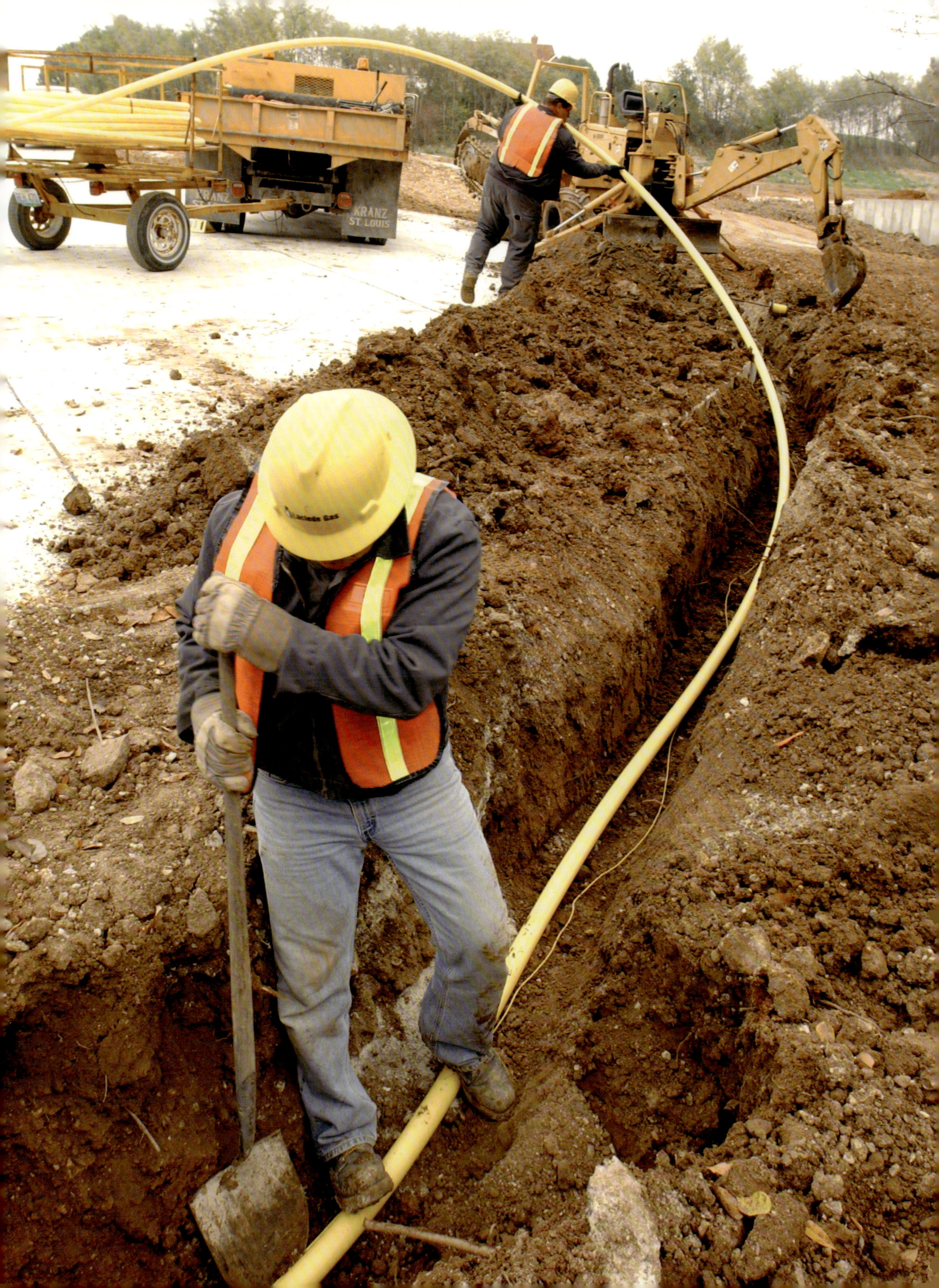
KRANZ
ST LOUIS
Laclede Gas

DOUG YAEGER

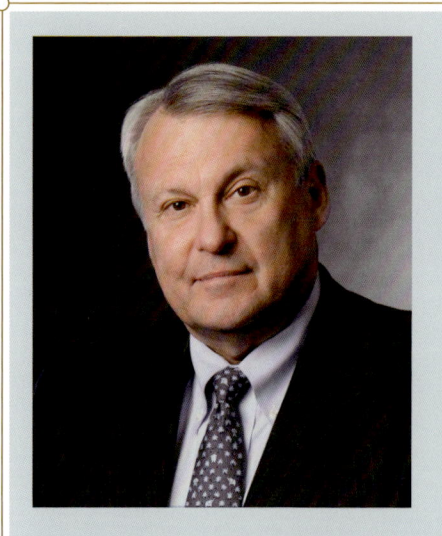

Elected president, chief executive officer and chairman of the board of Laclede Gas Company in 1999 at age 49, Doug Yaeger had already been in the interstate gas pipeline industry for nearly 20 years before joining Laclede in 1990. He spent the first two decades of his career at Mississippi River Transmission Company (MRT), rising to the position of executive vice president in the late 1980s.

"I spent a great deal of time in the marketing and sales departments," Yaeger said in a 2006 interview. "There were gas shortages in the early 1970s so the marketing function was defined by obtaining more supplies, so all of the pipelines had curtailment plans that would dictate which customer groups would get certain amounts of supply during shortage periods. We would forecast load for three days running when the weather was cold, and we would have to inform customers of their supply allocation."

A native of the St. Louis region, Yaeger graduated from Webster Groves High School before earning a bachelor's degree in marketing from Miami University of Ohio in 1971. He joined MRT (then the Mississippi River Fuel Corp.) and began his 35-year career in the natural gas industry. Yaeger earned an M.B.A. from St. Louis University in 1976.

While at MRT, Yaeger was exposed to some of the most critical issues in the long history of the natural gas industry in America. The 1970s and 1980s were watershed years for the industry, encompassing widespread shortages and a major deregulation initiative.

Yaeger joined Laclede in 1990 as vice president-planning. "At first, I didn't have much day-to-day responsibility, so I spent a lot of time at the Forest Park Operations Center learning the distribution side of the business," he said. "I also put in a lot of time with Bob Davis, who built much of the Laclede system."

In 1992, Yaeger earned a degree in the advanced management program at Harvard Business School.

When he came to Laclede, one of the first things Yaeger noticed was the pride and tradition providing reliable gas service.

"We continue to recognize that gas is our core competency, but we now look at other businesses if they make sense to our organization. And the people at Laclede have made that change without missing a beat," Yaeger said in a 2007 speech.

During the 1990s, Yaeger was successively promoted to senior vice president-operations, gas supply & technical services in 1992, then executive vice president-operations and marketing in 1995, followed by president & chief operating officer, as well as being appointed to the board of directors in 1997 and, chairman of the board, president & chief executive officer in 1999.

Throughout his career, Yaeger has been active in natural gas industry organizations and the St. Louis region. He serves on the board of directors of the American Gas Association and the board of the Missouri Energy Development Association (MEDA). In 2007, he became chairman of MEDA's board. He is on the board and is past chair of the Southern Gas Association. He also serves on the boards of the St. Louis Regional Chamber and Growth Association — a group that he chaired during 2003 and 2004 — the St. Louis Science Center Board of Commissioners and Webster University and was the president of Civic Progress from February 2005 through July 2007.

During his tenure at Laclede, he has assisted the company in transitioning from one that relied totally on MRT to supply all of its gas needs to a company that now has total responsibility for that function.

"We had to manage our own gas supply portfolio, nominating the gas for delivery, making sure it was delivered and finding supplies to purchase on the open market," Yaeger explained. "I know that those of us who were here at the time, myself included, had to learn an entirely new way of getting gas to our customers."

In the 21st century, Yaeger helped position Laclede for future change and growth. In October 2001, the company set up The Laclede Group as a holding company in order to give management more flexibility to look at new businesses.

"The acquisition of SM&P of Carmel, Indiana made sense since it is a pipe and main location provider, and its market is primarily in the Midwest," Yaeger said. "And one success story that I think everyone at Laclede Gas should take great pride in is Laclede Energy Resources, the company's non-regulated natural gas marketing unit. Both are key components of our holding company structure."

Doug Yaeger's tenure at the helm of Laclede Gas has been marked by change fully as momentous as that experienced by any of his predecessors who have headed the company during the past 150 years. Yaeger is never more positive than when he notes that his successors will be working to make Laclede a vital, successful part of St. Louis 150 years from now.

as developers and builders continued to develop opportunities presented by available land.

Acquiring SM&P

The restructuring that resulted in the formation of The Laclede Group provided separation between the regulated natural gas business and unregulated subsidiaries such as Laclede Energy Resources, Inc., Laclede Development Company and Laclede Pipeline Company. The formation of The Laclede Group meant that Laclede Gas could concentrate on continuing to provide reliable and safe natural gas energy, while the parent entity could explore other opportunities with flexibility for financial and operational growth.

Yaeger noted that "Laclede Gas was so heavily regulated that the concept of the holding company gave us room to maneuver in looking at different businesses."

The formation of The Laclede Group required new thinking. "We needed to be market-driven instead of regulatory-driven in finding unregulated businesses," Yaeger said. "We recognized that gas is our core competency, but we wanted to look at other businesses if they make sense to our organization."

The Laclede Group was formed to enable the company to pursue acquisitions in unregulated industries, acquisitions that made sense from an earnings perspective and in areas where the company had some expertise. Like the hunt for natural gas wells a quarter-century before, the search came to fruition in 2001 when The Laclede Group reached an agreement to purchase SM&P Utility Resources, Inc., one of the largest underground facility-locating companies in the United States, from NiSource, Inc., for $43 million.

The company, headquartered in Carmel, Indiana, performed more than 10 million locates a year and generated almost $130 million in revenue in 2001. SM&P employed 2,000 people in 10 states, from Ohio west to Kansas and from Texas north to Minnesota.

Locating companies' principal function is to mark the placement of underground facilities for major providers of natural gas, electric, water, cable television and fiber optic services so that construction work can be performed without damaging such buried facilities.

At the time, SM&P was one of the two largest companies in an industry that had four major players. Laclede had been familiar with both the industry and the management of the company. In addition, SM&P performed almost 25 percent of all the outsourced locating work in the country. As such, it demonstrated a constant revenue stream that was not seasonal and that diversified the performance of The Laclede Group and enhanced its cash flow.

The acquisition was a significant first step in achieving Laclede's goal of creating a growth component for shareholders with significant, sustainable, non-regulated earnings. SM&P also gave Laclede a significant business interest outside of the company's traditional Missouri service area.

The Business Development Group Takes Shape

At the time The Laclede Group successfully completed the acquisition of SM&P in 2001, the holding company's new Business & Services Development Group

2001
The Laclede Group purchased SM&P Utility Resources, Inc. from NiSource, Inc.

SM&P Utility Resources, Inc., headquartered in Carmel, Indiana, performs more than 10 million locates of underground facilities per year in 10 midwestern states.

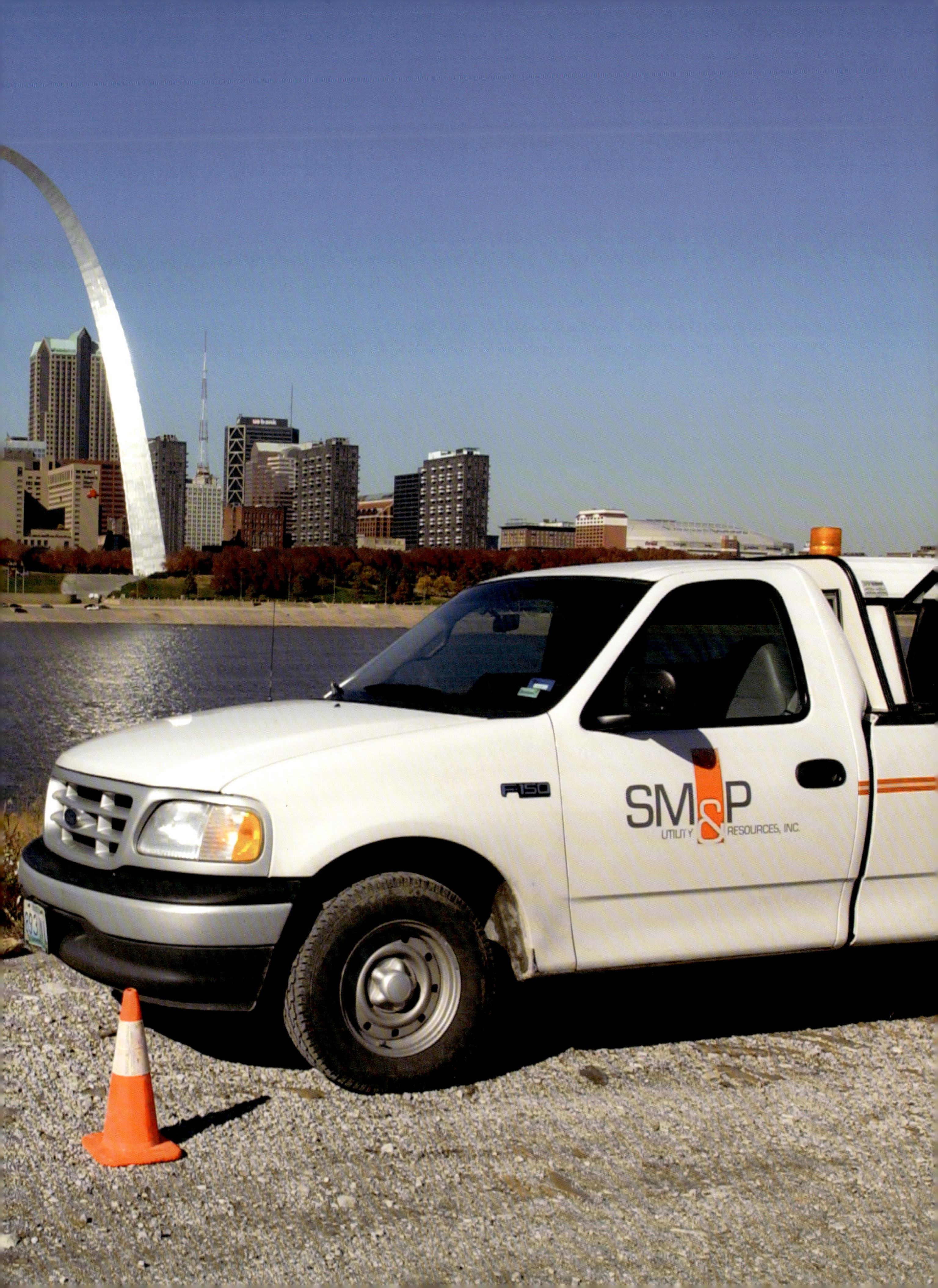
F150
SM&P
UTILITY RESOURCES, INC.

2001
Laclede successfully saturated St. Louis with more than 85 percent of the total heating market and more than 90 percent of new home construction.

was already working to assess opportunities for expansion that made sense both strategically and financially. Laclede would continue to be what it had always been, a reliable provider of heating energy. And its core business would remain the safe and reliable distribution and delivery of natural gas.

But there were limits to Laclede's ability to grow solely as a regulated utility. Laclede successfully saturated St. Louis with more than 85 percent of the total heating market and more than 90 percent of new home construction. The growth of Laclede's core business would not be enough to sustain and improve the value that the utility wanted to deliver to its shareholders.

To that end, the Business & Services Development Group was assigned the task of reviewing possible acquisitions by taking a close look at the structure of new deals and evaluating markets the company might enter. The group also was asked to evaluate if prospective acquisition candidates demonstrated a strategic fit with The Laclede Group and provided a proper return in proportion to the risk being assumed.

The Business & Services Development Group began conducting workshops to help department managers create three-year business models as part of the ongoing process of the strategic planning program started in 2001. The new group provided managers with a growth strategy for the years 2002-2004, and it furnished the company with a structure for communicating and translating strategy and results. One of the benefits of the strategic planning process was that it involved employees and department managers in Laclede's efforts to achieve company-wide goals.

With the formation of The Laclede Group, the company was finally free to develop opportunities for financial growth, separate and apart from the heavily regulated Laclede Gas. In the future, the focus for expansion would be a slow and steady process of sustainable growth in areas familiar to The Laclede Group, and in which such growth was feasible from an operating and financial standpoint.

Laclede Energy Resources

Another business opportunity pursued by The Laclede Group involved the company's expertise with deregulated gas marketing activities. Laclede Energy Resources (LER) emerged as a regional force in the gas marketing business during the early years of the 2000s. The holding company subsidiary was established to manage customers' natural gas needs and to market natural gas to both large retail and wholesale customers in the Midwestern United States.

The vast majority of LER's retail customers are large commercial and industrial customers located in the St. Louis metropolitan area. In addition, LER serves a number of large industrial customers in Iowa, Illinois, Arkansas and Louisiana. Also included in its customer base are industrial and commercial businesses, natural gas utilities and other wholesale customers. LER offers customers a variety of flexible pricing alternatives and provides various energy management services.

Laclede Energy Resources was another innovative way in which The Laclede Group could identify and provide non-regulated products and services to address the needs of customers, while offering stronger margins for the benefit of The Laclede Group's shareholders.

The Dividend Record

As The Laclede Group moved through the first decade of the 21st century, the company could point with justifiable pride to its financial performance. Total annual operating revenues more than tripled in the six years from 2000 to 2006, with net income almost doubling over that same time period.

The Laclede Group continued with the objective of expanding the Laclede Gas service area in a disciplined manner. In February 2006, Laclede Gas purchased certain assets of Fidelity Natural Gas, the natural gas distribution system serving Sullivan, Missouri. The purchase added approximately 1,300 new customers to Laclede's Missouri Natural Gas (MONAT) operating division.

Laclede Gas also focused on technology adaptation. The implementation of an Automated Meter Reading (AMR) system in 2007 essentially ended the need to estimate customers' bills, allowing the company to obtain actual customer usage information from a remote location. Since the transition involved every Laclede Gas customer, the installation of the AMR devices was one of the most visible activities undertaken by Laclede Gas.

The health of Laclede Gas and the non-regulated subsidiaries of The Laclede Group were reflected in the company's earning statements. Utility stocks, as a rule, are solid investments that don't experience wide swings in their share price. But they do generate a solid stream of income to shareholders in the form of dividends. The Laclede Group and its predecessor, Laclede Gas, have posted a history of paying dividends continuously since 1946. In the future, the company hopes to continue its long-standing policy of providing investors with a solid dividend return while pursuing new growth opportunities.

The future will likely present Laclede with new challenges and opportunities. But with 150 years experience in providing St. Louisans with low-cost energy solutions, Laclede will be up to the task for many years to come.

Automated Meter Reading (AMR) is a technology which allows for consistent and accurate collection of information from a natural gas meter, virtually eliminating the need to estimate customers' bills.

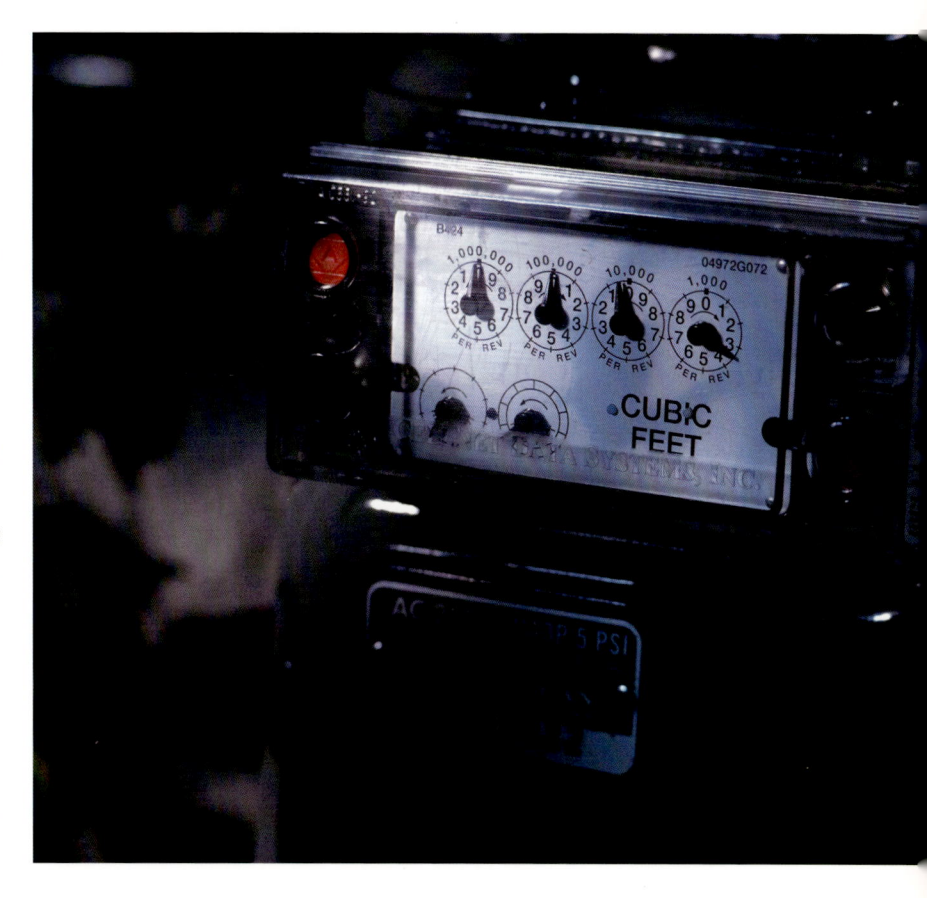

Throughout 2007, banners were hung on every streetlight surrounding the company's headquarters at 720 Olive, as well as the Old Post Office, in celebration of Laclede's anniversary.

CHAPTER 15

Building the Future on the Past

When Laclede Gas was formed on March 2, 1857, St. Louis was a riverboat town on the edge of the western frontier and no one could have predicted then how St. Louis and Laclede Gas would grow and evolve.

2004
Doug Dunphy, who retired in 2004, and was the fourth generation member of his family to work at Laclede Gas Company.

From humble beginnings as a town of 160,000 residents on the banks of the Mississippi River known as the last stop for pioneers anxious to make new lives in the west, the area has grown to a region of more than 2.5 million people. Similarly, Laclede Gas has developed from a small company that installed and fueled gas streetlights to the largest natural gas distribution utility in the State of Missouri — providing natural gas to more than 650,000 homes and businesses for heating, cooking, manufacturing and other uses.

Although much has changed in St. Louis and the natural gas industry during the past 150 years, one thing has remained constant at Laclede Gas: the pride and dedication of its employees. Laclede's employees are what make the company so successful. No organization lasts a century-and-a-half without a tradition of service that carries forward from one generation of employees to another. In fact, many of Laclede's past and present employees are the second and third generations of their families to work at Laclede. Impressively, there have been employees whose families have been part of the Laclede family for four generations and more than a century.

One example of this longevity is 2004 retiree Doug Dunphy and his family, a dedicated group that has personally experienced many of the changes over Laclede's long existence. Dolan, Doug's great grandfather, went to work for the company in the 1880s. Dolan's daughter's husband, Tom Dunphy, started in the meter shop at the turn of the 20th century. Doug's father, Bill Dunphy, found employment during the Great Depression in 1933, and Doug joined the company as a car washer in 1966. Doug retired from the Transportation Department with more than 36 years of service under his belt, not including 15 months spent with the First Air Cavalry in Vietnam in 1967 and 1968.

The commitment of its employees has allowed the Laclede to adapt to change, while anticipating and addressing the energy needs of the residents and businesses throughout metropolitan St. Louis. In addition, the company and its employees have had a significant impact on the St. Louis region as a whole. Traditionally, the Laclede family has been very active in and generous to various charities and civic organizations, including United Way, March of Dimes, Dollar-Help, Inc. and Susan G. Komen Race for the Cure. Many civic organizations, such as the Regional Chamber and Growth Association and Civic Progress have also benefited from the leadership and participation of the company and its employees.

As the company continues its journey in the 21st century, it will no doubt encounter challenges and changes as dramatic as those that it overcame during earlier periods. As the country's energy needs evolve and change, and natural gas supply and pricing issues continue to confront utilities around the country, Laclede and its employees will need to develop innovative ways to supply the energy that customers require at affordable prices. If past performance is any indication, they are, no doubt, up to the challenge.

Laclede was instrumental in the expansion of Lambert-St. Louis International Airport, not only monitoring pressure readings and flow rates, as seen here, but also the relocation of mains and fuel runs for the new parking garages and runway construction.

INDEX

A

Abernathy, Ronald 158
Adolphson, Capt. John 88
Adriatic Sea 89
Agricultural and Mechanical Fair 15
Alberta 112
Allentown, PA 35
Allyn, Lt. Robert V 89
America 64
American Bar Association 24
American Gas Association 107,119,144,176
America's Gilded Age 75
American Express Company 49
American Industrial Syndicate Ltd. Of London ... 42
American Iron & Steel Institute 126
American League 60
American Light & Traction Company ... 43,48,51,52,75,76
American Steel Foundries 62
Anadarko Basin 139
Anheuser-Busch Breweries 160
Anheuser, Eberhard 24
Appalachian Mountains 32,41
Arkansas 168,180
Arlen Properties of New York 129
Arlen-St. Louis Company 128
Army Air Corps 92,147
Army of the Potomac 34
Ashland, KY 41
Asia 87
Atlanta, GA 35
Atlas Corporation 80,86
Aubuchon, Andy 89
Aubuchon, Urvan 89
Automated Meter Reading (AMR) 181

B

Bagnell Hydroelectric Plant 71
Ball, Max 105,108
Baltimore, MD 13,49
Bank Panic of 1837 13
Bannister, Rex 103,139,162
Bastogne 87
Bates, Edward 24
Bavarian Brewery 24
Bayne, Henry 50
Beckham County, OK 139
Bedous, France 12
Beggs, John I. 50,52,76
Bell Telephone Company 57
Belleau Wood 65
Belmont, August 43
Binghamton, New York Gas Works 43
Birth of a Nation 60
Bi-State Development Agency 164,165
Blue Flame Family Protection Plan 141
Boatmen's National Bank 95
Bodine, Samuel 42
Boeing 166
Bonne Terre, MO 122
Bonus Marchers 80
Bonwit-Teller 86
Boone County, MO 23
Boonville, MO 19,159
Boston 49,50
Boston Braves 82
Boston Gas Light Company 32
Bredell, Edward 16
British Columbia 112
Broadhead, James O. 24
Brooklyn, NY 82
Brooklyn Dodgers 60
Brooklyn Union Gas Company 33,35
Browns 60
Burgess, Al 105,139
Burma 89
Busch, Adolphus 24,52
Bush, George Walker 52,172
Bush, George Herbert Walker 52
Business & Services Development Group 177,180
Byllesby, Henry M. 77
Byllesby, H. M., & Company 77

C

Caddo Parish, LA 52
Cahokia 12
Cahokia Steam Plant 71
California 86
California Trail 18
Canada 10,112,115
Cardinals 60
Carmel, IN 177
Carondelet Coke Station 69,71
Carondelet Gas Light Company 16,22,31
Carondelet Shipyards 23
Carter, Jimmy 134,136
Carthage Gas Field 112
Catalan Street 87,99
Central Institute For The Deaf 94
Central Service Building 88
Cervantes, Mayor Alphonso J. 129
Chateau Thierry 65
Chattanooa Gas 121
Chemical Building 39
Chester, IL 11
Chicago, IL 10,30,49,104,107,112
Childress, L. Wade 87,88,89,92,94,95
Chouteau, Auguste 11,12
Chouteau, Marie Therese 12
Chouteau's Pond 14
Cincinnati, OH 49,61
Cincinnati Gas & Electric Company 49,51
Circuit Court of St. Louis 26
Citizens Gas Trust 33
Cities Service Company 77
City Water Department 39
Civil War 17,18,19,21,23,41
Clark, Dr. Edward L. 108
Clark, William 11
Clarke, Harley 74,80,85,86
Clean Cities Program 166
Cleveland, OH 3,76
Cleveland Electric Illuminating Company 49
Clinton County, Oklahoma 139
Clover, Henry A. 16
Coffin, Charles 76
Cohen, Arthur G. 129
Collins, RIP 82
Cologne, Germany 104

Colorado 112
Columbia Carbon Company 83
Columbia Exposition of 1893 27,39
Columbia, IL 96
Columbia River 10
Columbia Terminals Company 94
Columbus Gas Works 41,43
Columbia Gas System 112
Combination companies 94
Commonwealth Edison 77
Compressed natural gas (CNG) 163
Concord, NH 35
Consolidated Gas Company of New Jersey 43
Continental Europe 27
Convair 86
Convent Street 53
Conversion & Surveys, Inc. 97
Cowdery, Edward C. 50,51
Cown, Bill C.P.I. Corporation. 141
Cromwell, William Nelson 50
Crowell, William DeForest 57
Cutlery Factory 26

D

Daugherty, Harry 77
Davis, Ralph 105
Davis, Bob 118,176
Davy, Sir Humphrey 113
Dean, Daffy 82
Dean, Dizzy 82
Denver Gas & Electric Company 43
Derrick, H. Reid 111,116,117,118,121,129
Detroit City Gas Company 43
Detroit Edison 49,50,76
Detroit Tigers 82
Des Moines, IA 35
DeSoto, MO 122
Dickason, Lt. Harry H. 89
Dickmann, Bernard F. 84
District of Columbia 32
Division of Smoke Regulation 84
Dodd, William S. 27
Dollar-Help, Inc. 152,153,184
Donnelly, Bill 118
Dresser Couplings 113
Duecker, Elmer J. 88
Duecker, Staff Sgt. Elmer 88
Duke of Sutherland 42
Dunphy, Bill 184
Dunphy, Dolan 184
Dunphy, Doug 184
Dunphy, Tom 184
Durocher, Leo 82

E

Eads Bridge 23,25,44
Eads, James Buchanan 25
Emerson McMillin Observatory 43
East River 43
East River Gas Company 43
East St. Louis 44,62,80
East Vixen 139
Edison, Thomas 28,35,49,75,77
Edwards, AG & Sons 122

Eiffel Tower 126
Electric Bond & Share Company 76
Emanuel, Albert 74
Emanuel, Victor 74
Emerson McMillin & Co., Bankers 43
Emery Roth & Sons 129
Empire Alarms, Inc. 140
Eureka Board of Aldermen 158
Eureka, MO 158,159
Europe 87
Evans, G.B. 72,85
Excelsior Stove Factory 26

F

Fairground Park 15
Farmington, MO 122,123
Fayette, MO 23
Federal Clean Air Act 163
Federal Energy Regulatory Commission (FERC)
. . . . 144,145,162,168
Federal Reserve Bank of St. Louis 57
Federal Power Commission 104,106,133,162
Federal Reserve Bank of St. Louis 122
Federal Trade Commission 77
FERC Orders 436 & 500 168
Ferris Wheel 36
Festus, MO 122
Fidelity Natural Gas 181
Field School 147
Findlay, OH 41
First Air Cav 184
First National Bank 95,129
Fisher, Jr., Robert E. 158
Flat River, MO 122
Fletcher, Thomas C. 19
Florida 76
Florida Power & Light 76
Foshay, Wilbur 77
Florissant Arch 108
Florissant, MO 107,108,115,118,139,147
Follmer, Adele 127,128
Forest Park Center 121
Fort de Chartres 11,12
France 60,64,88
Franklin County 103,158,160
Frazier-Davis Construction Co. 98
Fredericktown, MO 122
Freeport Oil Company 139
French and Indian War 10
Frisch, Frankie 82
Fulton Gas Shortage 157
Fulton, MO 157

G

Galleria Shopping Center 163
Gamble, Archibald 16,19
Gamble, Hamilton R. 16,19
Gardner, Samuel 16,19
Gas Age Magazine 111
Gas Bubble 144,145
Gas Cooling Technology Conference & Exposition . . . 160
Gashouse District 82
Gashouse Gang 82
Gas House Workers Union 85

150 Year Anniversary **187**

Gas Light Company of Baltimore 32
Gateway Arch 123,126,128
Gateway City 29
Gateway Mid-America Partners 141
General Electric Company 76
Germany 14,60,64
Gettysburg of the West 19
Gibson, Charles 16,19,24
Goldsmith, Sir Julian 42
Goldstein, Dr. M. A. 94
Gosling, E. P. 85,86
Graham, Frank 82
Grand, Joseph H. 122
Grand Rapids, Michigan Gas Light Company 43
Granite City, IL. 62
Granite City Steel 62,87
Great Britain 60,64
Great Depression 77,89,184
Great Flood of 1993 159
Great Lakes Carbon Corporation 99
Griffith, D.W. 60
Guadalcanal 87
Guggenheim, Charles 126
Gulf Interstate Company 112
Gulf of Mexico 132

H
Hammond, IN 35
Harding, Chester 16
Harrod C. L. 93
Harvard College 50
Hassenridder, Delmer 162
Hermann, MO 23,159
Herrscher Dome 107
Hill of Chapultepec 14
Hogshooter Field 83
Holding Company Act of 1935 94
Hollins, Henry Bowly 31,42
Holman, Charles 50,51,72
Home Service Department 70
Hoover, Herbert 77
Hooverville 80
Hornsby, Rogers 82
Hough, Laura R. 23
Howe, Burt 74
Hughes, James 16
Hurricane Katrina 169
Huttig, Charles H. 52

I
Illinois 33,77,86,87,107,145,167,168,180
Illinois Basin 63
Illinois & Missouri Pipeline Company 69
Illinois River 10
Independence, MO 12
Indiana 33,77,83,145,167
Indianapolis, IN 63,93
Indianapolis Power & Light 86,93
Insull, Martin 74
Insull, Samuel 71,72,77,80,86
Iowa 33,168,180
Iran 132
Ireland 14
Iron Mountain Railroad 15

Ironton Gas Works 41
Ironton, OH 41
Israel 132
Italy 89
Iwo Jima 87

J
Jackson, Battle of 19
Jackson, Claiborne 18
Japan 87,88
Jaudes, Bob 133,134,162
Jefferson City, MO 15,18,23,102,159
Jefferson County 122,158,160
Jefferson National Expansion Memorial 81,126
Jefferson, Thomas 11,126
Jenks, Downing B. 106
John Hancock Mutual Insurance Company 129
Johnson, Lyndon 132

K
Kahle, George A. 30
Kansas 76,83,159,177
Kansas City, MO 15,83,159
Kansas Natural Gas Company 83
Kasserine Pass 87
Keiser, Charles W 23
Keiser, John Pinkney 23,28
Keokuk Hydroelectric Project 71
Keyes Ordinance 45
King Louis IX 11,12
Knapp, Evelina Merseole 31
Komen, Susan G., Race for the Cure 184
Koppers Co. 64
KSD-TV 108
Kukuljan, Jacob 89
Kukuljan, Staff Sgt. Richard L. 89

L
Laclede Airport Park 141
Laclede Communication Services 141
Laclede Development Company 105,140,177
Laclede Energy Resources 140,168,177,180
Laclede Gas Building 129
Laclede Gas Company . . . .
9,80,95,96,97,98,99,101,102,103,104,105,106,107,108,109,
110,111,115,116,117,118,119,120,121,122,123,126,127,128,
129,130,131,132,133,136,137,138,139,140,141,143,144,145,
146,147,148,151,152,153,155,156,157,158,159,160,161,162,
163,164,165,166,168,169,170,172,173,174,176,177,180,181,
182,183,184
Laclede Gas Family Services 141
Laclede Gas Light Company . . . .
16,19,22,23,30,39,42,45,46,47,48,49,50,51,52,53,54,55,56,
57,58,60,61,62,63,64,65,67,68,69,70,71,72,73,74,75,76,78,
79,80,81,82,83,84,85,86,87,92,94,95
Laclede Gas Security Systems 141
Laclede Group, The 171,173,177,180,181
Laclede Honor Roll 88
Laclede Investment Corporation 140
Laclede Pipeline Company 177
Laclede Power & Light Company 71,74,95
Laclede Venture Corporation 141
Lafayette Park 14
Lake Michigan 10

188 Laclede Gas Company

Lake Superior 50
Lambert Airport. 141, 185
Lee, Robert M. 159
Legends Resort 158,159
Lehman Brothers 43
Lehman, Ernest 43
Leong, Don. 159
Lewis, Merriwether 11
Lexington, Battle of 18
Liberman, Lee
. . . . 27,91,92,99,102.107,111,121,122,129,134,147,162
Life Magazine. 84
Lindell Railway Company. 29
Liguest, Pierre Laclede. 8,9,10,11,12
Lincoln, Abraham 34
Lionberger, Isaac. 22,26,27,31
Locust Building 127
Lone Star Gas Company 83
Louisville,KY 49
Louisiana. 80,132,137,139,168,180
Louisiana Purchase 11,126
Louisiana Purchase Exposition. 39
Lowe, Thaddeus S. C. 34
Lowe, Theodore S.B.C. 75
Lower Manhattan. 82

M
Main Line 2 96
Manchester, NH. 35
Manter, Frances H. 16,19
Manufacturer's Bank 95
Maquoketa Shale 109
Marbury, William 103,104,106,122
March of Dimes 184
Marquette, Michigan 50
Martin, Peper 82
Martin, Peper & Martin 122
Maryland Heights, MO 163
Massachusetts 50,76
Mauran, Russell, Crowell 57
Maxent, Gilbert Antoine 10,12
McDonnell Aircraft Corporation 119
McGwire, Mark 82
McKinley High School 162
McMillin, Andrew 40
McMillin, J. H. 40
McMillin, Marion 40
McMillin, Milton 40
McMillin, Murray 40
McMillin, Osirus Emerson
. . . . 40,41,42,43,44,48,49,50,51,52,76
Medwick, Joe 82
Mee, Greg 159
Mega-NOPR. 168
Memorial Plaza 80
Menlo Park. 29
Memphis & St. Louis Packet Company 23
Mercantile-Commerce Bank & Trust Company 94
Mercantile-Commerce National Bank 94,95
Merchant Marine 105
Metropolitan Board of the YMCA 94
Meuse Argonne 65
Mexico. 112
Meyer, Lois Ann. 122

Miami University of Ohio. 176
Michigan-Wisconsin Pipeline Co. 112
Mid-Atlantic States 33
Middle East. 132
Middle West Companies 74
Middle West Utilities. 74,75,77
Midway 87
Midwest Missouri Gas Co. 122,174
Mills Ranch Prospect. 139
Milwaukee, WI. 49,50,76
Milwaukee Electric Railway
and Light Company (TMERL) 50,76
Milwaukee Gas Light Company 43,50
Minneapolis, MN 29,77
Minnesota. 177
Minnesota Power & Light 76
Mississippi Delta 80
Mississippi River 10,15,29,54,61,62,68,69,80,96,98,184
Mississippi River Barge Line 127
Mississippi River Corp. 106
Mississippi River Fuel Company 83,92,96,103,104,176
Mississippi River Transmission Corporation (MRT)
. . . . 139,140,169,176
Mississippi Valley 159
Mississippi Valley Bank 95
Mississippi Valley Barge Line Company 94
Missouri 83,103,105,145,159,167,168,184
Missouri Department of Natural Resources. 163
Missouri Energy Development Corp. (MEDA) 176
Missouri Highway & Transportation Dept. 163
Missouri Historical Society. 162
Missouri Industrial Gas Company 83
Missouri Legislature 22
Missouri Natural Gas (MONAT) 122,123,174
Missouri-Pacific Railway 68,106
Missouri-Pacific Railroad Building 57
Missouri Pipeline 156
Missouri Public Service Commission
. . . . 71,72,86,94,99,102,104,108,162, 173
Missouri River 111,156,159
Missouri Supreme Court 103
Mitchell, Sidney Zollicoffer. 76
Monroe 109,137
Monsanto Chemical Company. 119
Montreal Heat, Light & Power Company 71
MoPac 106
Morgan, J. P. 31,77
Morgan, Randal 76
Mormon Commonwealth. 147
Moss, Myron. 129
Moten, John Jr.. 120,146,148
Mound City Line 29
Mt. Zion Church 19
Mrazek Van & Storage. 129
Municipal Electric Lighting & Power Company 39,45
Museum of Westward Expansion. 126
Musial, Stan 82
Munroe, Charles A. 71,72,80
Murfreesboro, Tennessee. 94
Muskegon, Michigan 48

N

Nachefski, Phillip 89
Napton, W.B. 24
Napoleon 11
Nashville, TN 35
National Park Service 81
Natural gas desiccant system 160
Natural Gas Pipeline Company of America 112
Natural Gas Act 104,169
Natural Gas Policy Act of 1978
. . . . 134,144,147,162,167,168
Nebraska 159
Nebraska Power Co. 76
NESCO 62
Netherlands 132
New Madrid 19
New Mexico 112
New Orleans, LA 10,11
New York 99
New York City 12,48,49,52
New York Gas Light Company 32
New York Times 31
Niedringhaus brothers 62
Nixon, Richard 133
Norman, OK 139
Normandy 88
North American Company 35,48,49,61,75,76,94
North Converse Field 139
North Dakota 159
North District 119
North Missouri Railroad 15
Northeast Airlines 86
Northern Pacific Railway 49
Northwestern Mutual Life Insurance Co. 95
Northwestern University 103
Novatny, Donald 162

O

Odlum, Floyd Bostwick 86,94
Ogden Corp 75,80,86
Ohio 33,83,145,167,177
18th Ohio Infantry Regiment 41
Ohio River 10,61
Ohio State University 43
Oil, Chemical & Atomic Workers of America (OCAW) . 136
Okinawa 87,89
Oklahoma 68,83,139
Oklahoma Natural Gas Company 83
Old Cathedral 12
Old Courthouse 126
Old Judge Coffee Building 26
Omaha, NE 42
Omaha Beach 87
Omni Hotel 161
Onion Bayou 139
Ontario 23,115
Order No. 636 145,168,169
Ordinance of Secession 18
Oregon 77
Oregon Trail 12,18
Otto, Robert W.
. . . . 85,96,101,102,103,104,105,107,108,111,118,119,121,147
Organization of Petroleum Exporting Countries (OPEC)
. . . . 132

Osage River 71
Otis, Elisha 38
Owens, Lorraine 89

P

Pacific Gas & Electric 49,51,76
Pacific Ocean 10,89
Pacific Power & Light 76
Pacific Railroad 15
Page, George Shepherd 42
Panhandle Eastern Pipeline Company 112,156
Panhandle-Hugoton Field 83
Panic of 1913 61
Peace River Gas Fields 112
Peale, Rembrandt 32
Peleiliu 87
Penatangueshene, Ontario 23
Pennsylvania 28,63,76
Pennsylvania Power & Light 76
Pentagon 172
People's Gas 72,118
Peper, Christian 122
Permian Basin Gas Fields 112
Perryville Field 96
Perryville, Louisiana 83,109
Peters, Lovett "Pete" 104
Phenol 64
Philadelphia, PA 13,35,160
Philadelphia Gas Works 33,76
Phoenix Light, Heat & Power Company 39,45,71
Phoenixville, PA 35
Pickard, B. F. 89
Pike, Zebulon M. 11
Pintsch Compressing Company 48
Pintsch, Julius 48
Pittsburgh, PA 23,61,63
Ploesti 87
Poplar Bluff, MO 122
Portland, OR 76
Potomac Electric Power 76
Price, David 115
Public Utility Holding Company Act of 1935 77,86

Q

Quick Meal gas ranges 30

R

Raeder Place Building 26
Railway Exchange Building 57
Reagan, Ronald 141
Reconstruction Finance Corporation 85,86
Reitz, Tom 174
Renneck, Capt. Eugene 89
Renneck, Marie 89
Republican National Committeeman 50
Residential Conservation Service 146
Residential Insulation Financing Program 146
Richmond Heights 94
Rickey, Branch 60,82
Riggin, John 16
Ringin, John 30
Rising Star Award 160
River Des Peres 61,98,159
Riverport Casino Center 163

RKO Studios 86
Robinson Field 60
Robinson, Jackie 60
Rockefeller, John D. 41,50
Rock Hill Oil Company 105
Rock Island Lines 106
Roger Mills Country, Oklahoma 139
Roosevelt, Franklin Delano 77,86
Roosevelt, Teddy 64
Roxana Petroleum Corporation 68
Royal Bank of Canada 71
Rural Electrification Administration 113
Rust, H.B. 72
Russia 64

S

Saarinen, Eero 126
Sabine Parish, LA 139
Salomon & Company 52
Salt Lake City, UT 92,147
Salvation Army 159,162
San Antonio Gas & Electric Company 43
San Antonio, Texas 48
San Antonio Traction Company 43
San Juan Basin Gas Fields 112
Santa Ana 14
Santa Fe Trail 18
Santa Fe Railroad 106
Sarah Street 54
Saudi Arabia 132
Savannah, GA 35
Schaeffer, Beatrice 103
Schnucks 160,161
Scott Army Air Corps Base 92
Scott, Dred 16
Scott, Eddie 89
Scott, Winfield 14
Securities & Exchange Commission 77,94,104
Shah of Iran 141,144
Shaw, P. B. 86
Shaw's Gardens Apartments 159
Sheldon, George R. 50
Shell Oil 166
Sherman, William Tecumseh 19
Shockley, R. Ray 129
Shrewsbury Gas Plant 95,119,120,164
Shulman, Bob 99
Siemens, Werner 38
Sigma Chemical 160
Sioux City Gas Light Company 41,42
Sioux City Heat, Light & Power Company 41
Smith, Capt. Henry W. 23
Smith, Luther Ely 126
SM&P Utility Resources, Inc. 177
Soldan High School 147
South District 119
Southern Light & Traction Company 43
Southern Plains 83
Spanish-American War 27
St. Anthony Falls 29
St. Charles County 156,160,174
St. Charles Gas Company 121,122,123,156,174
St. Charles Gas Division 157
St. Charles, MO 159

St. Joseph, MO 147
St. Louis, MO 76,118
St. Louis Cable & Western Company 29
St. Louis Cardinals 60,82
St. Louis Centre 161
St. Louis City Directory, 1857 17
St. Louis City Police Department 164
St. Louis Civic Center 119
St. Louis County Gas Company
. . . . 93,94,95,102,111,119,147,162
St. Louis Gas Light Company 13,14,16,22,30,31,42,76
St. Louis Girl Scouts 70
St. Louis Globe-Democrat 109
St. Louis Heat and Power Company 31
St. Louis & New Orleans Anchor Line 23
St. Louis Post-Dispatch 52,70
St. Louis Regional Clean Air Partnership 164
St. Louis Regional Commerce & Growth Association . . 147
St. Louis Regional Chamber & Growth Association . . . 176
St. Louis Science Center 163,176
St. Louis Star-Times 99
St. Louis Symphony 147
St. Louis Terminal Association 68
St. Louis Transit Company 29,39
St. Louis Union Station 161
St. Louis United Way Campaign 162
St. Louis University 13,104,176
Ste. Genevieve, MO 12,122
St. Paul Gas Light Company 43
St. Peter Sandstone 108,109
Standard Oil Company of Indiana 68
Standard Oil Company of New Jersey 83
Stanford Law School 92
Station "A" 39,44,48,53,54,65,69,95,147,162
Station "B" 31,53,54,65,95,118
Station "C" 44
Station "E" 54
Statue of Liberty 126
Stith, Henry 60,65
Stone & Webster 92,94
Stonebridge Mobile Home Court 159
Stupp Brothers Bridge & Iron Co. 104,105,106
Stupp, Erwin 105,106
Stupp, Jack 106
Stupp, Johann 104,105
Stupp, John Jr. 106
Stupp, Robert 106
Sullivan, Louis 38
Sullivan, MO 181
Sunbury, PA 28
Sverdrup & Parcel, Inc. 98
Syracuse, NY 61

T

Taft, William Howard 64
Taney, Roger 16
Teheran 144
Tesla, Nikola 75
Texas 68,76,132,177
The Gas Record 63
Thomson, Elihu 75
TNT 64
Toluene 64
Toluol 64

Transcontinental Gas Pipeline Co. 112
Traverse City, MI 103
Tree of Lights Campaign........................... 162
TriNitroToluene 64
Tripartite Agreement 30
Tucker, Charles A. 50
Twain, Mark 159
Tyrolean Alps 24

U

U. S. Federal Mediation & Conciliation Service 136
U. S. Naval Base, Pearl Harbor 87
U.S. War Department 64
Union Army Corps of Aeronautics 34
Union Depot Railway Company 29,44
Union Depot Electric Company...................... 45
Union Electric Company............ 49,85,92,93,94,95,157
Union Electric Light & Power Company.............. 71
Union Light, Heat & Power Company................. 39
Union Station..................................... 68
United Carbon Company 83
United Gas Improvement Company (UGI).... 34,35,42,76
United Railways Company 49
United States 64,65,112,132,133
United States Custom House & Post Office 38
United States Department of Energy 164,166
United States Postal Service 164
United Way....................................... 184
University of Missouri 103,122,147
Upper Louisiana................................... 10
Utah Power & Light................................ 76
Utilities Power & Light Corporation 74,75,80,84,85,86

V

Valley Forge 37
Vanderbilt, William K.............................. 31
Veiled Prophet Parade 27
Vietnam 184
Vicksburg, MS 35
Vicksburg, Siege of................................ 19
Villard, Henry..................................... 49
Virginia 33
Virginia Polytechnic Institute..................... 121

W

Wachsler, Lt. Harry 88
Wainwright Building............................... 38
Wal-Mart Stores.................................. 160
Wall Street 75,76,77
Walker-Busch Syndicate 52,53,71
Walker, G. H. 52
Walnut Street Cathedral 23
War Chest 94
Washington Avenue................................. 29
Washington, D.C. 19,24,49,80,106
Washington Gas Light Company..................... 33
Washington, MO 103
Washington University....................... 147,162
Webster Groves High School 176
Weekly Reveille................................... 14
Weiland, Harry.................................... 89
Wells, Erastus 14
Wells, Rolla 39
Welsbach Commercial Company.................... 43

Weslbach Mantles............................... 27,37
West Virginia 61,63,83
Westerheide, Kathy 103,109,111
Western Front..................................... 64
Western Gas Light Company 43
Westport, Battle of................................ 19
2nd West Virginia Cavalry 41
Wetherall, Helen.................................. 70
Wetmore, Charles..............................50,51
Wheeler County, Texas 139
Williston Basin Interstate Pipeline Company......... 115
Wilson, Joseph B................................86,94
Wilson, Woodrow 64
Wilson's Creek, Battle of 18,19
Wisconsin 77
Works Progress Administration 126
World's Fair Ground 39
World's Fair, 1904 37
World Series 82
World Trade Center.............................. 172

Y

Yale University............................. 122,147
Yaeger, Doug.......... 145,146,157,168,172,173,176,177
YMCA of Greater St. Louis........................ 162
Youghiogheny River Valley 63

LACLEDE GAS

OF THE LACLE
USE GAS

FUTU